IMAGES
of America

PORT JEFFERSON

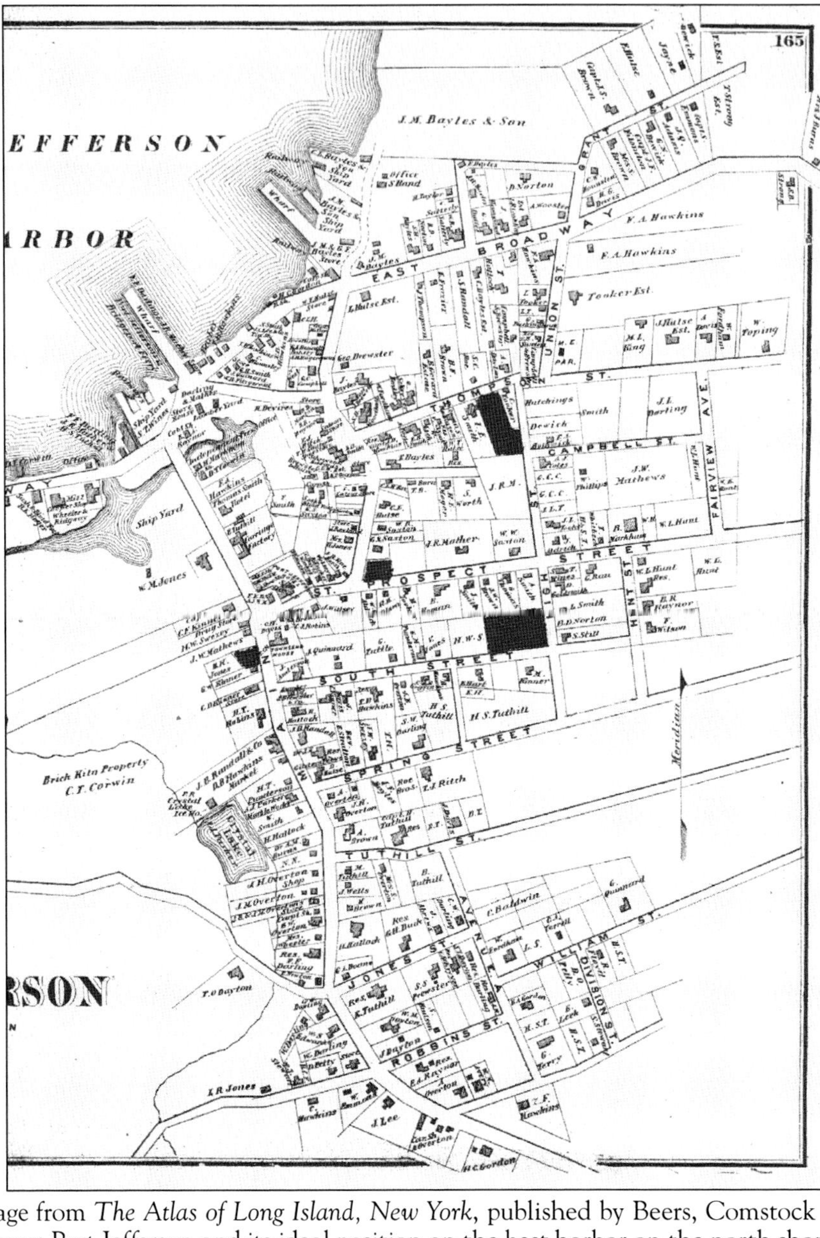

This page from *The Atlas of Long Island, New York*, published by Beers, Comstock & Cline in 1873, shows Port Jefferson and its ideal position on the best harbor on the north shore of Suffolk County. Some of the large marshy areas that inhibited the village's growth in the early years can be seen on the central left side of the map. (Courtesy of the Port Jefferson Free Library.)

ON THE COVER: The schooner yacht *Resolute*, with Port Jefferson residents Sereno T. Dayton as captain and Charles F. Kinner as first officer, was a frequent visitor to Port Jefferson in the 1870s and 1880s. After the decline of commercial sailing, the shipyards of the village turned more and more to the building, outfitting, and repairing of pleasure yachts. The workmen in the foreground are shipyard employees, perhaps preparing to work on the yacht. The *Resolute* was renamed the *Ramona* in 1892. (Courtesy of the Historical Society of Greater Port Jefferson.)

IMAGES
of America

PORT JEFFERSON

Robert Maggio and Earlene O'Hare
of the Port Jefferson Free Library
and Port Jefferson Village

ARCADIA
PUBLISHING

ISBN 978-0-7385-9817-8

Published by Arcadia Publishing
Charleston, South Carolina

Printed in the United States of America

Library of Congress Control Number: 2012945312

For all general information, please contact Arcadia Publishing:
Telephone 843-853-2070
Fax 843-853-0044
E-mail sales@arcadiapublishing.com
For customer service and orders:
Toll-Free 1-888-313-2665

Visit us on the Internet at www.arcadiapublishing.com

To Frances Child and Randall Woodard, who have kept alive the rich history of Port Jefferson and shared it with us, we gratefully dedicate this book.

Contents

ACKNOWLEDGMENTS

We are truly indebted to the following people and organizations for their knowledge of Port Jefferson and their willingness to share it with us: the Incorporated Village of Port Jefferson, particularly Mayor Margot Garant and Jill Nees-Russell, for their support, and Kenneth Brady, for his comprehensive knowledge of Port Jefferson and its history; the Historical Society of Greater Port Jefferson, especially Mildred Michos, Laura Warren, Beth Pranzo, Teri Powers, and Sandra Swenk, for providing us with the majority of images for this book and for the history behind them and for fact-checking our work; Frances Child, for graciously lending us her family photographs and sharing the memories of the Bayles family and of life in Port Jefferson at the turn of the 20th century; Randall Woodard, for his inexhaustible treasury of personal stories and anecdotes and his knowledge of Port Jefferson families; Nancy Orth and Wolf Schaefer of the Belle Terre Archive, for their images, personal knowledge, and research into the often misrepresented history of Belle Terre. We also wish to thank our acquisitions editor at Arcadia Publishing, Rebekah Collinsworth, for answering our many questions.

Finally, we would like to thank the staff of the Port Jefferson Free Library, for their patience and support, especially Robert Goykin, library director, for his encouragement; Valerie Schwarz, for taking the present-day photographs, and Nicole Greenhalgh, for their help and expertise in scanning, formatting, and organizing the images that we had collected; Samantha Winter, for preserving the images from the library's own collection; and most especially Linda Gavin. Without her impetus and her wide-ranging connections with the community, this book would never have happened.

Unless otherwise noted, all images appear courtesy of the Historical Society of Greater Port Jefferson.

INTRODUCTION

The people of Port Jefferson, a village on Long Island's North Shore, are justly proud of their community's long and varied history. In their Algonquian language, the Native Americans of the area called the place Suwassett, meaning "land of small pines," and relied on its fish, shellfish, and waterfowl for food and wampum, although their major settlements were elsewhere. In 1655, the original English settlers of Brookhaven Town bought from the Native Americans the area stretching from the town's western border to the east side of Port Jefferson Harbor, but the first permanent European settler to build a home in the "drowned meadow," John Roe, an Irish shoemaker, did not arrive until 1682. The settlement was called Drowned Meadow because the area that now comprises most of the commercial district was a marsh that flooded with every high tide. That flooding, and the steep hills and deep ravines that surrounded the marsh, made farming difficult, and the village grew slowly. In fact, by 1800, there were only a handful of houses.

But the village was blessed with the finest harbor on the North Shore, and its fortunes were to change dramatically with the arrival of shipbuilder John Willse in 1797. The sloop he built that year, the *Jay*, was to be the first of more than 500 ships built in Port Jefferson over the next 120 years. The shipyard owners' names—Jones, Mather, Darling, Bayles—are among the most prominent in village history. William L. Jones began filling in the "drowned meadow" by building an 18-foot-wide elevated road across its center in 1837. This was the beginning of today's Main Street. The Bayles family yards turned out at least 142 vessels, and the Mather yards 50 or more, including the largest sailing ship built in Port Jefferson. As shipbuilding increased, the village's traditional name no longer seemed to fit its progressive image. In 1836, residents voted overwhelmingly to change the name from Drowned Meadow to Port Jefferson. Shipbuilding reached its zenith in 1845–1860, when there were 10 to 12 yards producing as many as 14 vessels annually. Collateral businesses—blacksmiths, chandlers, wood-carvers, and sailmakers, among others—also flourished during this time. The shipping industry, bringing in coal, lumber, grain, and machinery and leaving with produce and finished goods from Long Island farmers and artisans, was thriving, too. In 1852, Port Jefferson was made an official US port of entry, one of only two on Long Island.

Almost every family in the village had at least one or two members involved in shipbuilding or sailing. The shipyard owners and ship captains built large and gracious homes, but even the workers used their carpentry skills to build more modest but equally pleasing houses on the village's steep and winding streets. Most of these homes still exist, contributing to Port Jefferson's beauty.

The village also became a transportation hub. The Long Island Rail Road arrived in 1873. The Bridgeport & Port Jefferson Steamboat Company was formed in 1883 to connect the two communities with a ferry, which still runs today. Tuthill's Carriage Manufactory was founded in 1850 and produced wagons, coaches, and buggies known for quality throughout the New York area.

Times were changing, however. Commercial sailing vessels were becoming obsolete; the shipyards that survived turned more and more to the production and refurbishing of luxury yachts. The village had one last moment of shipbuilding glory during World War I, when the US Shipping Board took over the Bayles, the Mather & Wood, and the John Hawkins yards, building barges, tugboats, freighters, and a tanker. One of the freighters, the *Cloverock*, at 5,000 tons and 374 feet, was the largest vessel ever built here. At the end of the war, however, shipbuilding on a large scale was gone for good. Even the building of yachts ceased, because the alterations that the shipping board made to the yards rendered them unsuitable for the building of pleasure vessels, although the repair and refurbishing of yachts continued.

The decline of the shipbuilding industry forced Port Jefferson to reinvent itself in order to remain vital. The town's salvation would once again be found in the waters of the harbor. Port Jefferson decided to promote itself as a tourist destination. Among the many attractions offered were bathing in the harbor, dancing to live music at the California Grove pavilion, and attending a show at Athena Hall. There were also festivals, including Old Home Week, a seven-day celebration of boat races, ball games, water and field sports, hot-air balloons, and moonlight cruises.

In the end, though, this latest incarnation proved to be ephemeral. Port Jefferson would remain a typical small American town for the majority of the mid-20th century. Local commerce was represented by a large number of automobile dealerships and dining establishments, along with an ever-changing cast of small businesses.

The town's fortunes would begin to change once the post–World War II suburban migration started. Port Jefferson's location and desirable housing stock made it a popular choice for those wishing to relocate. Consequently, its population began to grow. But this burgeoning suburban sprawl would prove to be a double-edged sword.

With the increase in population on Long Island came an increased demand for energy. The Long Island Lighting Company opened a power plant on the west side of the harbor in 1948. A number of oil and natural gas companies erected storage tanks along the waterfront, where their tankers off-loaded their cargo. The car dealers left and relocated to the south of Port Jefferson to be closer to the communities developing in central Long Island.

The residents became concerned that their community's identity was being lost to the overcommercialization of the harbor and waterfront and the loss of local businesses. They appealed to the presiding government body, the Town of Brookhaven, but received little satisfaction. By the early 1960s, a majority of the population had become so frustrated that a proposal was made to allow Port Jefferson to become an incorporated village, which would enable it to have the authority to decide its own fate. A vote was held in December 1962 and, by a two-to-one margin, the proposal was approved. Port Jefferson officially became an incorporated village on April 12, 1963.

Today, Port Jefferson is once again thriving, as it balances its dual roles as both a residential community and a welcoming destination for visitors. The industrial development along the waterfront has all but disappeared, replaced by parkland and berthing for boaters. But its rich history is not forgotten. The harborside Village Center building was once part of the Bayles Shipyard, and the annual Dickens and Maritime Festivals hearken back to similar celebrations a century ago.

A note about street names: Port Jefferson street names have changed in the time period covered by this book: Main Street north of East Main Street was known as Jones Street; East Main Street was simply Main Street; East Broadway between East Main and Main Streets was known as Water Street, and then Surf Avenue. In the interest of clarity and consistency, we have used present-day street names throughout this work.

One

EARLY SETTLERS

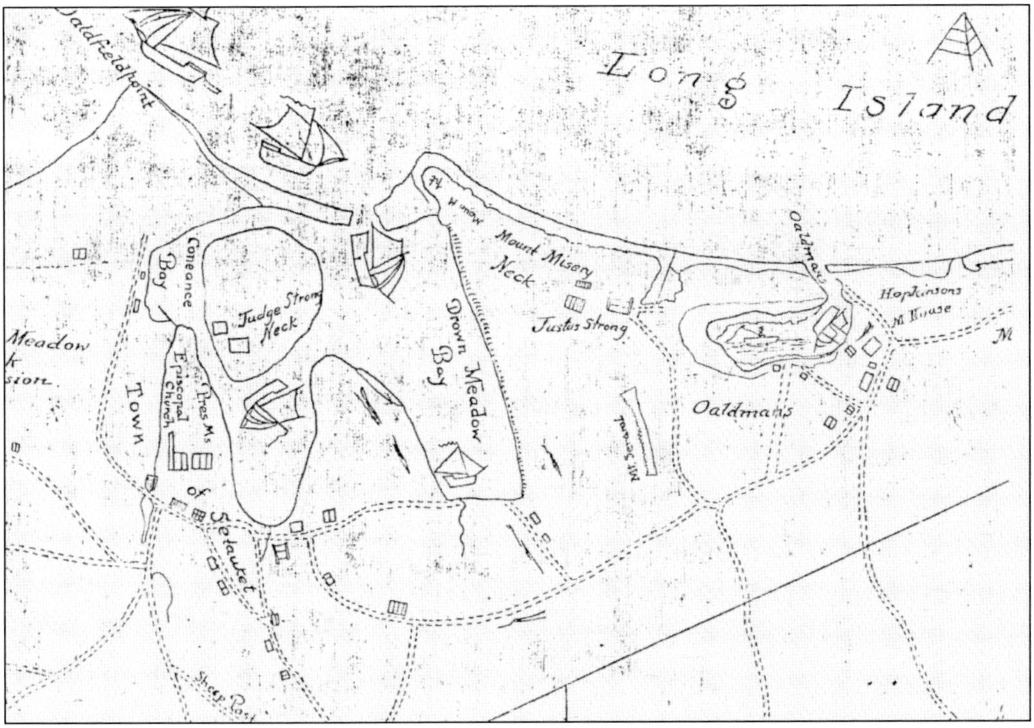

This portion of a map drawn according to a survey of the town of Brookhaven by Isaac Hulse in 1797 shows Drown Meadow Bay (Port Jefferson Harbor) and the Strong estate on Mount Misery Neck. The two houses on the road south of Drown Meadow Bay are probably the John Roe houses on Main Street. Port Jefferson was still very sparsely settled more than 100 years after Roe arrived.

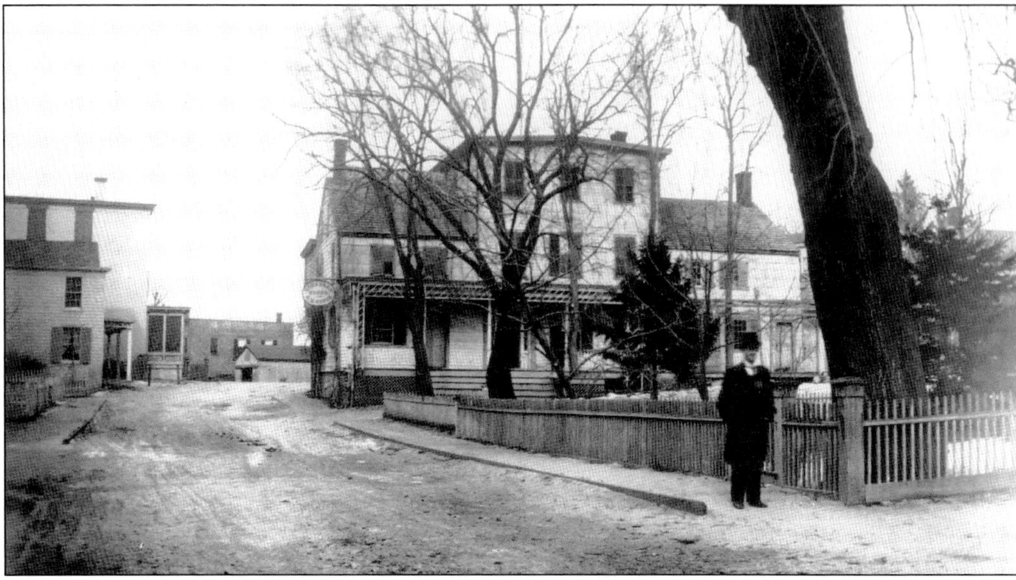

John Roe, Port Jefferson's first European settler, arrived in 1682 and built a house near the southeast intersection of today's Main and East Main Streets. He later built a similar-sized addition to the house around 1700. In 1840, the house was acquired from the Roe family by Henry Townsend for his hotel. Caleb Davis bought the hotel in 1867 and split it in two, constructing a three-story addition between the two halves. When Main Street was widened around 1898, the left side of the house, as seen in the above photograph (probably the 1700 addition), was moved to Sheep Pasture Road. There, it was discovered by former village trustee Robert Sisler, who was instrumental in having it moved to West Broadway and restored to its original appearance. Since 1982, it has served as an information center (below), staffed by the Port Jefferson Chamber of Commerce. (Both, courtesy of Port Jefferson Free Library.)

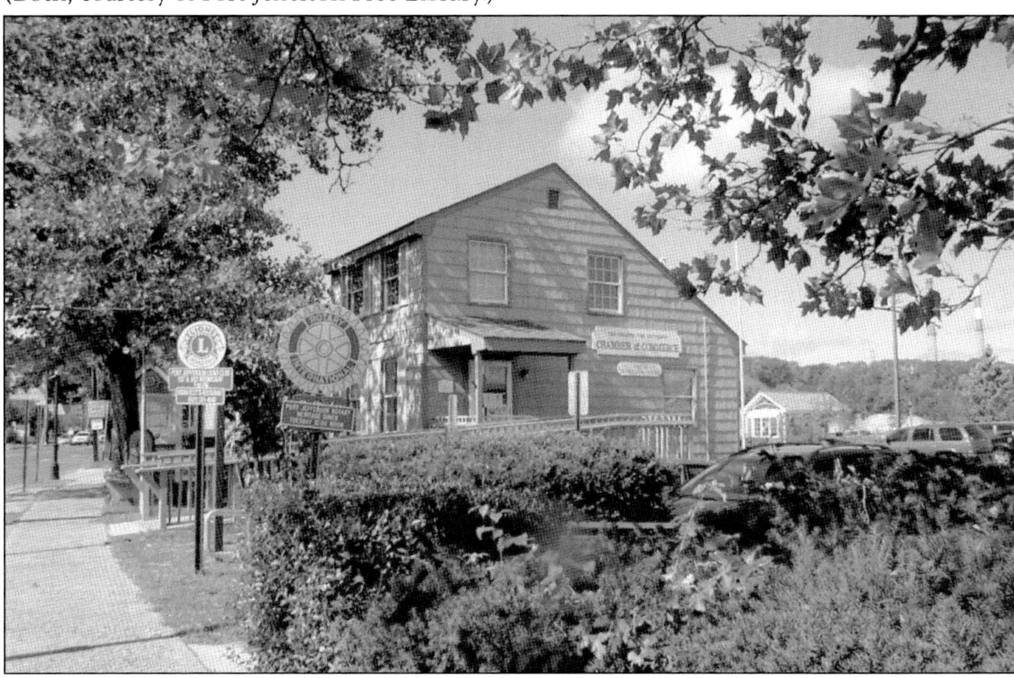

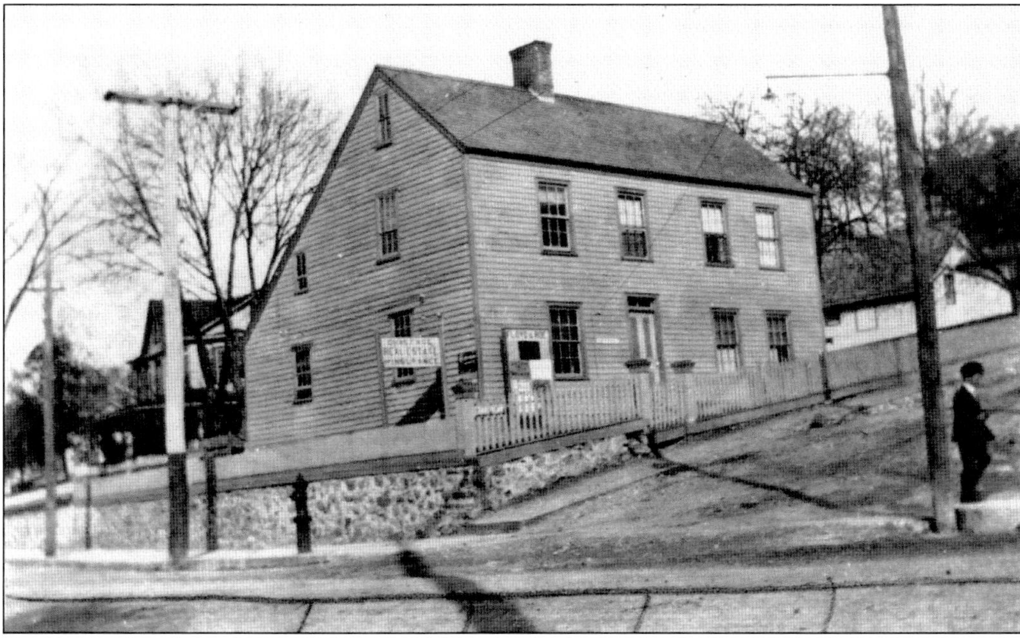

The saltbox pictured here, dating to 1730, is another of Port Jefferson's earliest houses. It was built by John Roe, a grandson of the first settler. In the early years of the 20th century, it was still being used by the Roe family, as indicated by the sign "Chas. F. Roe—Real Estate." The house was destroyed by fire in the early 1920s.

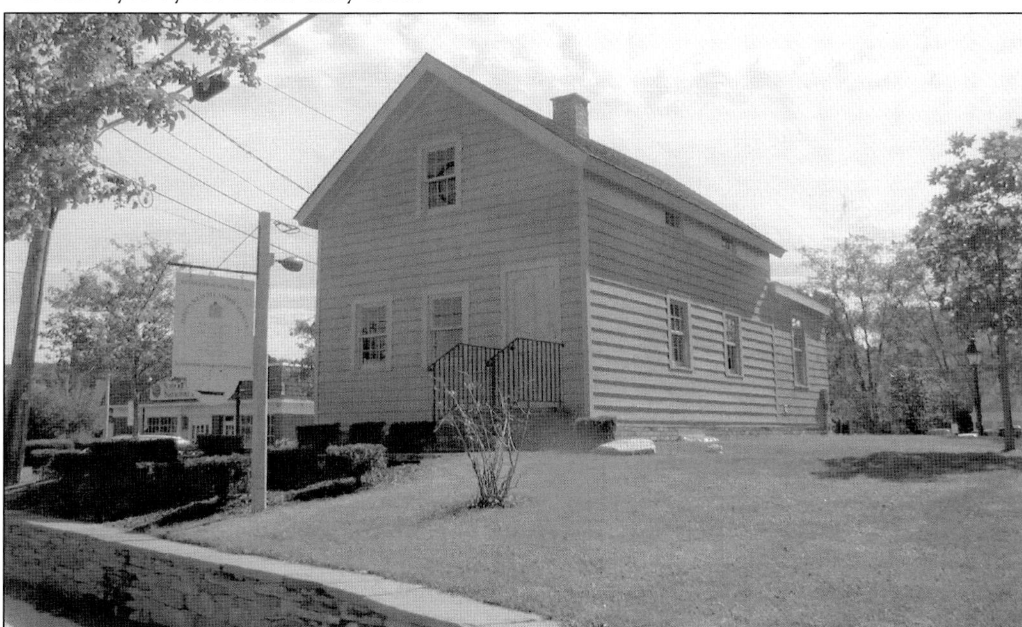

Another of John Roe's grandsons, Phillips Roe, built this house around 1755. It originally stood on the east side of Main Street, near Tuthill Street, but was moved across the road in 1849. Alterations in the early 20th century disguised its ancient appearance, but it was rediscovered by village trustee and historian Robert Sisler, moved to the corner of Barnum Avenue and West Broadway, and restored and opened to the public in 2010. (Courtesy of Port Jefferson Free Library.)

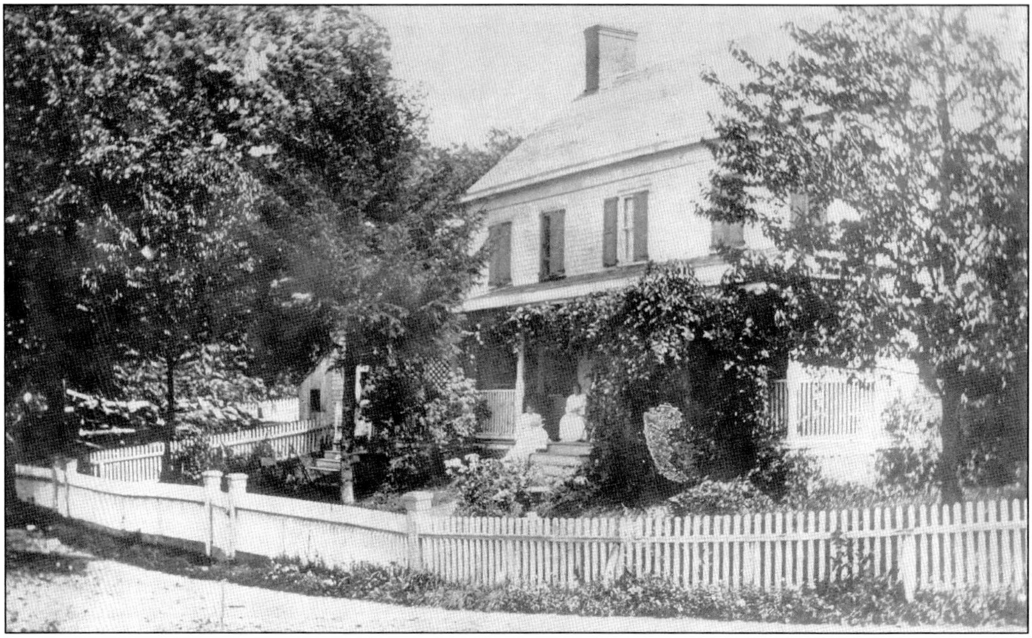

Several of the earliest houses are associated with the shipbuilding Bayles family. This house, known as the Bayles Homestead, was built in 1802 by John Willse, Port Jefferson's first shipbuilder, near the corner of East Broadway and East Main Street. James M. Bayles, son of Elisha Bayles, bought the house in 1835. The house faced the harbor and was conveniently adjacent to the family shipyard and the first Bayles chandlery. (Courtesy of Frances Child.)

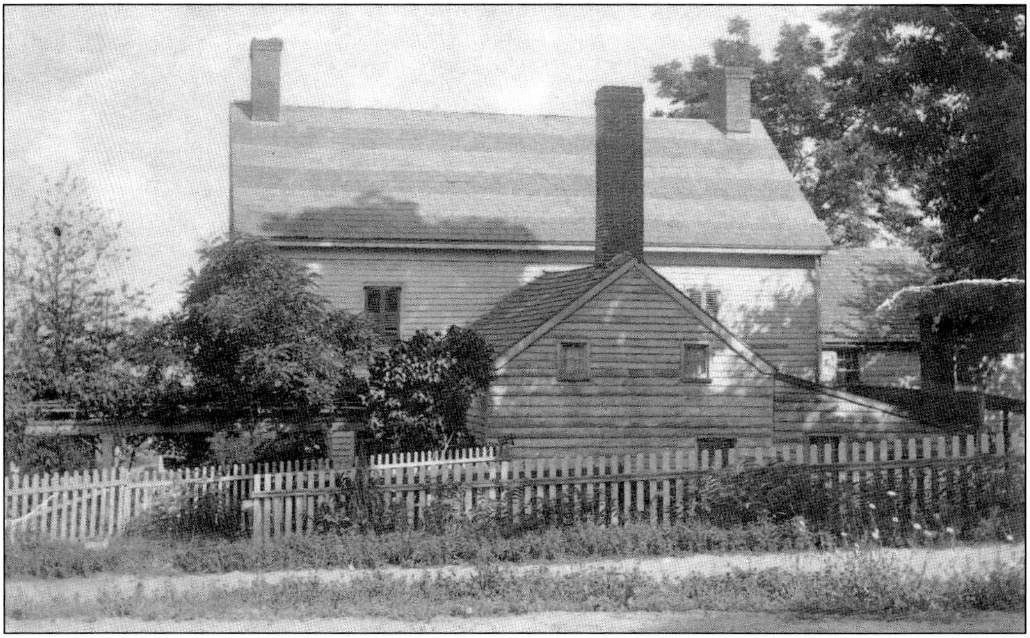

The rear of the Bayles Homestead, shown here, faced East Broadway. The house was torn down in December 1917 to make way for the US Shipping Board buildings. The site is now the Village Center. On the hill above the homestead, several of James M. Bayles's sons built their own homes; it is still known as Bayles Hill. (Courtesy of Frances Child.)

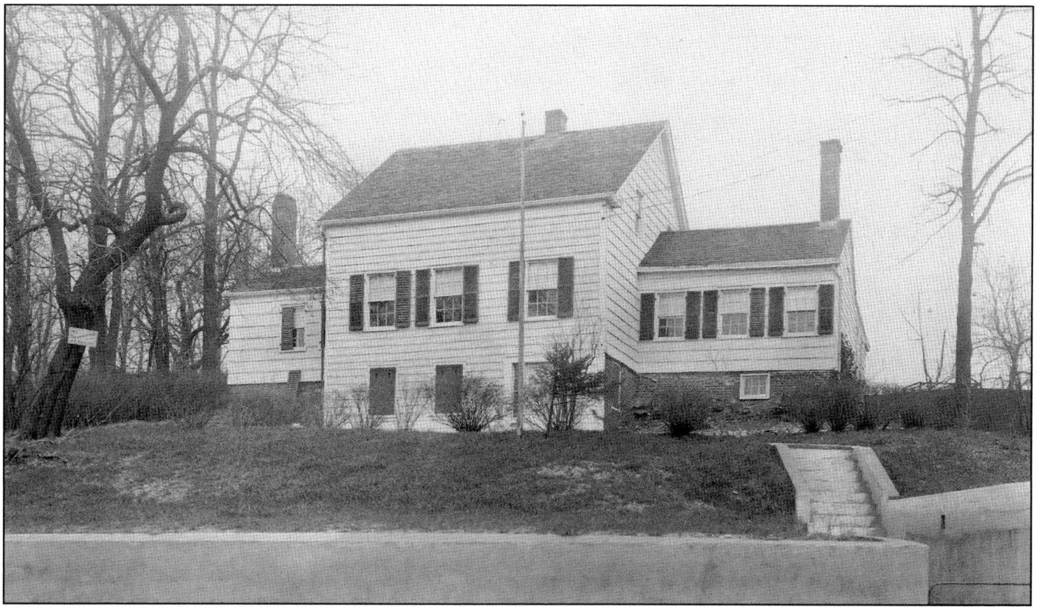

This home was built around 1802 by Elisha Bayles, the patriarch of the Bayles shipbuilding family. It is known as Cookie Hill, from the legend that a wife of a seafaring Bayles baked and sold cookies to supplement her income while her husband was at sea. The house still stands on the east side of East Main Street. (Courtesy of Frances Child.)

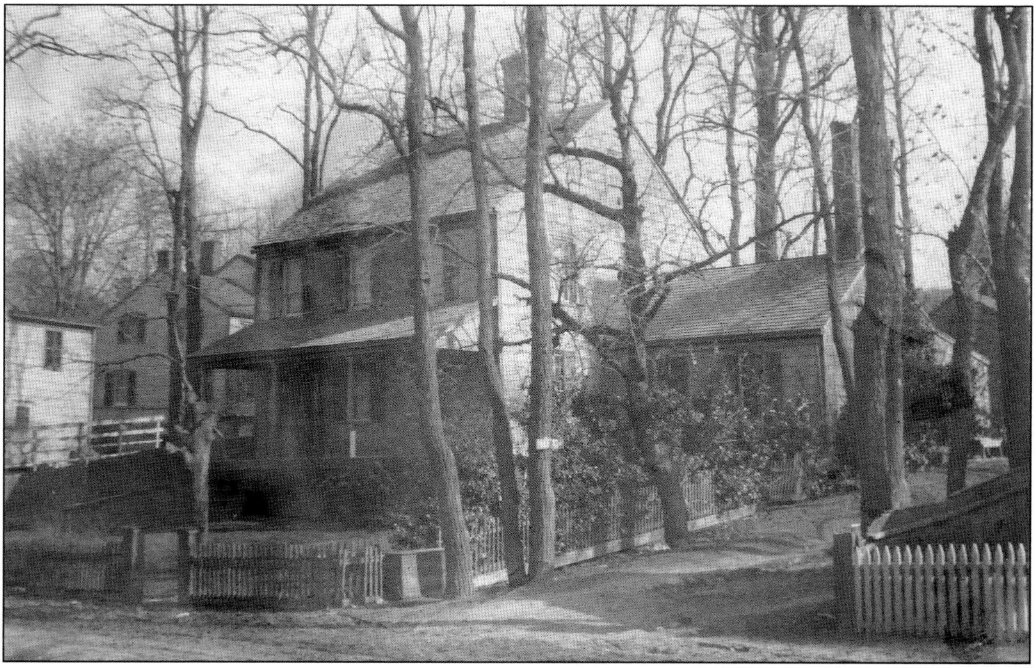

Thomas Bayles, the brother of Elisha, built the smaller, south wing of this house, which still stands at the corner of East Main Street and Vineyard Place, in 1812. It was later occupied by shipbuilder Lewis Hulse. Thomas Bayles is known to have built the sloop *Beaver* in 1816, while Hulse built nine vessels between 1821 and 1855. The building is still known as the 1812 House. (Courtesy of Frances Child.)

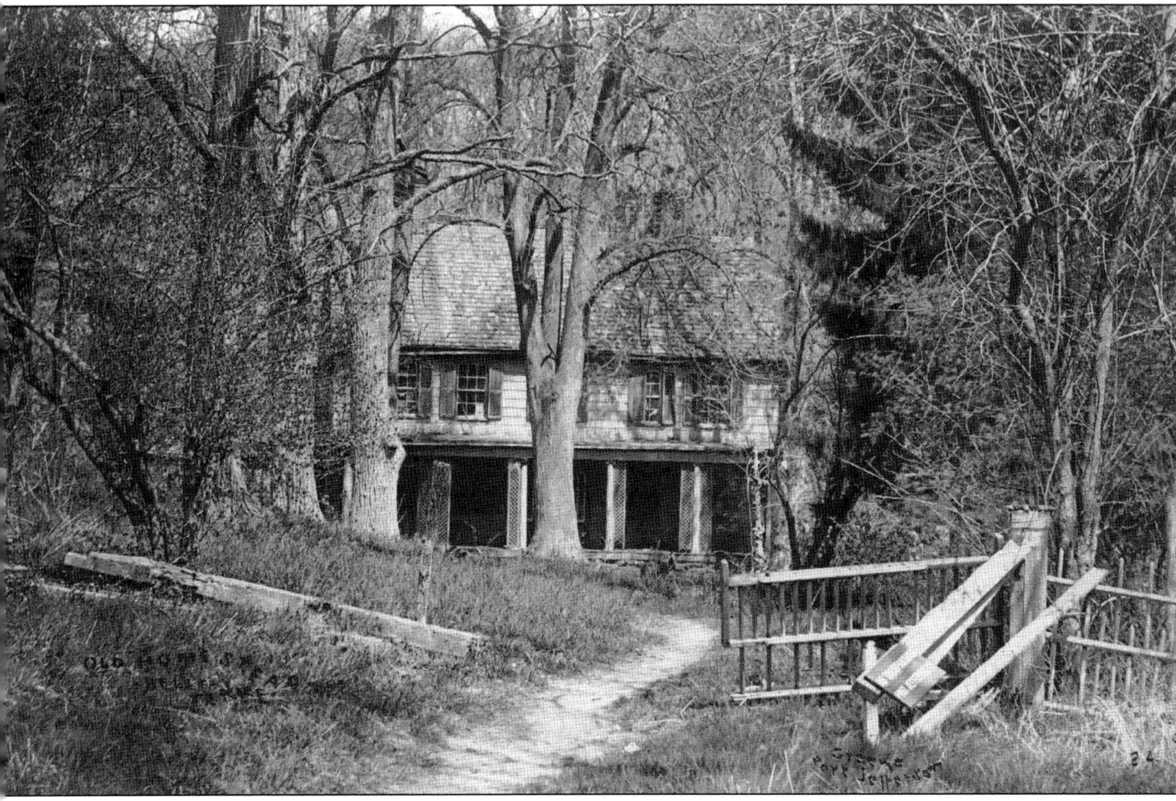

The Strong family came to Mount Misery Neck in 1729 and built this house, known as the Old Homestead, in 1796. It replaced an older house that had been struck by lightning while the family was eating. Fortunately, everyone escaped injury. Their 1,200-acre estate, called Oakwood, was sold to the developers of Belle Terre. After Belle Terre Estates went into receivership, the property was bought by the Seaboard Sand & Gravel Corporation, which, in the 1920s, renovated the house for use as a weekend retreat. It stood approximately at the corner of Winston Drive and Crystal Brook Hollow Road and was destroyed by fire in 1962. Oakwood Road carries on the name of the historic estate.

Two

Down to the Seas

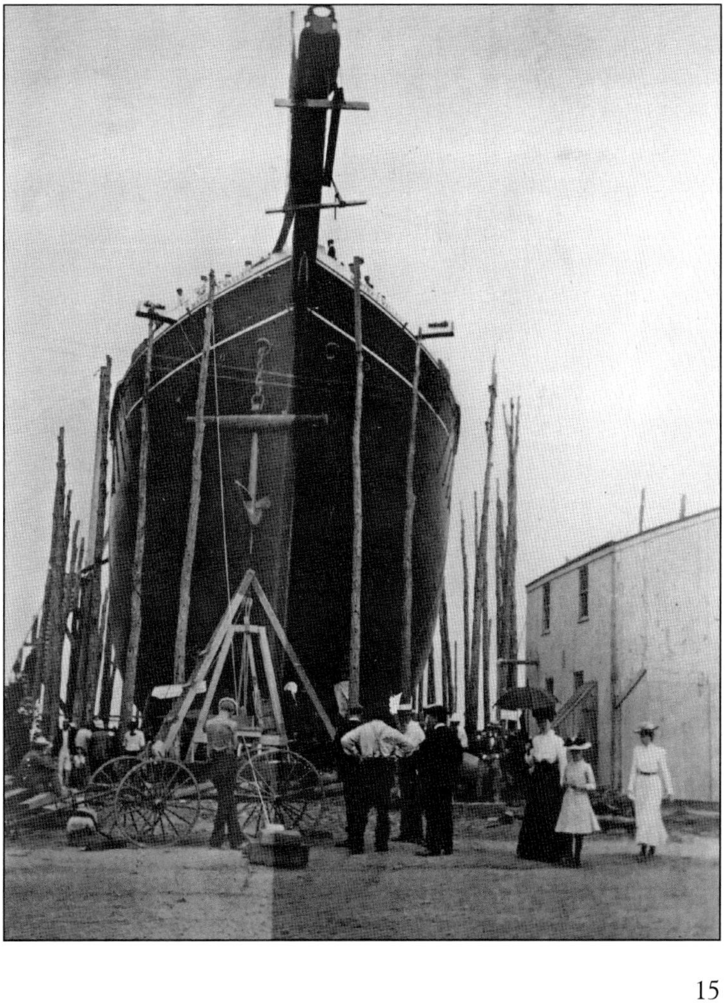

Although the Mather & Wood yard was primarily known for building steamships, it also built the *Martha E. Wallace*, which was not only the largest but also the last of the great schooners built in Port Jefferson. She was 218 feet long, with four masts and 16 sails made at the Wilson Sail Loft. Her 1902 launch was witnessed by 2,000 people. She would run aground in heavy seas eight years later off the coast of North Carolina and be destroyed.

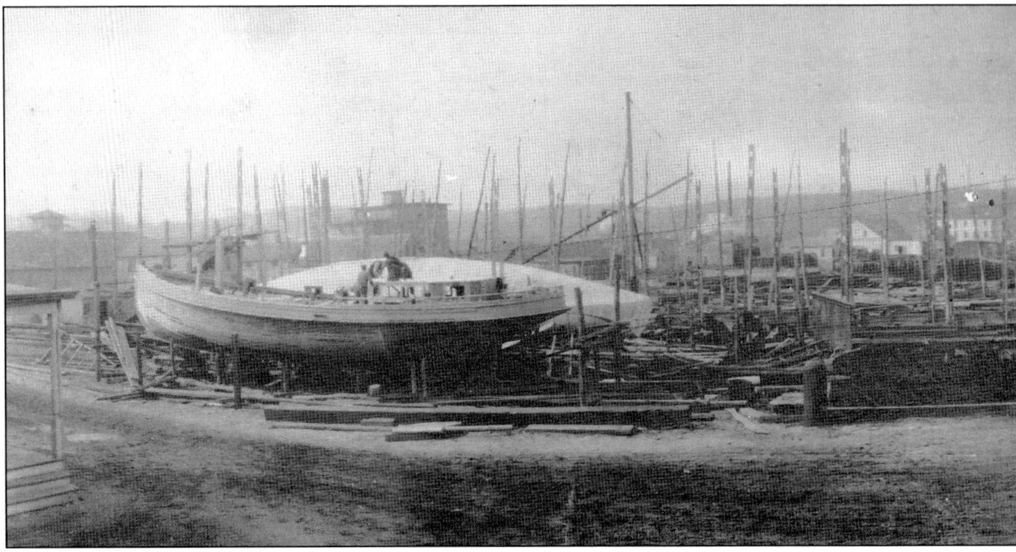

John Titus Mather was the son of shipbuilder John Richard Mather and grandson of Port Jefferson's first shipbuilder, John Willse. Sometime around 1879, he and partner Owen E. Wood built the Mather & Wood yard, shown here around 1890. Located at the foot of Main Street, it was known for rebuilding and overhauling vessels as well as for new construction. Mather's home on Prospect Street now serves as the headquarters and museum of the historical society.

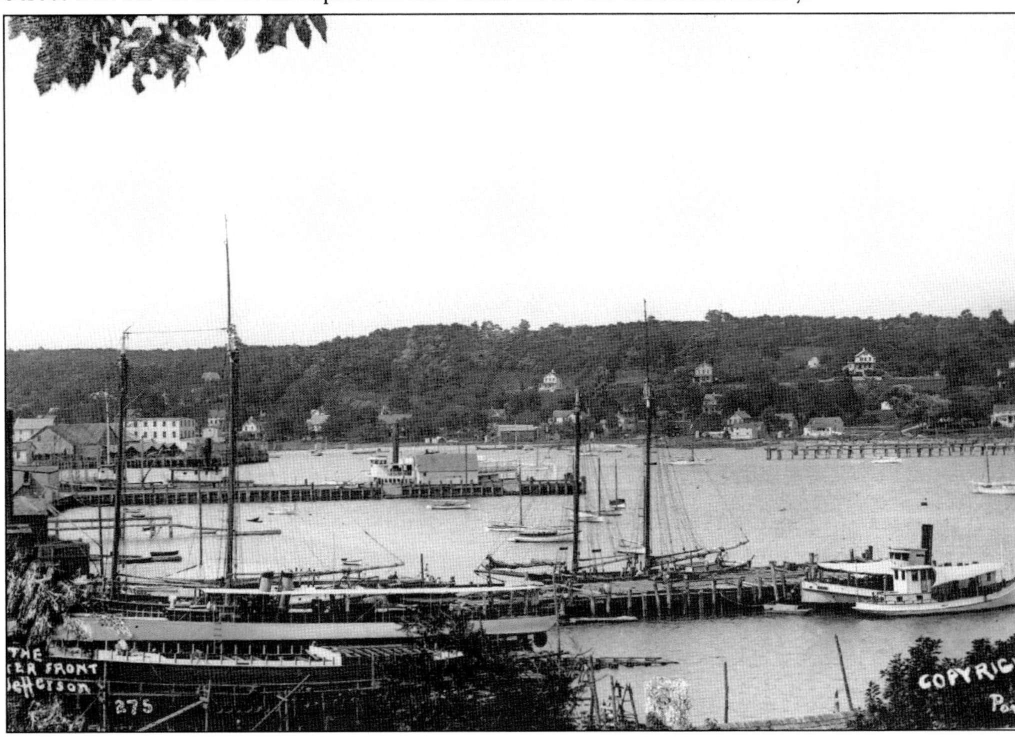

Over 140 wooden seagoing vessels were built at the James M. Bayles & Son Shipyard during its almost 90 years of existence. Among these ships were cargo-hauling schooners, whaling ships, and high-end yachts. The yard was located at the southeast end of the harbor. This c. 1910 view is looking to the west.

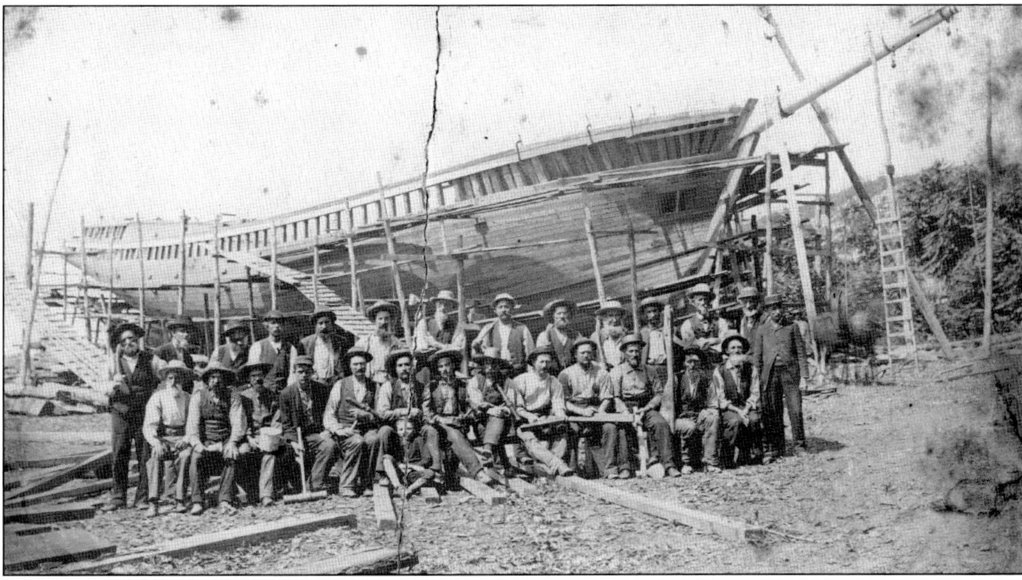

Bayles Shipyard workers pose for a group photograph in front of the hull of the schooner *Nettie Shipman* in 1884. It took an array of skilled artisans, including plankers, carpenters, joiners, caulkers, and adz men (who smoothed and shaved the rough planking), to produce each ship. The Bayles yard had a reputation for excellent workmanship and sound construction.

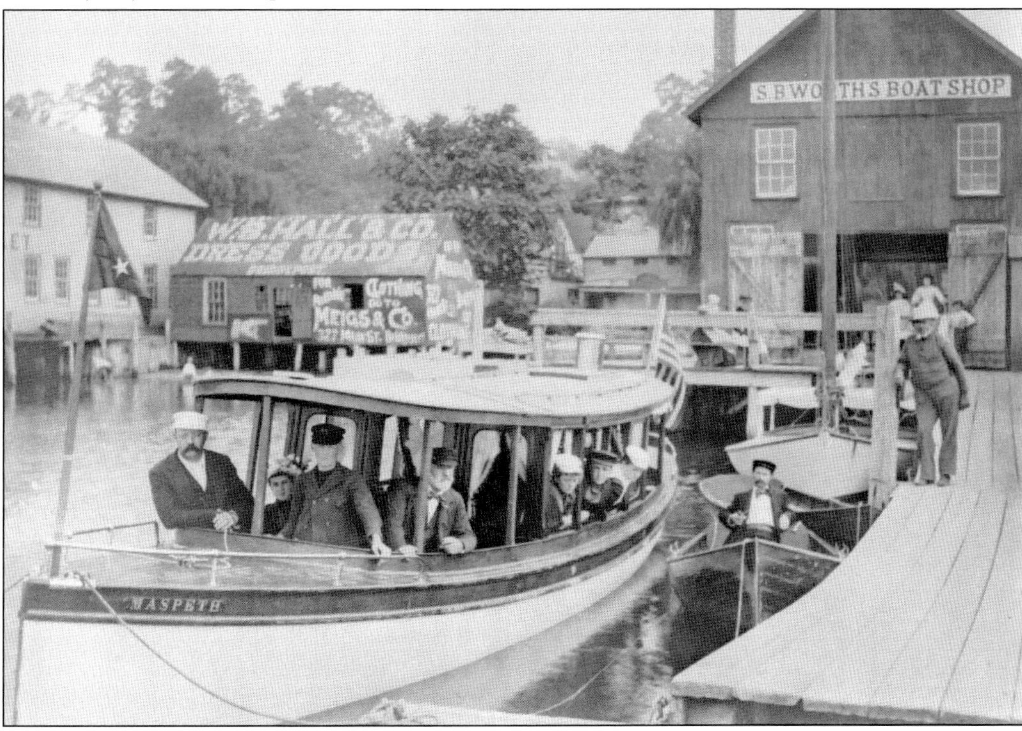

The *Maspeth* sits at its berth in front of Seth Worth's Boat Shop in the late 1800s. Worth was one of the more prominent small boatbuilders in Port Jefferson at the end of the 19th century. He built rowboats, dories, and yawls, to be loaded onto larger vessels and to be used by local fishermen and recreational boaters. (Courtesy of Frances Child.)

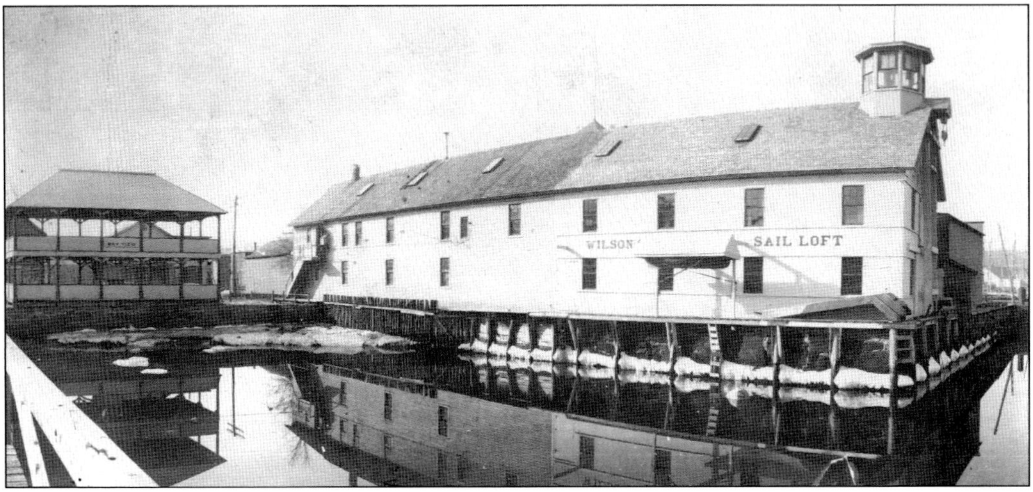

The Wilson Sail Loft (shown above around 1910) was located on the harbor on East Broadway, next to the Bayview Pavilion. Reuben H. Wilson, who founded the company in 1837, developed a vastly improved sail design, shaped like a bird's wing, which caught more wind and generated more speed. The schooner yacht *America,* equipped with Wilson's sails, challenged the best British yachts in 1851 and vanquished them all. The world's foremost yachting competition is still called the America's Cup, in honor of the schooner rigged with Wilson's sails. His desk and tools are on exhibit at the Port Jefferson Historical Society museum. (Both, courtesy of Frances Child.)

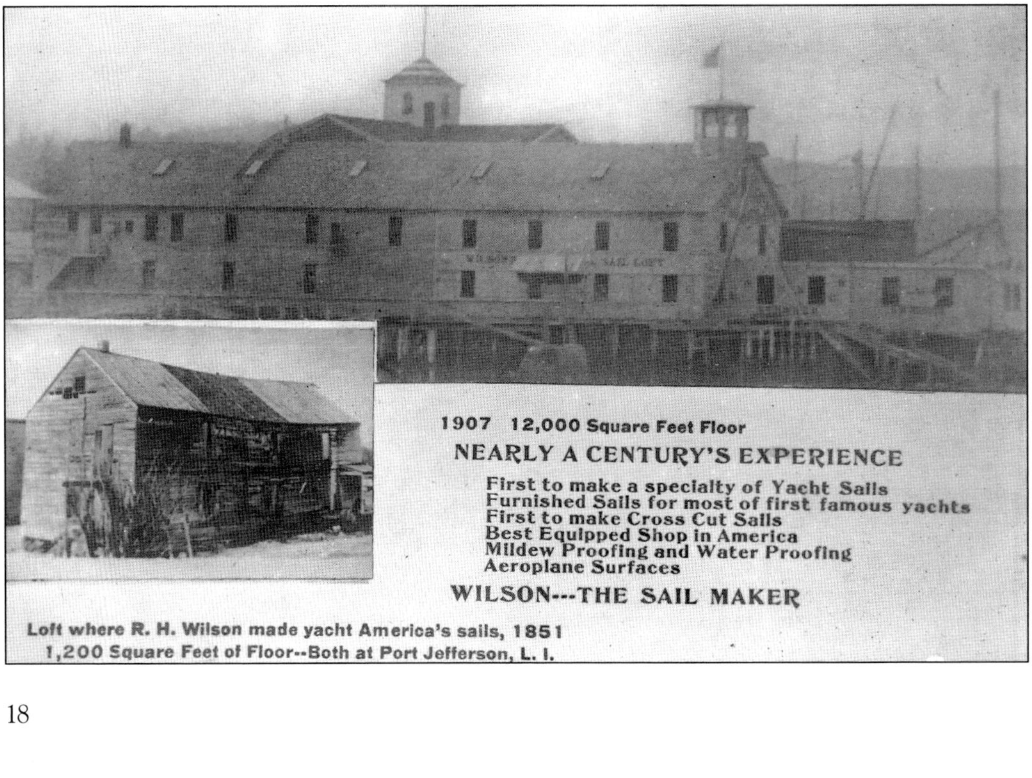

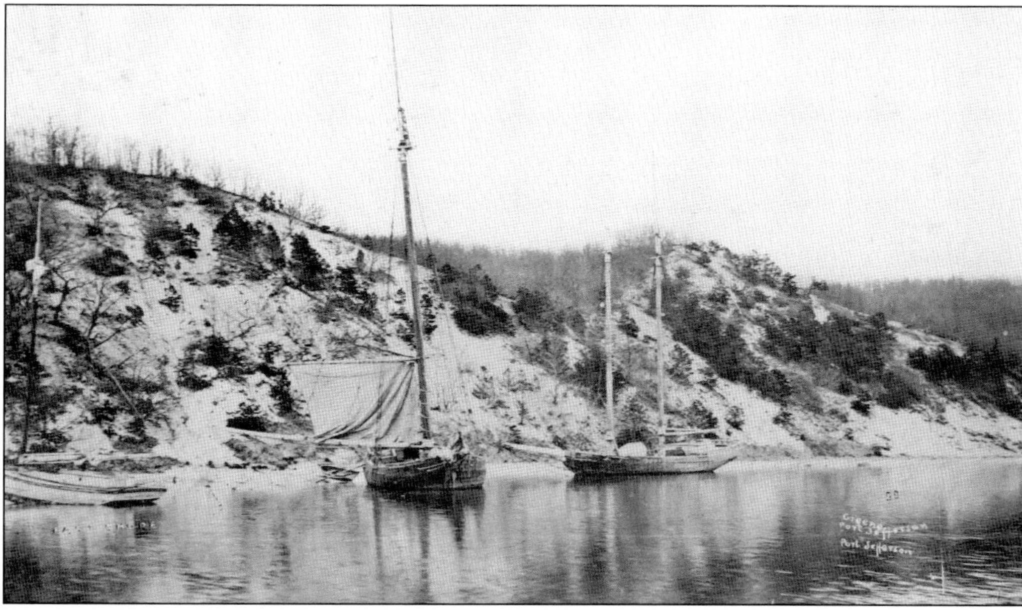

The packet sloop *Emperor* made weekly trips between Port Jefferson and New York City, transporting wood and produce and returning with merchandise for local retailers. James M. Bayles was believed to have gained his early sailing experience as a member of the *Emperor*'s crew. The sloop met her end on the east side of the harbor. Bathers used the remains as a diving platform. (Courtesy of Port Jefferson Free Library.)

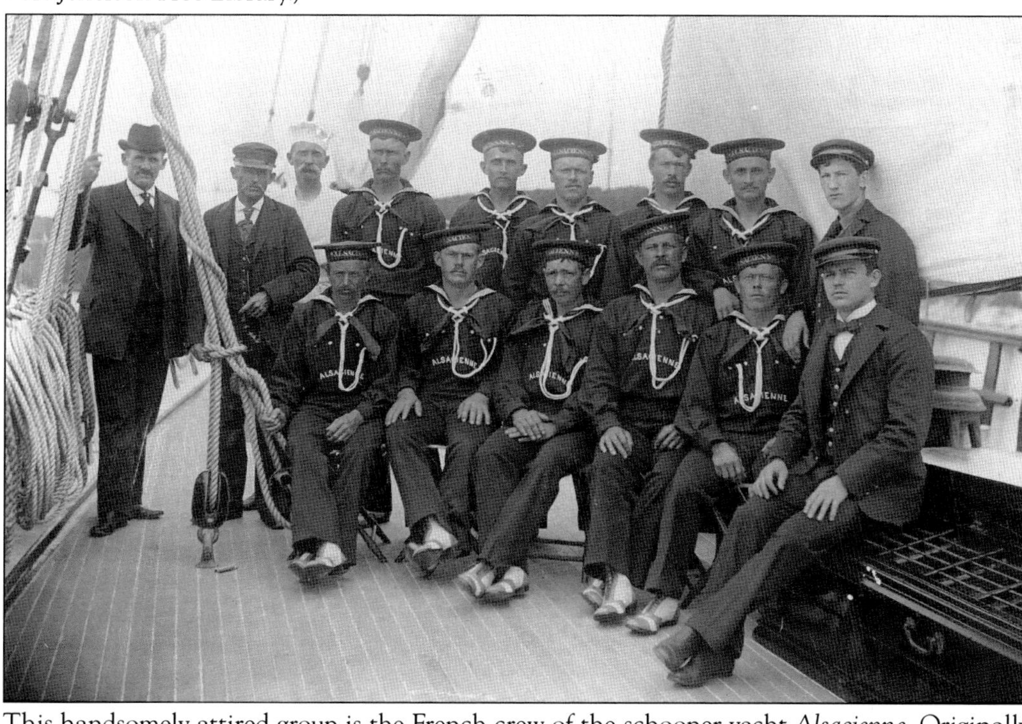

This handsomely attired group is the French crew of the schooner yacht *Alsacienne*. Originally the *Norseman*, the yacht was lavishly fitted out at the Mather & Wood yard in 1895, with Capt. Robert Dayton in command. She sank in a storm in Port Jefferson Harbor in November 1898.

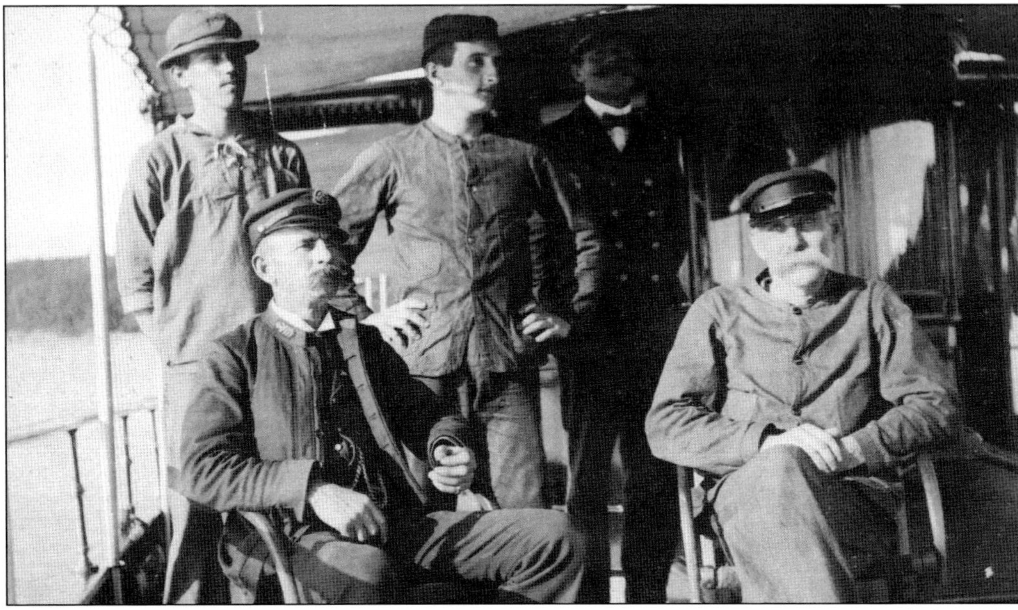

As the wooden shipbuilding industry went into decline, the Bayles yard depended on ship refurbishing in order to remain viable. The steam yacht *Sultana* was replanked, redecked, and had her interior reconstructed by the workers at Bayles in 1904. Pictured at left on the first row is her skipper, Wallace H. Tooker, one of the many skilled yachting captains of Port Jefferson.

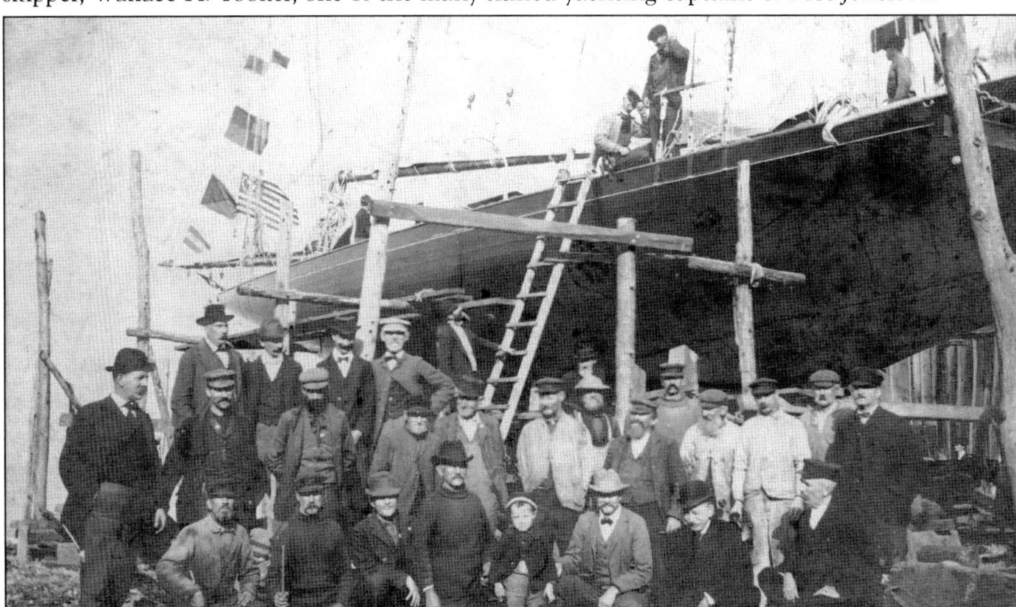

The Bayles Shipyard's expert workmanship was exemplified in the construction of the schooner *Palestine*. Commissioned by the Tinker family, this 100-foot vessel was the epitome of luxury, from her white mahogany-finished cabins to the East India teakwood of the rails, skylights, and deck hatches. Launched in 1904, she sailed the waters of Long Island Sound, the eastern Atlantic, and the West Indies. In the 1930s, she was converted to a fishing vessel. She sank off the coast of Rhode Island in 1956.

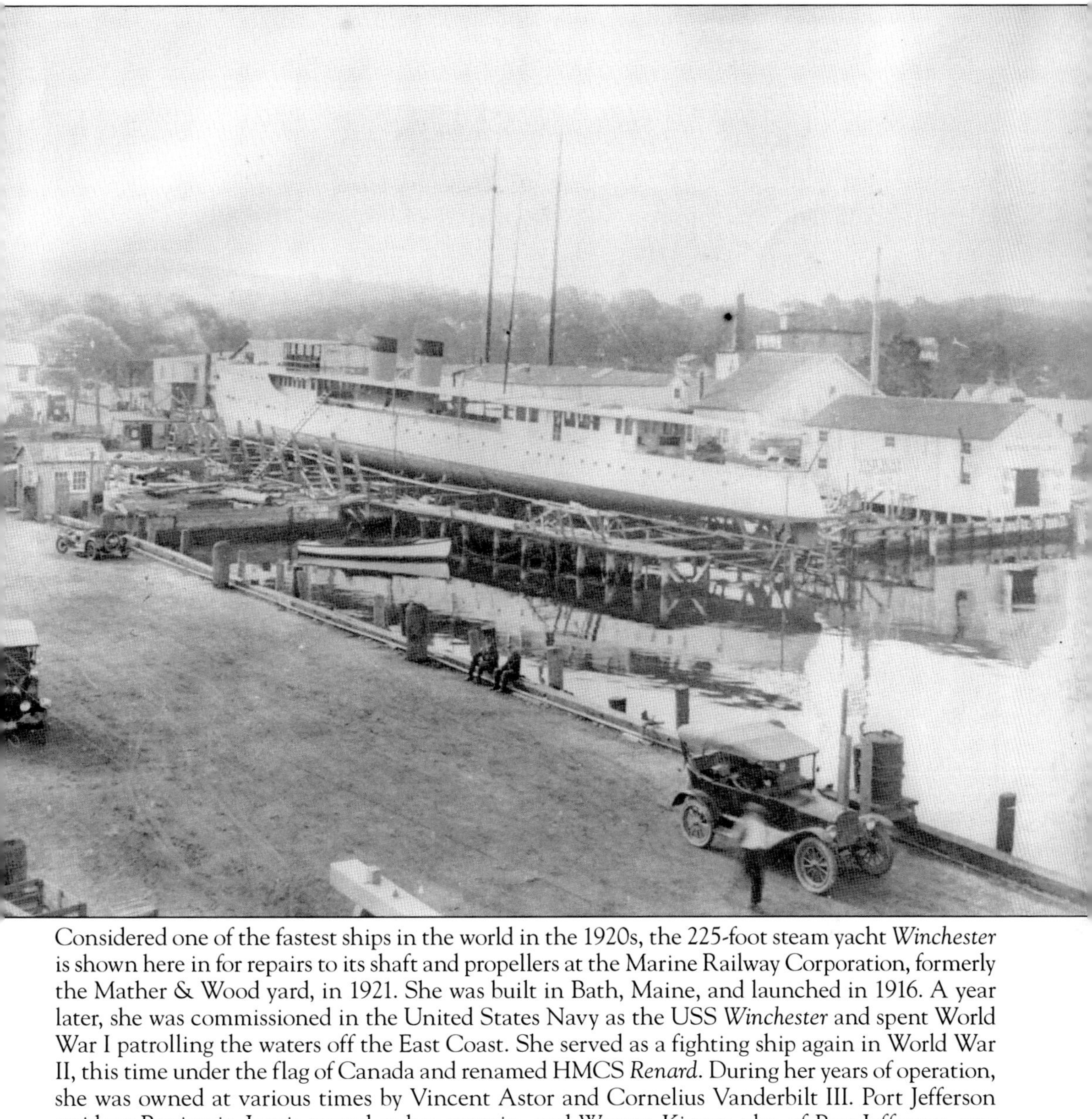

Considered one of the fastest ships in the world in the 1920s, the 225-foot steam yacht *Winchester* is shown here in for repairs to its shaft and propellers at the Marine Railway Corporation, formerly the Mather & Wood yard, in 1921. She was built in Bath, Maine, and launched in 1916. A year later, she was commissioned in the United States Navy as the USS *Winchester* and spent World War I patrolling the waters off the East Coast. She served as a fighting ship again in World War II, this time under the flag of Canada and renamed HMCS *Renard*. During her years of operation, she was owned at various times by Vincent Astor and Cornelius Vanderbilt III. Port Jefferson resident Benjamin Jarvis served as her captain, and Warren Kinsey, also of Port Jefferson, was her chief engineer. (Courtesy of Port Jefferson Free Library.)

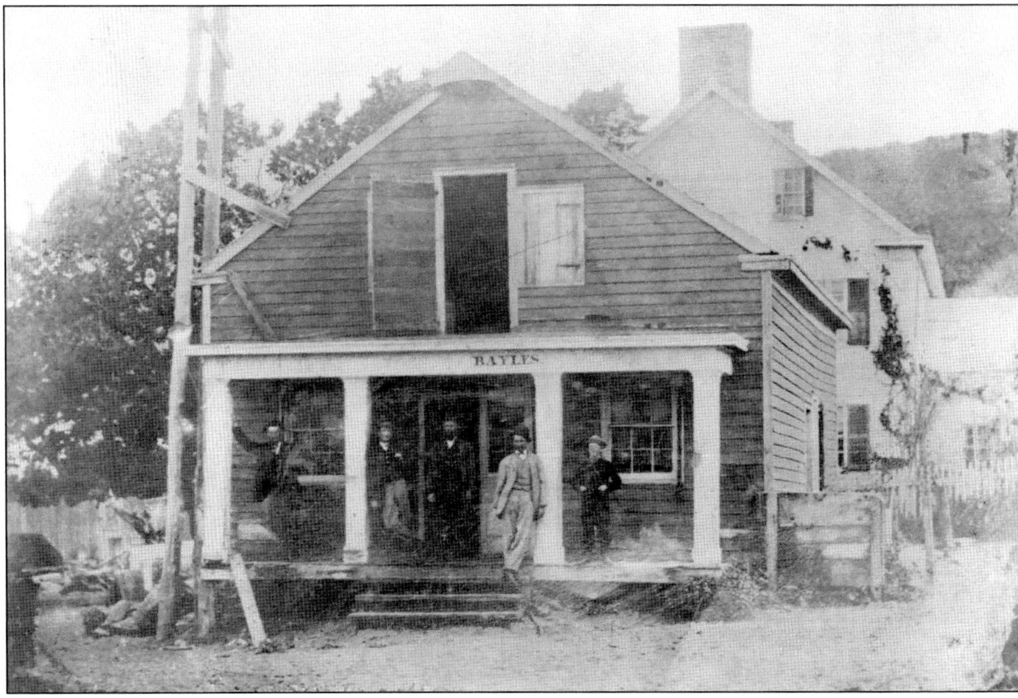

The original Bayles Chandlery was located on East Broadway, immediately west of the Bayles Homestead (seen in the rear). The chandlery was a "retailer of supplies and groceries prepared especially for ships." In later years, it was run by James M. Bayles's third and fourth sons, respectively, George Frank Bayles and Hamilton Tooker Bayles.

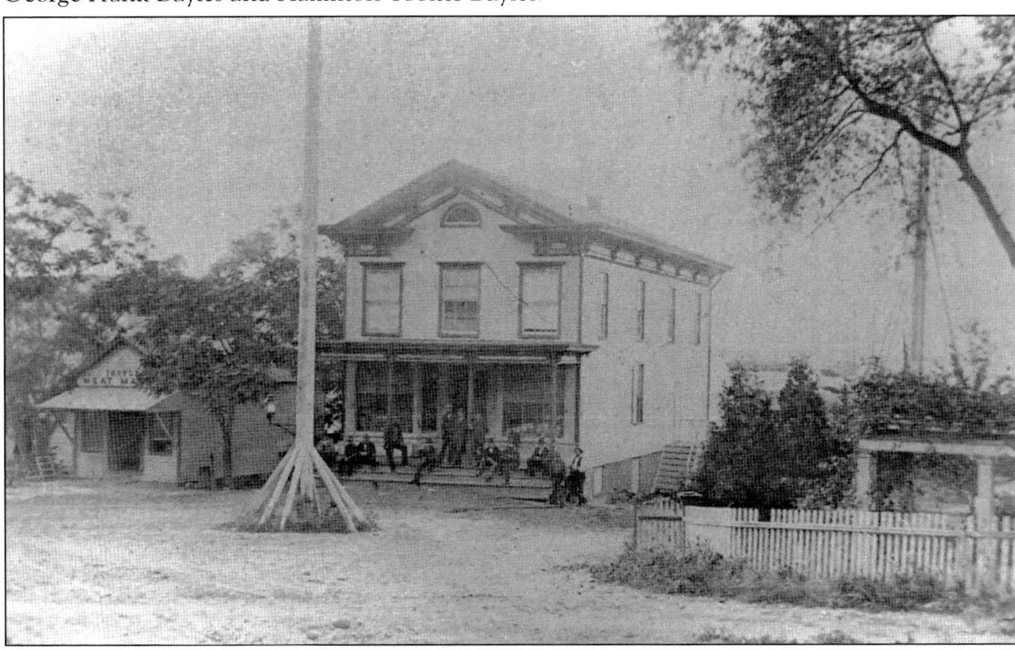

The second incarnation of the chandlery, seen here, was also used as a meeting hall and community center. Built in 1890 to the west of the original chandlery, it burned down in the disastrous fire of July 1897 that destroyed much of the waterfront.

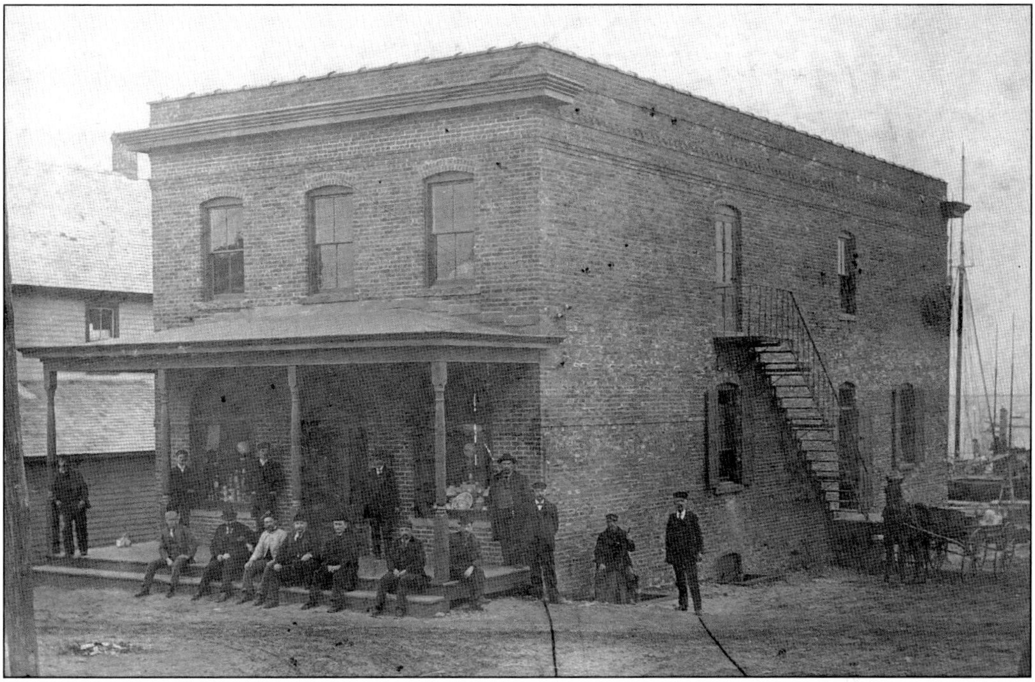

In a wise move, the third chandlery was constructed of brick. After the Bayleses sold the shipyard in 1917, the building served many uses, including as a storage facility, offices for an oil company and a lawyer, and as a local police precinct. It is now the Maritime Explorium.

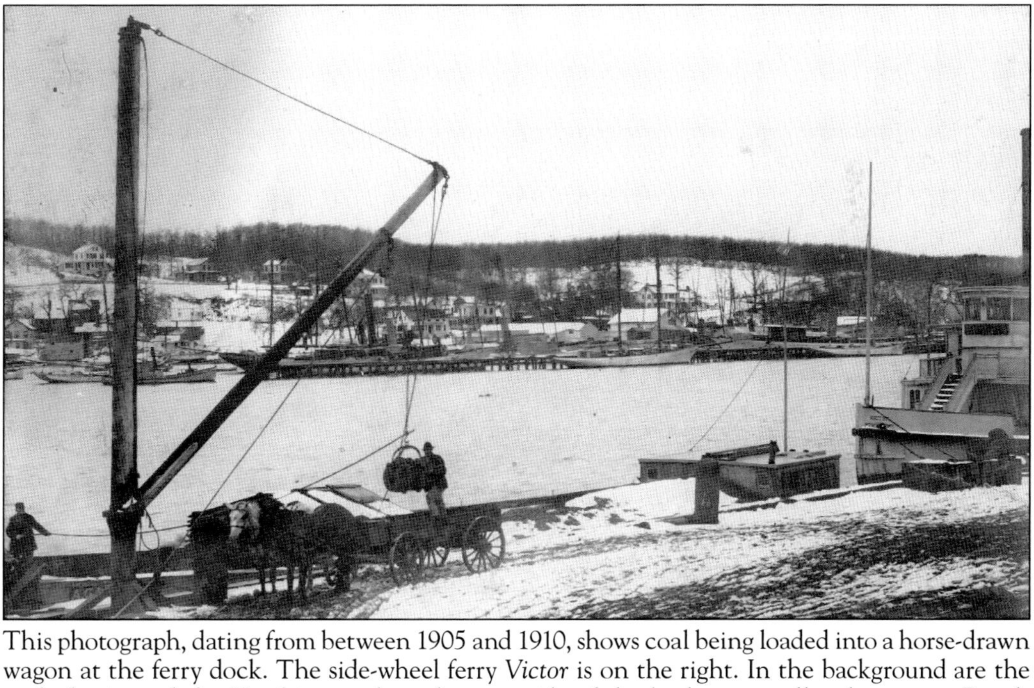

This photograph, dating from between 1905 and 1910, shows coal being loaded into a horse-drawn wagon at the ferry dock. The side-wheel ferry *Victor* is on the right. In the background are the yacht basin and the Hawkins yard on the west side of the harbor, as well as houses on Beach Street and Bayview Terrace.

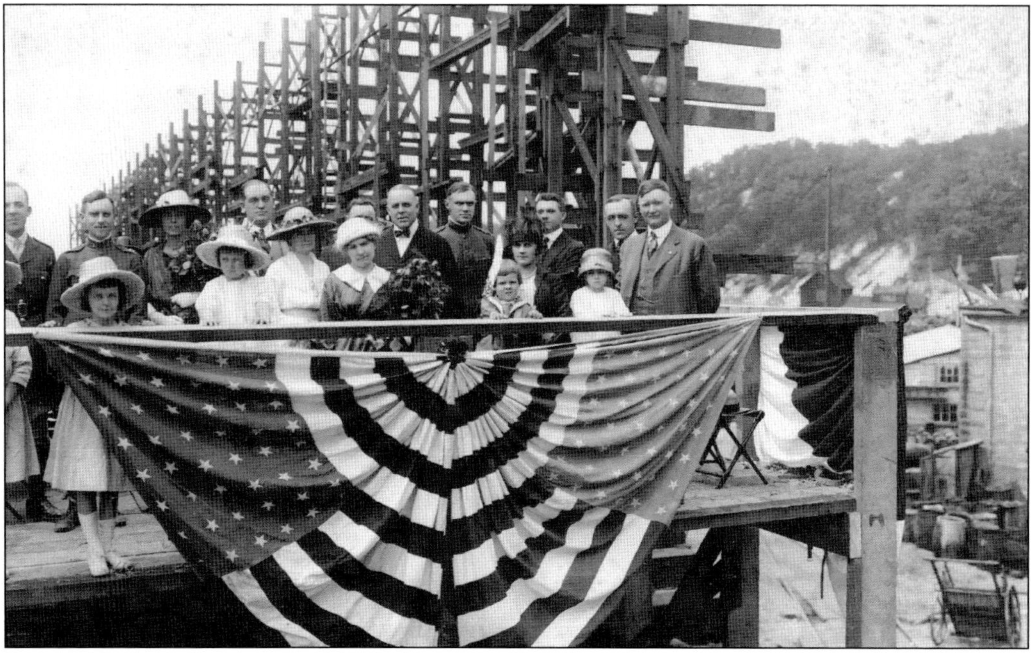

A crowd estimated at 5,000 gathered in Port Jefferson on "Launching Day," Saturday, May 31, 1919, to witness the 1:00 p.m. launching of the oceangoing tug *Bastrop* and the 5,000-ton freighter *Osiris* from the Bayles Shipyard. Nearly $7 million had been invested in the facility by the US Shipping Board since its purchase from the Bayles family. (Courtesy of Port Jefferson Free Library.)

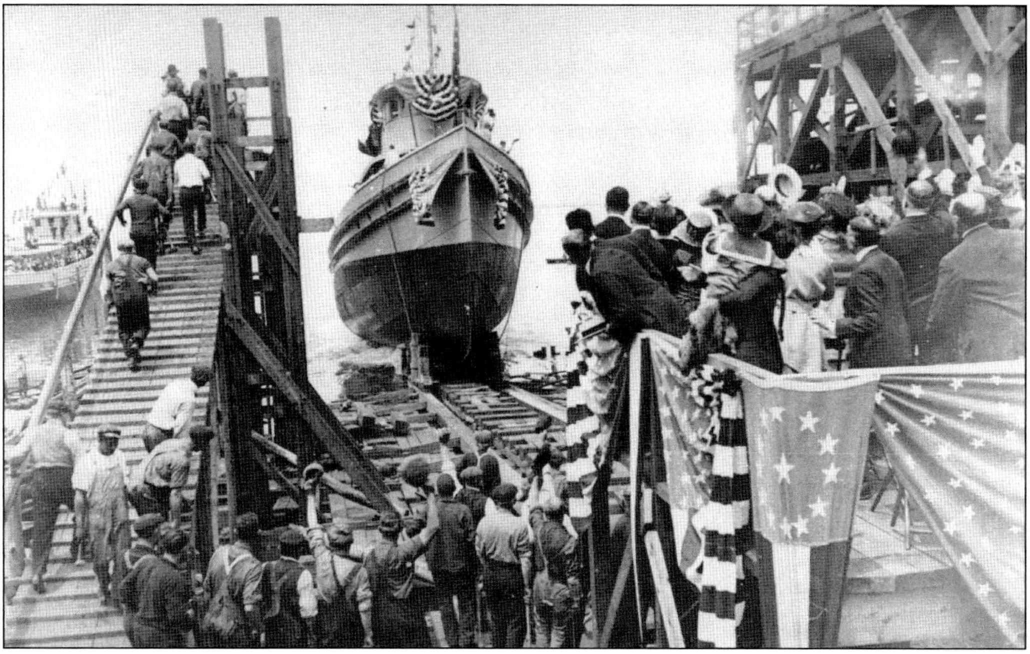

The 150-foot tug *Bastrop* was christened by Mrs. C.R. Dillon, wife of the resident agent in charge of the Bayles Shipyard for the Emergency Fleet Corporation of the US Shipping Board. The *Bastrop* was the sister ship of the *Basswood*, which had been launched in April 1919. In all, eight steel-hulled vessels were built at the shipyard. (Courtesy of Port Jefferson Free Library.)

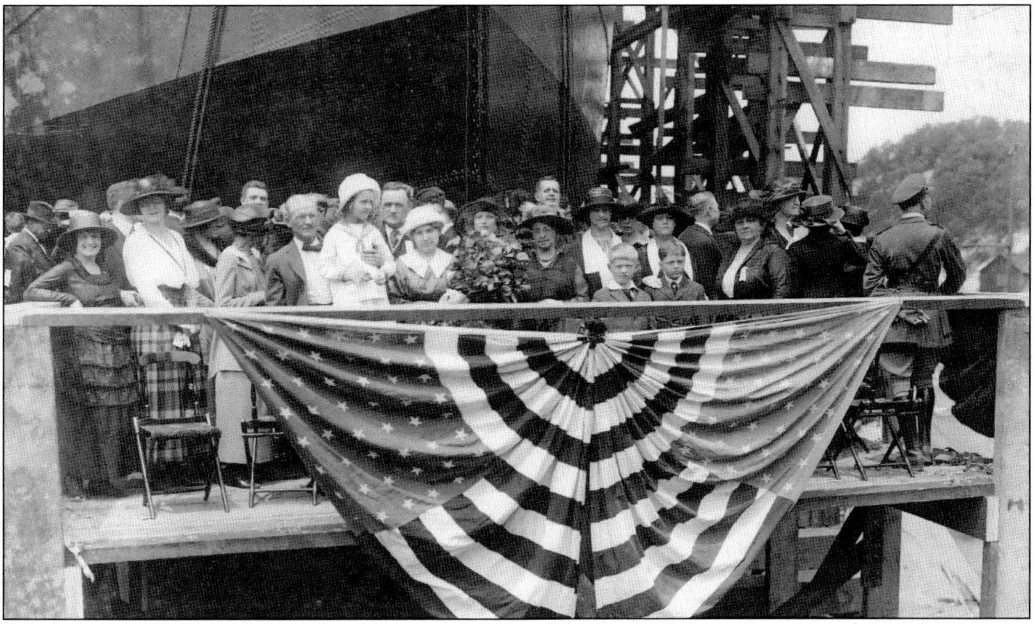

After the *Bastrop* went down the ways, the *Osiris* was christened at 2:30 p.m. by Ruth Magor, wife of Basil Magor, the district manager of the shipping board. The *Osiris*, one of three freighters launched from the Bayles Shipyard in 1919 and 1920, was sold to a Belgian company in 1920 and renamed the *Canonier*. (Courtesy of Port Jefferson Free Library.)

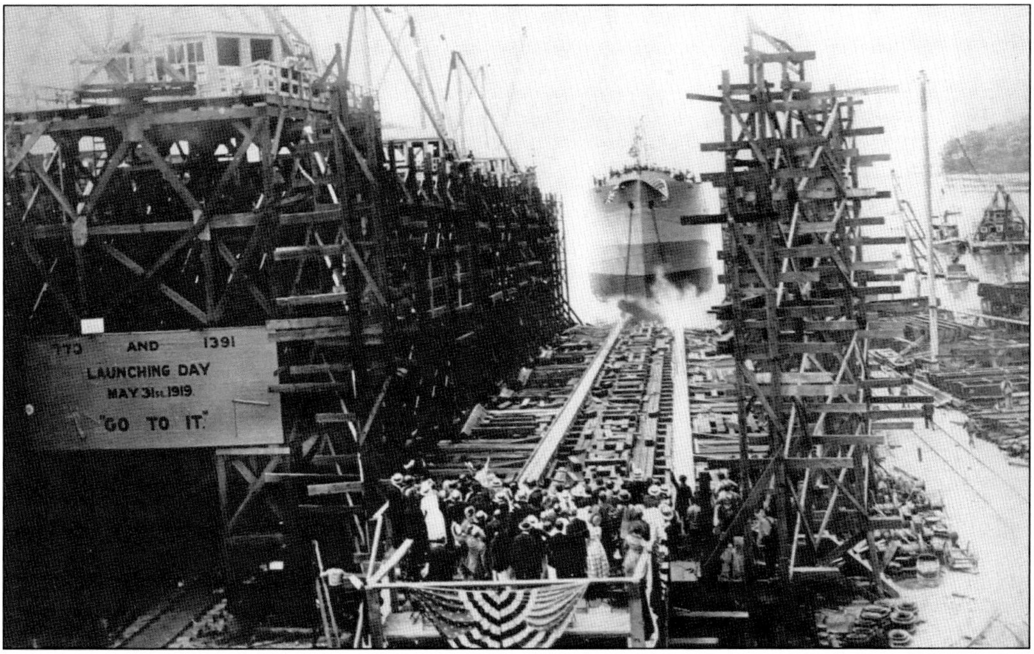

The launchings were accompanied by music from the Bayles Shipyard Band. When the ships hit the water, they received a "tremendous welcome" from the vessels in the harbor and the whistles of the shipyard. The guests, many of whom came from New York City, were invited to inspect the facilities and ask questions of the workers. A reception followed at the Plant Hotel (site of the present-day high school). (Courtesy of Port Jefferson Free Library.)

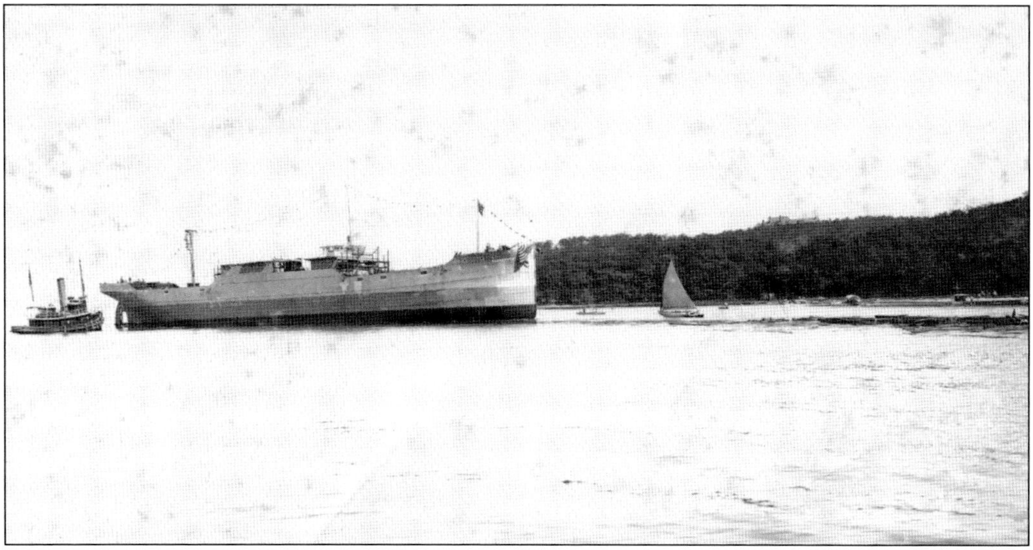

The freighter *Cloverock* was built in the Bayles Shipyard for the US Shipping Board and began service in 1921. After several name changes, it was sailing as the *Mount Taygetus* in September 1942 as part of a convoy headed to Great Britain when it was sunk by a German U-boat. (Courtesy of Port Jefferson Free Library.)

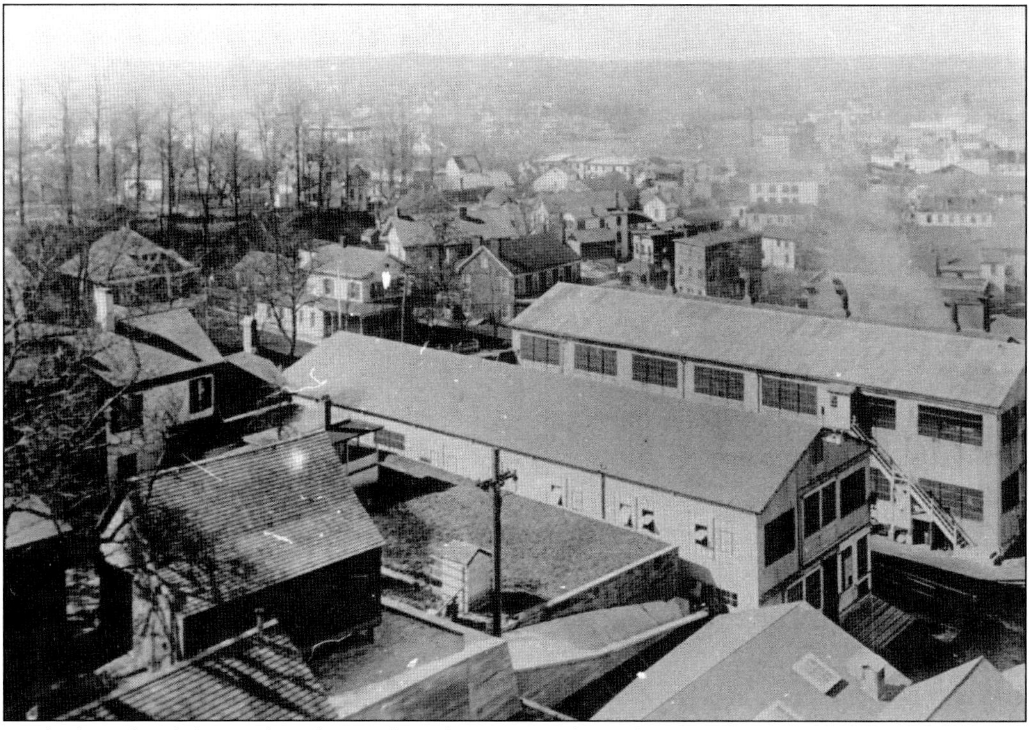

With the sale of the Bayles Shipyard to the New York Harbor & Dry Dock Company in April 1920, shipbuilding in Port Jefferson effectively came to an end. The new company soon found that the changes made to the shipyard by the shipping board rendered it unsuitable, and in 1923, it was sold to the Standard Oil Company, which demolished all of the buildings except the one on the far right. (Courtesy of Port Jefferson Free Library.)

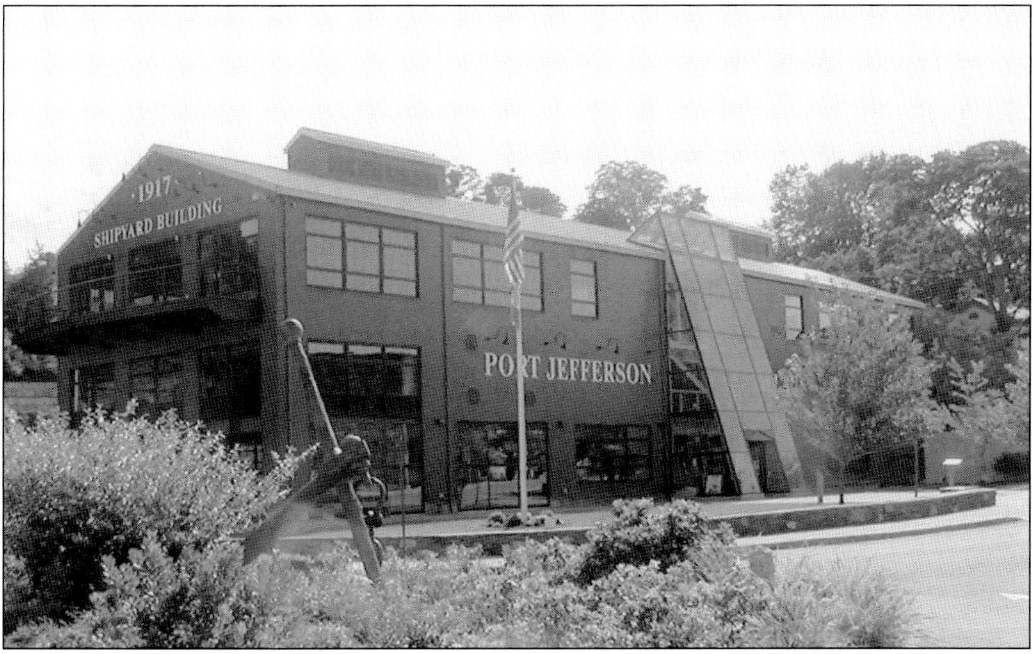

When the village purchased the oil tank property from Mobil in 1997, there was debate over the fate of the rusting corrugated steel building. Some considered it an eyesore and thought it should be demolished, but others saw its potential. The $2.5 million renovation began in December 2003, and the result, now known as the Port Jefferson Village Center, has become the "center" of the community. (Courtesy of Port Jefferson Free Library.)

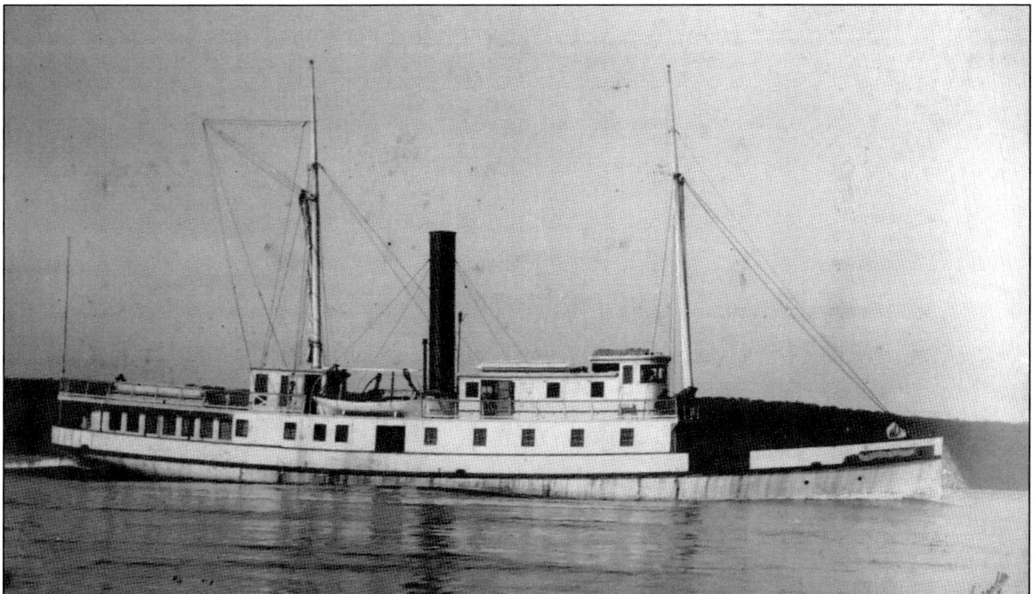

This view shows the ferry *Nonowantuc* icebound in Port Jefferson Harbor. Built at the Mather & Wood yard, she served the Bridgeport & Port Jefferson Steamboat Company from 1883 (the year of its founding) until 1902. Capt. Charles Tooker and his brother-in-law Capt. Elbert M. Davis organized the company, and circus impresario P.T. Barnum was one of the original stockholders.

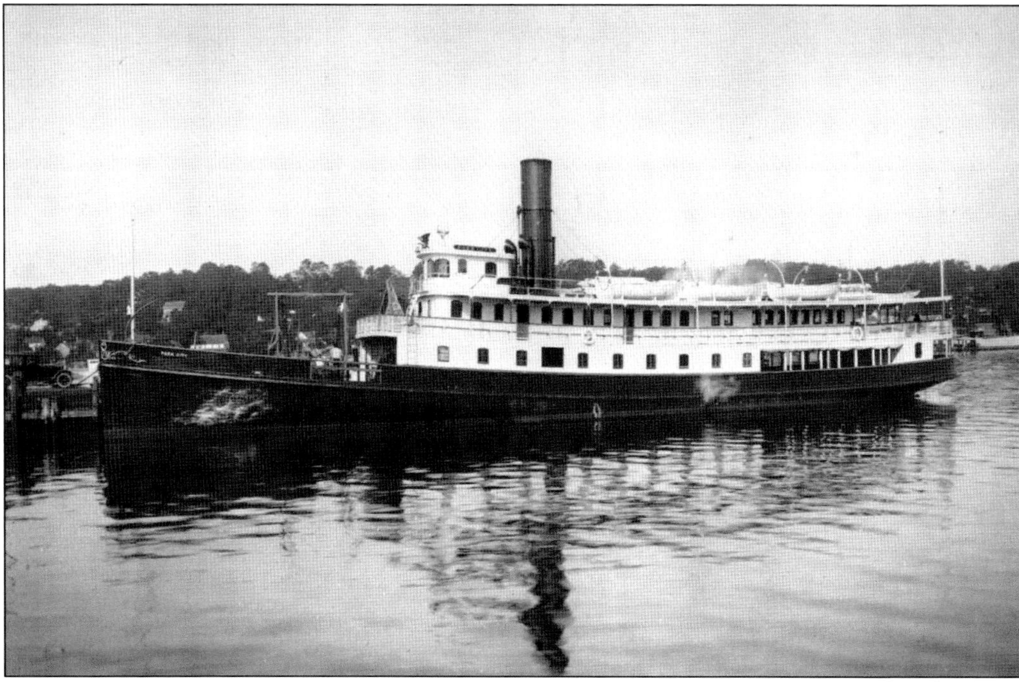

The ferry with the longest service was the *Park City*, built in the Mather & Wood yard in 1898. She survived the 1938 hurricane, but after she was finally sold in 1949, she sank in a storm off the coast of New Jersey on her way to Louisiana. The present *Park City* carries on the name.

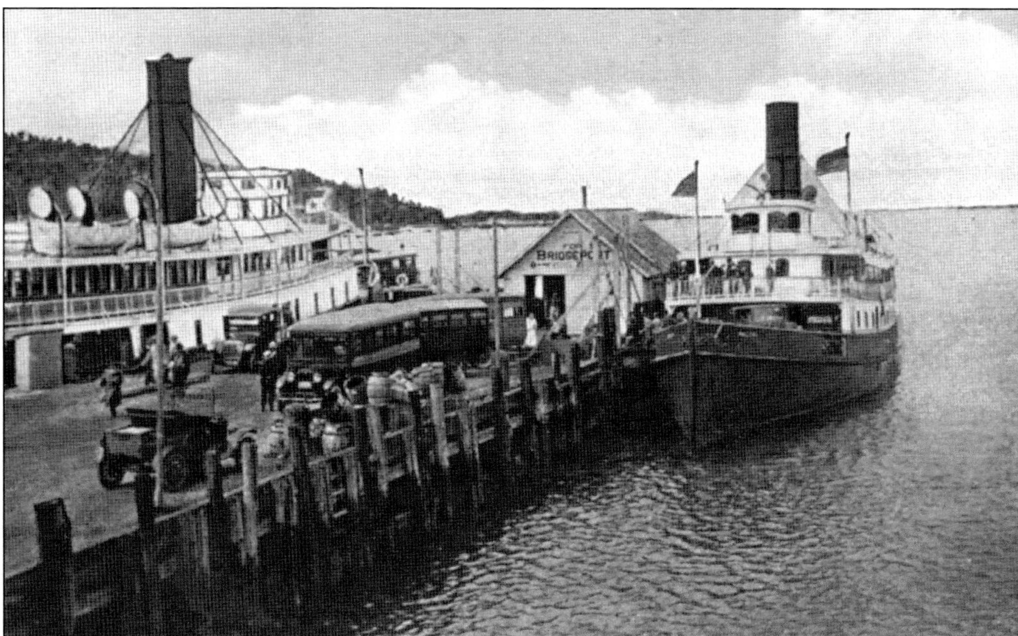

The *Long Island* (left) and the *Park City* are seen here. Christened after Bridgeport's nickname, the *Park City* acquired a nickname of her own, "The Lady of Long Island Sound." As the automobile gained a more prominent role, the *Park City* underwent a refurbishing. A turntable was installed in the fantail to ease the loading and unloading of cars.

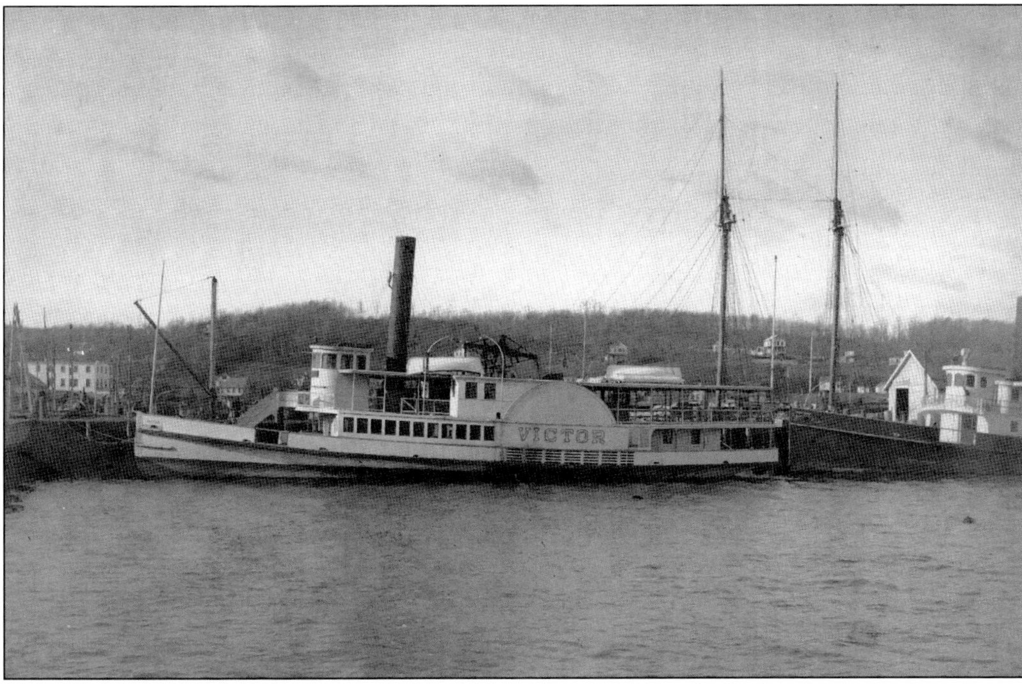

The side-wheeler *Victor* was part of the fleet from 1905 to 1910. She had a previous existence as a US Navy vessel, the USS *John L. Lockwood*, patrolling the waters off the Southern coast during the Civil War. She is shown here docked at Steamboat Landing.

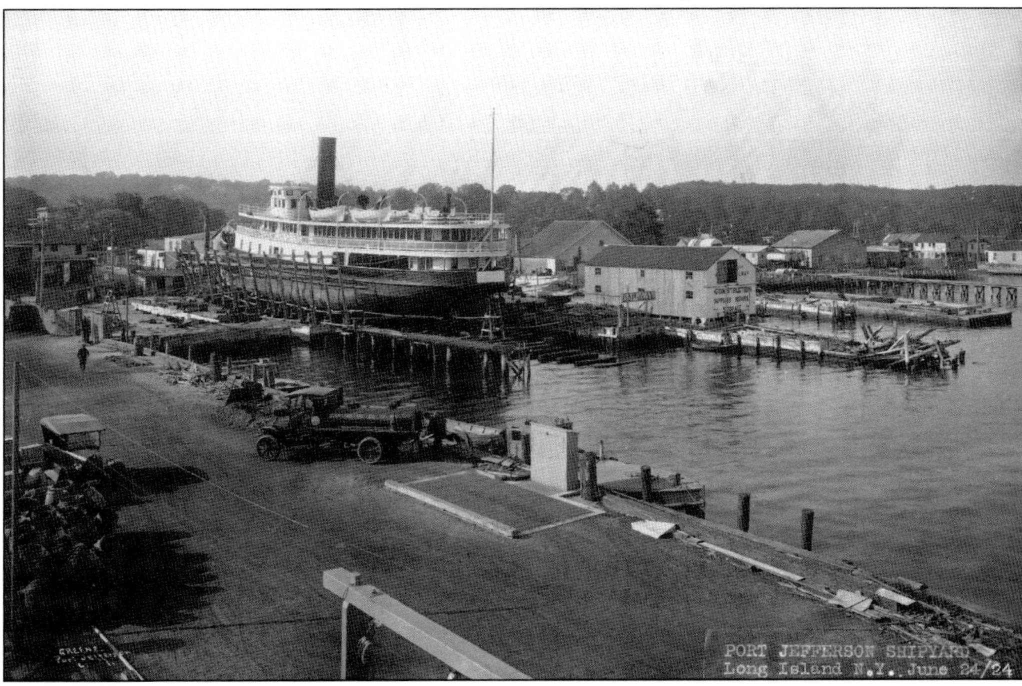

The steam-powered ferry *Long Island*, a former New York City prison ship, alternated trips between Port Jefferson and Bridgeport with the *Park City* from 1924 to 1936. She is pictured here in dry dock in June 1924 at the Port Jefferson Shipyard, the former Mather & Wood yard.

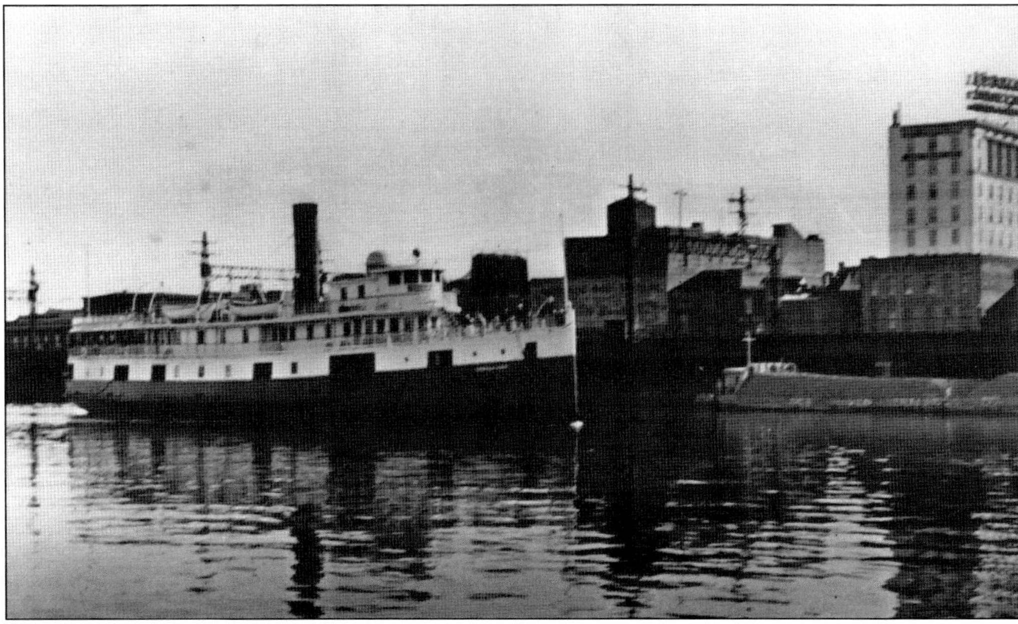

The *Priscilla Alden* was part of the ferry fleet from 1936 to 1946, alternating with the *Park City*. She is shown here in Bridgeport Harbor. The wooden hull of this vessel now lies submerged in the shallow waters of Mount Misery Cove.

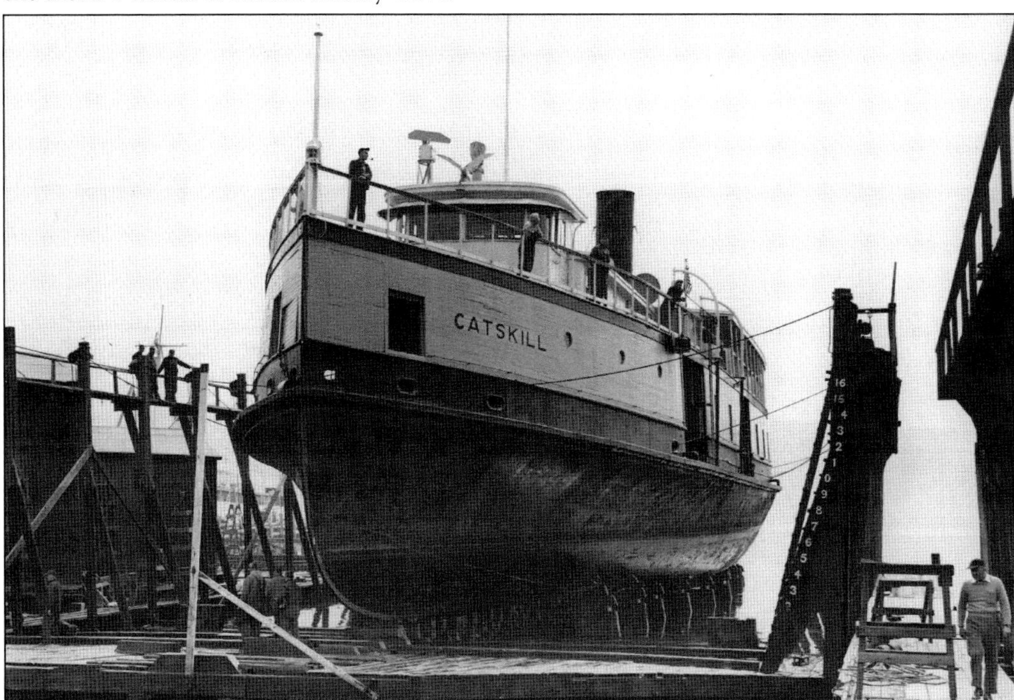

Shown here in dry dock, the steel-hulled and steam-powered *Catskill* served from 1946 to 1967. It had previously operated as a freighter on the Hudson River, and then ferried passengers between Orient Point, Long Island, and New London, Connecticut. After being sold in 1967, it was abandoned in Jamaica Bay and scrapped in 1975.

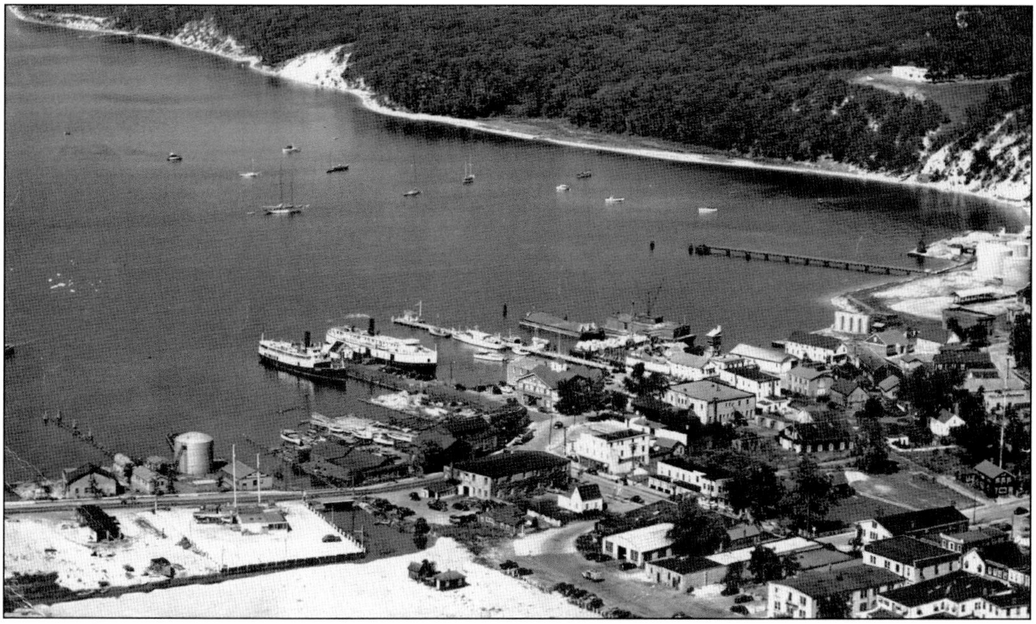

The *Park City* (left) and the *Catskill* are docked in this 1948 aerial photograph of the harbor. Main Street is the thoroughfare running diagonally down the center from the harbor to the lower right. Newcomb Brothers Garage, with the cupola, sits just to the right of the ferries. Teddy's Hotel is the white building just below the garage at the corner of Main Street and East Broadway. Note the oil storage tanks on the right.

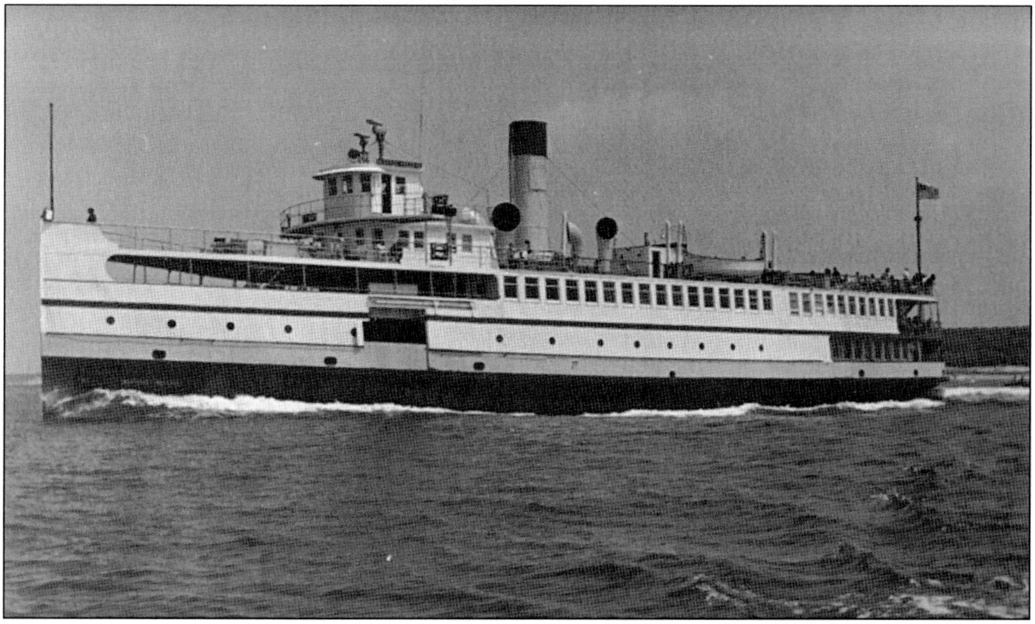

The *Martha's Vineyard* was launched from Bath, Maine, in 1923 to serve the Massachusetts islands. Converted from steam to diesel in 1959, she was bought by the ferry company in 1968 and served until 1985. Plans to reconvert the power plant to steam for excursion service in Massachusetts fell through, as did plans to use her for dinner cruises in Boston Harbor. The venerable vessel was docked at the Charlestown Navy Yard in Boston when she sank in 1990. She was then scrapped.

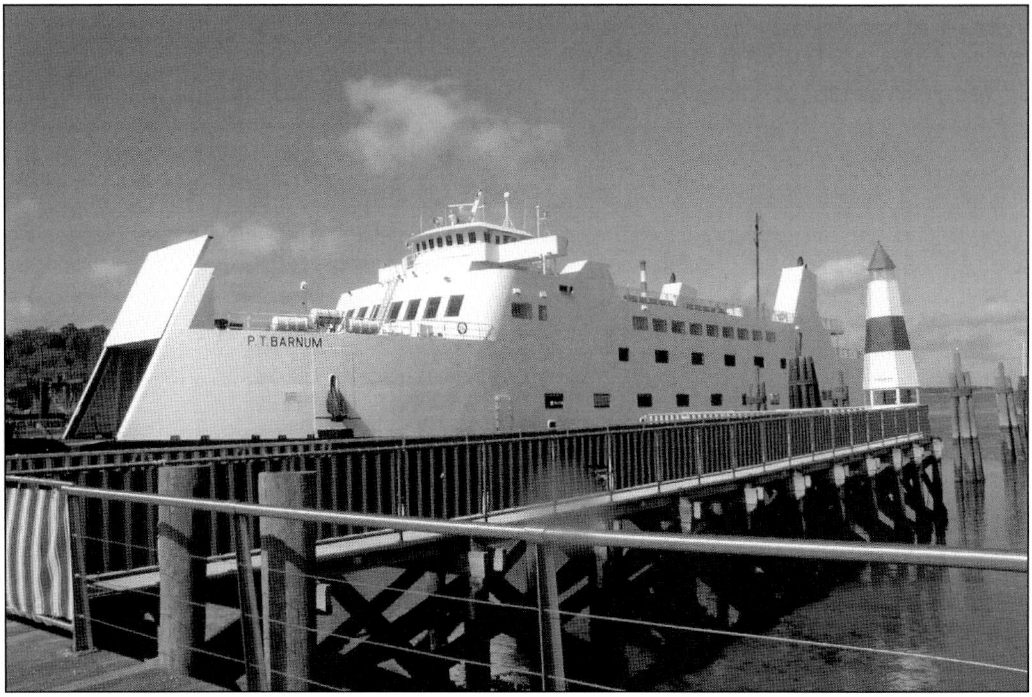

The *P.T. Barnum*, named in honor of the famous showman who served as the first president of the ferry company, began service in 1999. She is 300 feet long and is capable of holding 120 vehicles and 1,000 passengers. The *Park City* (1986) and the new *Grand Republic* (2003) ferries round out the current fleet. (Courtesy of Port Jefferson Free Library.)

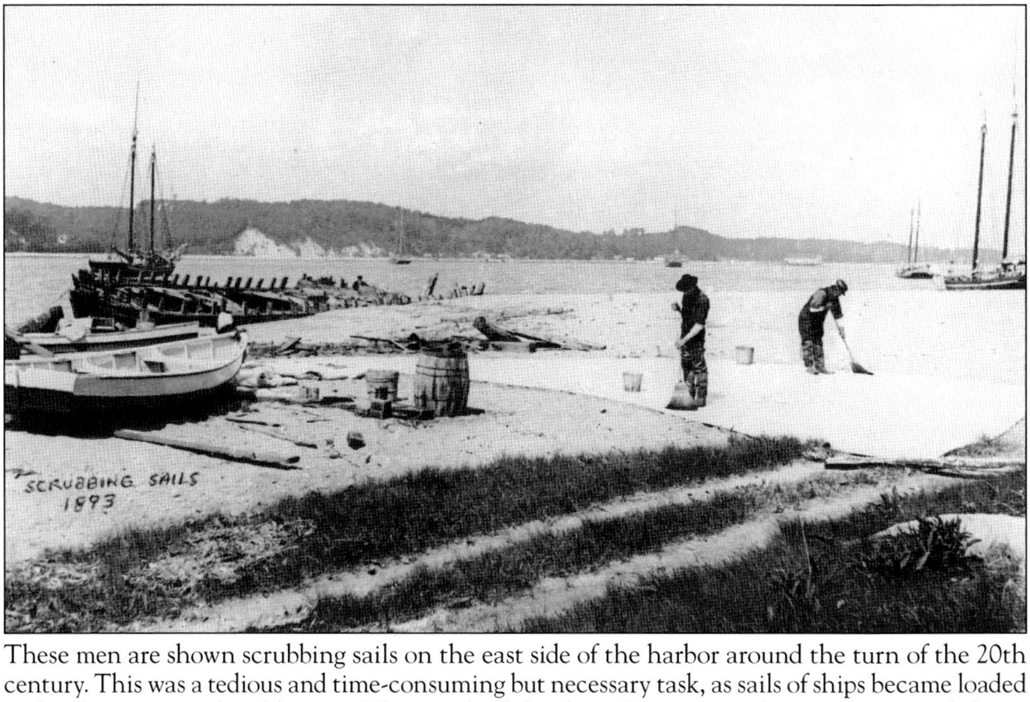

These men are shown scrubbing sails on the east side of the harbor around the turn of the 20th century. This was a tedious and time-consuming but necessary task, as sails of ships became loaded with salt, grime, and mold stains. The wreck of the sloop *Emperor* can be seen at center left.

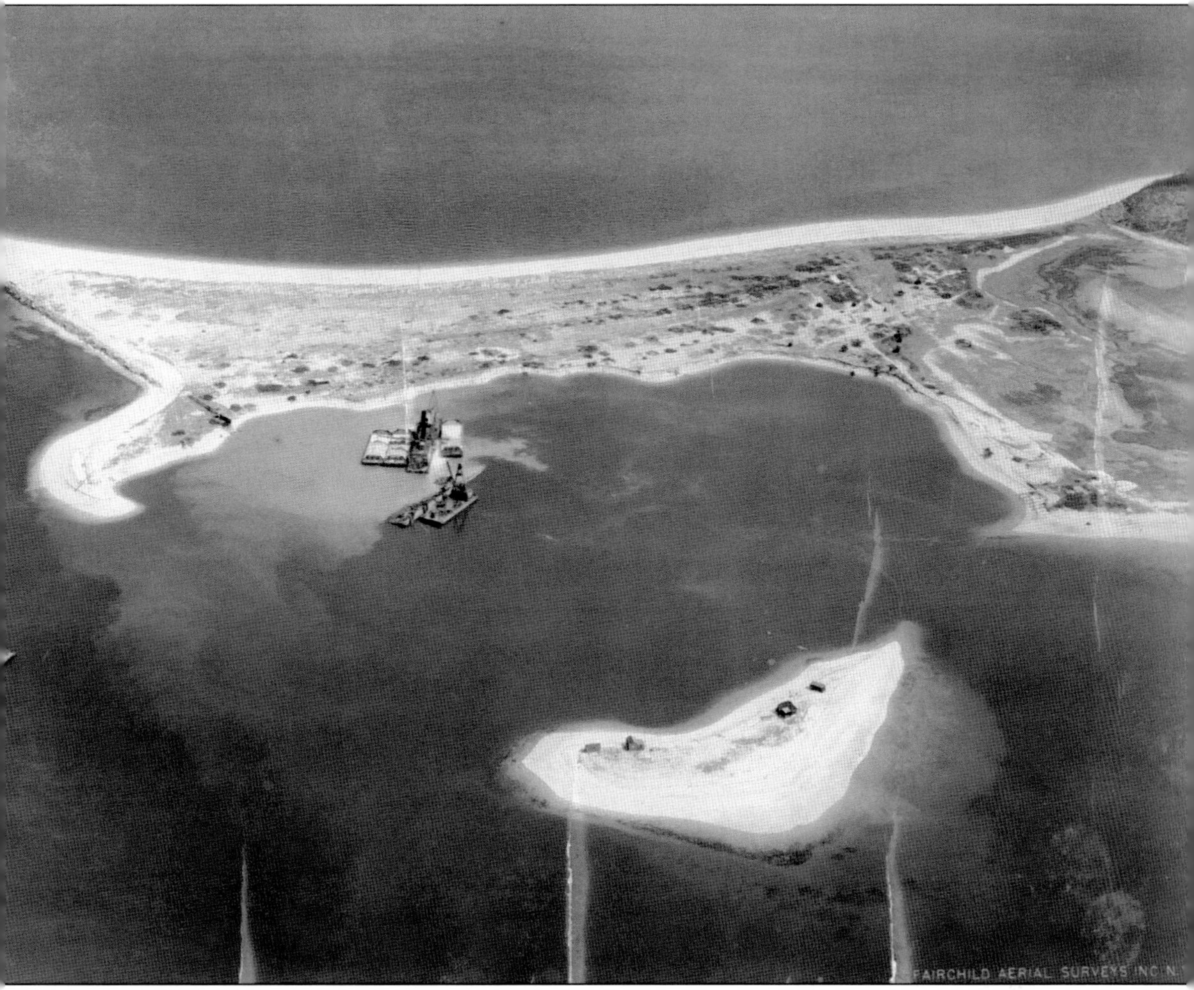

The mining and dredging of sand and gravel, which supplied materials for construction, roofing, iron smelting, glassmaking, sandpaper, and roads, started in Port Jefferson Harbor around the turn of the 20th century. At the industry's peak in the 1920s and 1930s, as shown in this photograph, three gravel companies with four dredges operated in the harbor. Unloading docks were also a feature of Port Jefferson throughout the 20th century, on the west side of the harbor and even in the heart of the village. Although the industry supplied employment at a time when shipbuilding on a large scale had ended, it was never without controversy. Large parts of Mount Misery Neck and Strong's Neck were gouged out by the dredgers, and many felt that the dredging companies had too cozy a relationship with the Brookhaven town trustees (the companies paid nothing for the sand and only 5¢ a yard for the gravel). A desire to expel the dredging companies was in large part responsible for the incorporation of Belle Terre.

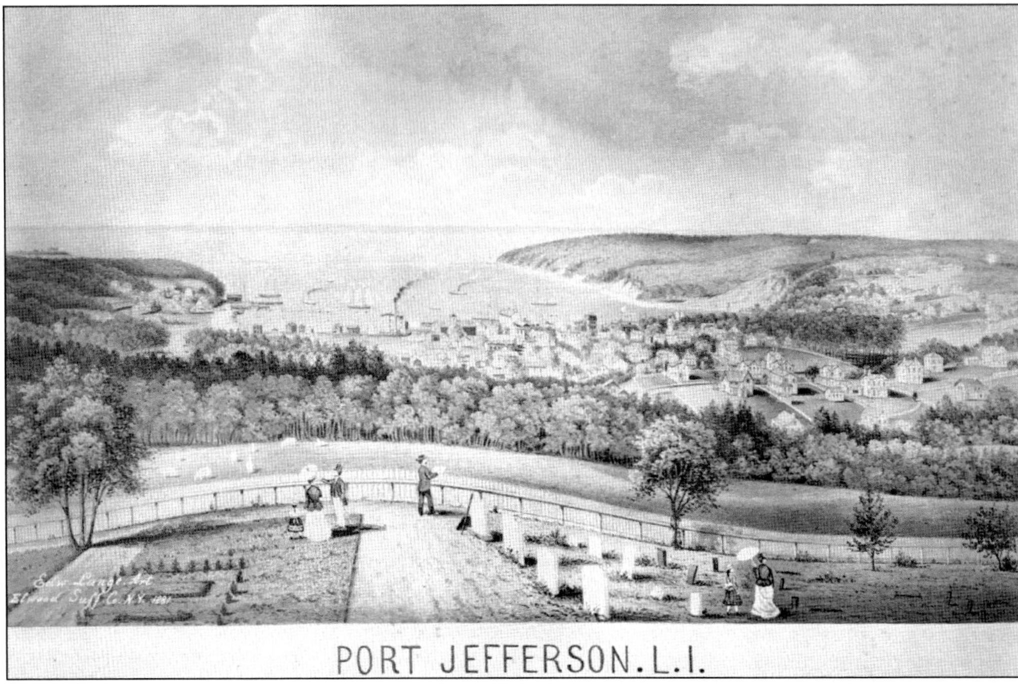

This 1881 drawing by noted Long Island artist Edward Lange depicts a group of well-dressed people enjoying the view of Port Jefferson Harbor from Cedar Hill Cemetery, which had been established in 1859. Among the buildings on the waterfront, the flour mill with the smokestack (on the left) and the American House hotel, the three-storied building with a mansard roof (to the right), stand out.

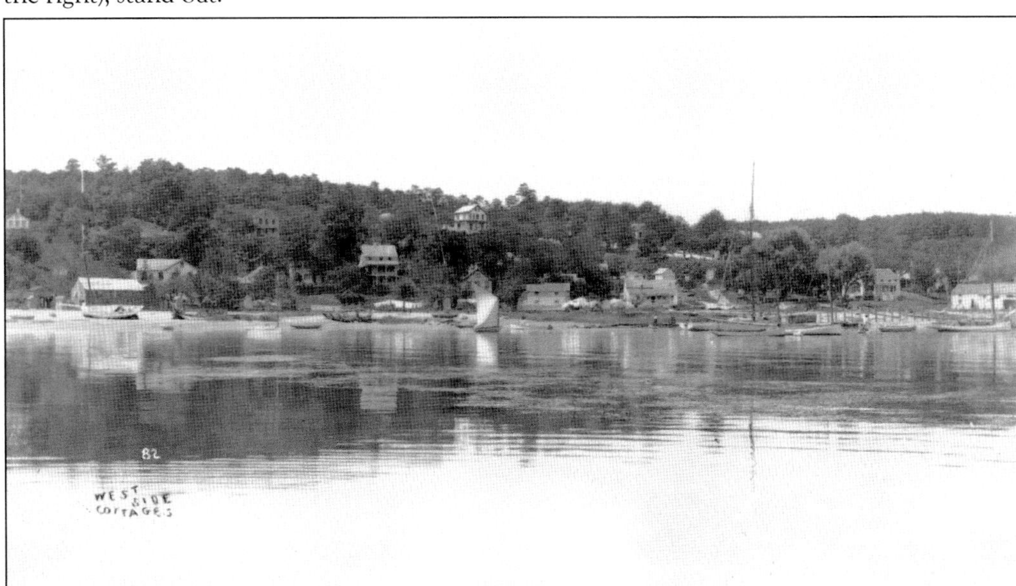

Looking west across the smooth waters of the harbor, this photograph, taken by Port Jefferson photographer Arthur S. Greene around 1897, shows the cottages on the west side. A number of yachts are pulled up on the shore and in the basin. Until 1890, the west side of the harbor was technically part of Setauket.

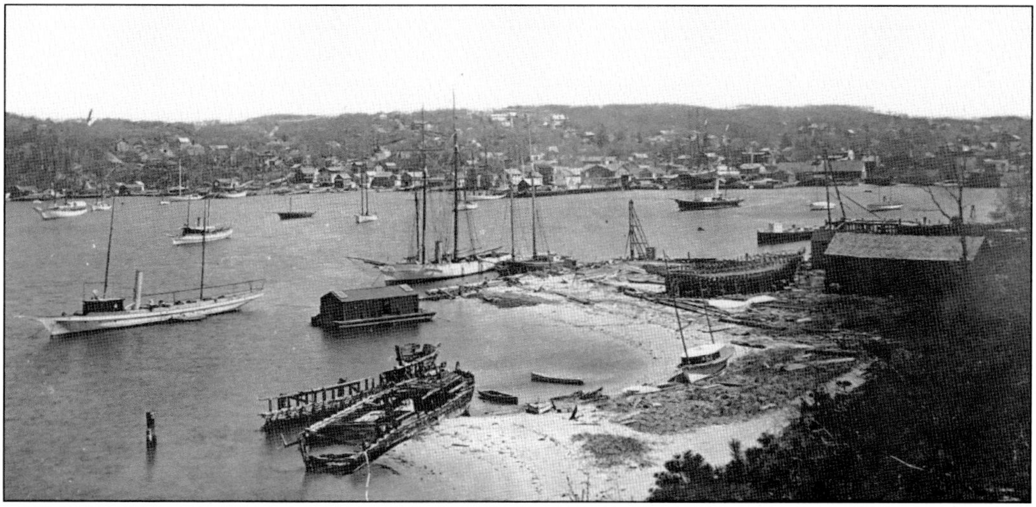

This interesting 1901 view of the harbor from the west side, looking southeast, shows steam yachts and schooner yachts in the foreground. A yacht is under construction in the Hawkins yard. In the background, East Broadway ascends the hill to the left; the F.F. Darling Store, with cupola, is in the center; and the tower of the old Victorian schoolhouse is on the right.

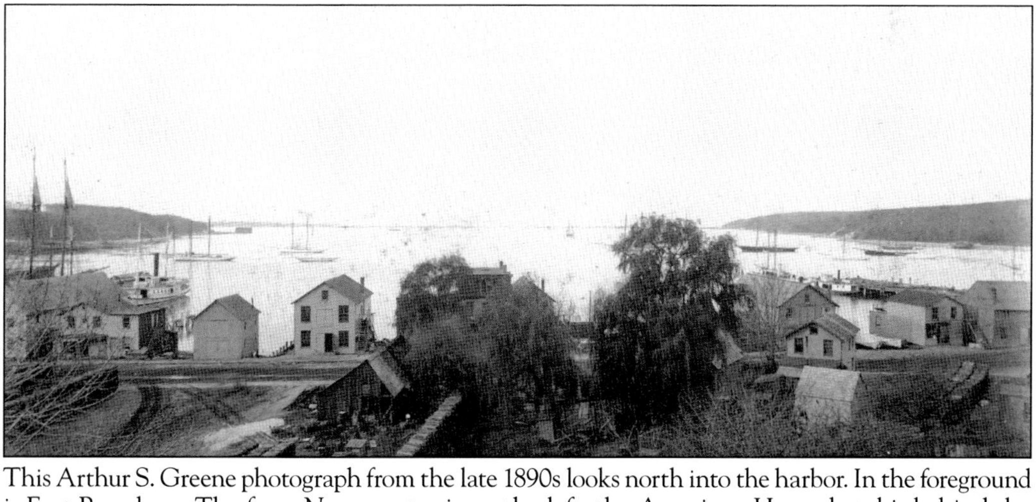

This Arthur S. Greene photograph from the late 1890s looks north into the harbor. In the foreground is East Broadway. The ferry *Nonowantuc* is on the left, the American House hotel is behind the trees in the center, and Bayles Dock is on the right. Note the neatly stacked woodpile.

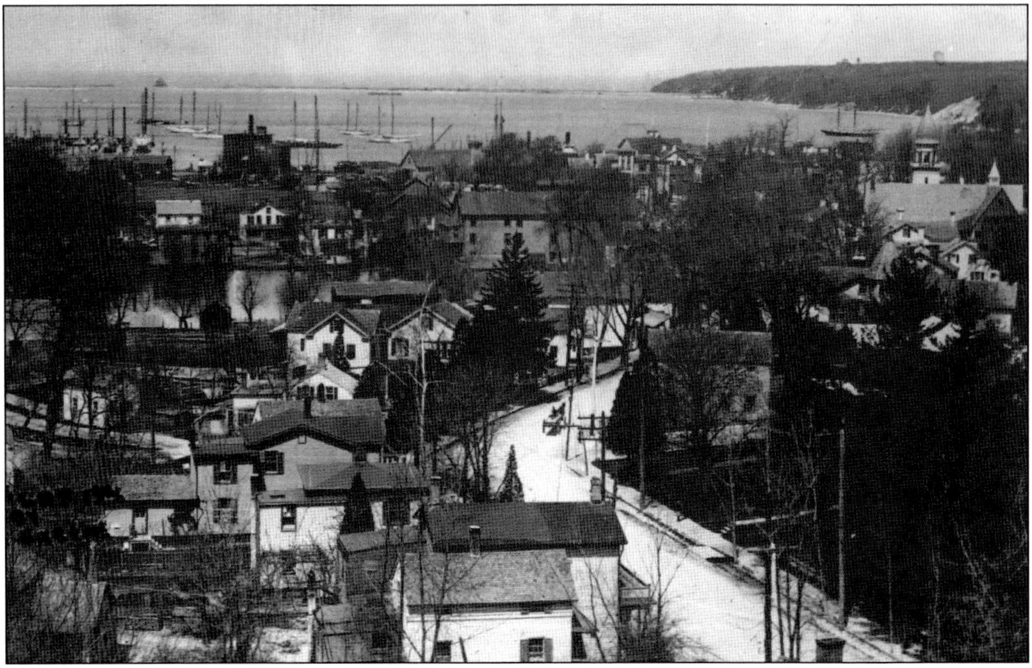

This 1906 view of Port Jefferson is remarkable for its comprehensiveness and clarity. Main Street runs through the foreground of the photograph, with Barnum Avenue bending toward the left. Parker Pond lies at center left, with Athena Hall to its right. Above and to the left of the Methodist church steeple on the right is the silhouette of the newly built Belle Terre Club.

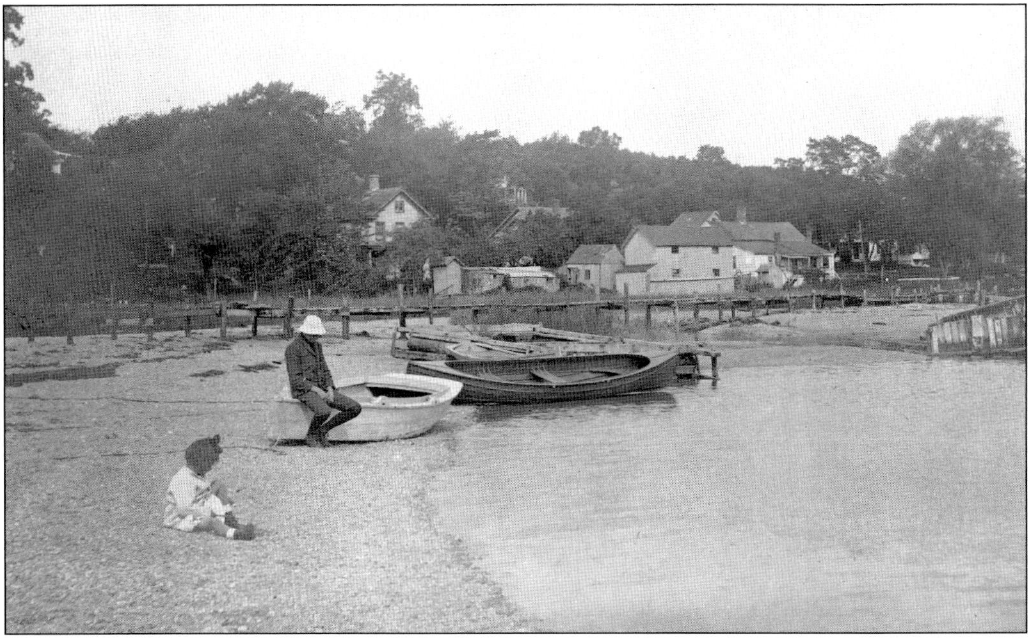

In this photograph from the early 20th century, a contemplative pair, man and child, sits on the west shore of the harbor, at the approximate location of the present-day boat ramp. In the background, houses on Beach Street and, above it, Bayview Terrace can be seen. The Darling and Robbins families were the first residents of this neighborhood.

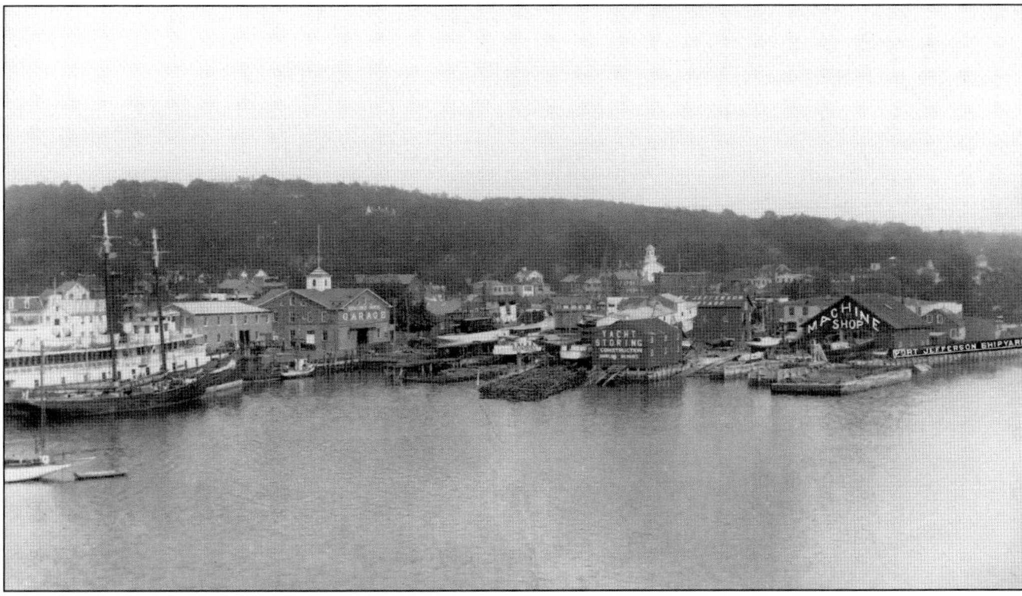

Visible in this c. 1920 photograph looking south from the harbor toward the waterfront are the *Park City* and a schooner tied up at the ferry dock, the Newcomb Brothers Garage (the old F.F. Darling store), and a yacht in dry dock at the Port Jefferson Shipyard. In the distance are the steeple of the Baptist church and the cupolas of the First National Bank and the Presbyterian church.

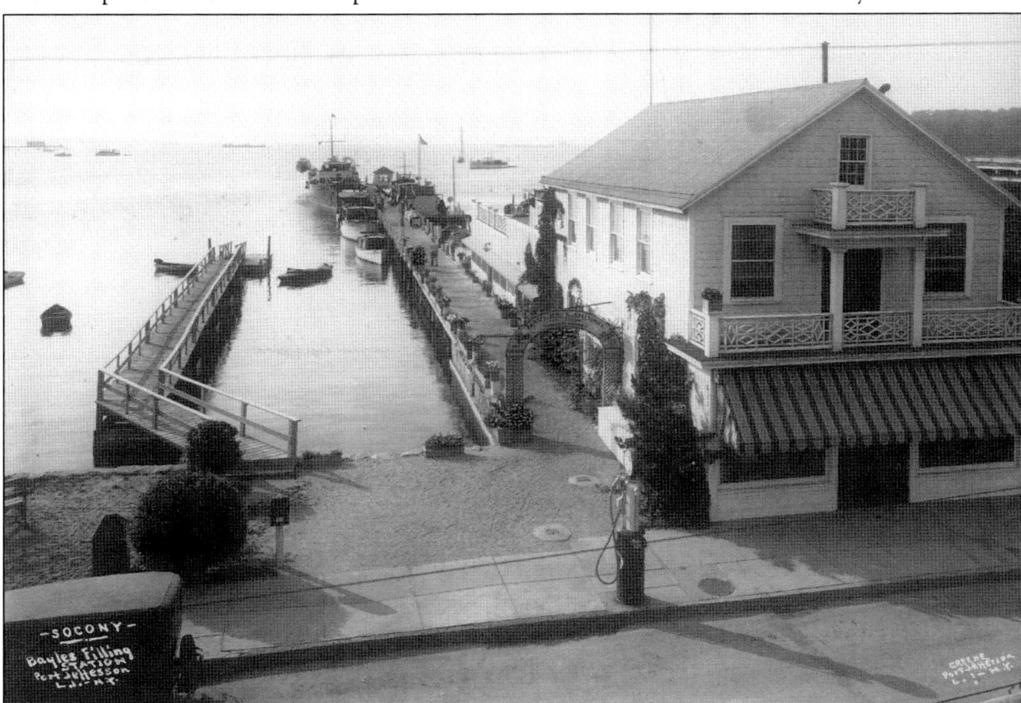

This 1936 photograph shows large and small boats tied up at Bayles Dock. At over 400 feet in length, the dock and its filling station could accommodate all the boaters, stopping to relax or fill up, that Port Jefferson attracted. The building on the right housed Mary Bayles's gift shop and is now part of Danford's Hotel and Marina.

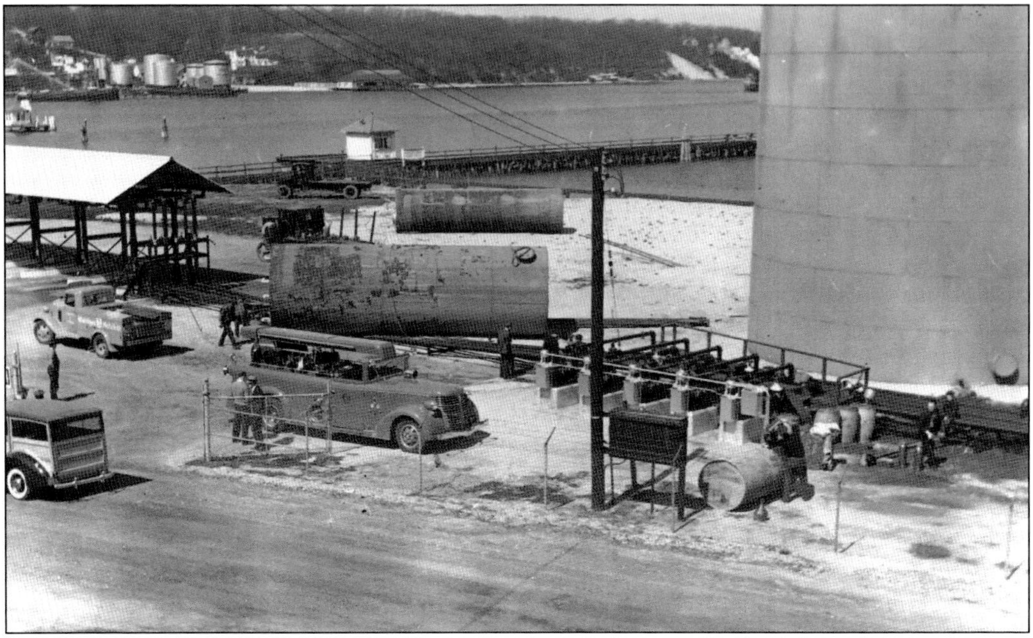

Pictured here in 1939 are oil tanks from the Mobiloil storage facility being dismantled to make way for larger tanks. The commercial development of the waterfront is evident by the array of storage tanks on the west side of the harbor. The Mobil property was purchased by the village in 1997 and is now the site of Harborfront Park.

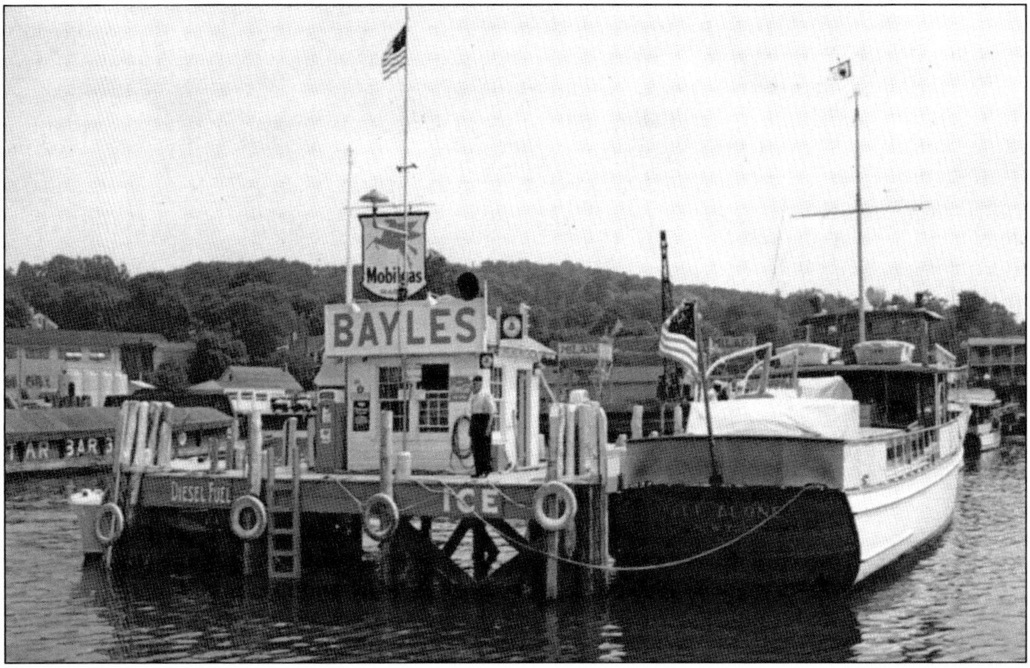

In this c. 1960 photograph, a yacht is tied up at Bayles Dock. In the background, the 1917 Bayles Shipyard building and the third chandlery building can be seen on the left, the Harborview Hotel is on the right, and the McLain Stone sand and gravel yard is in the center, where Danford's Hotel now stands.

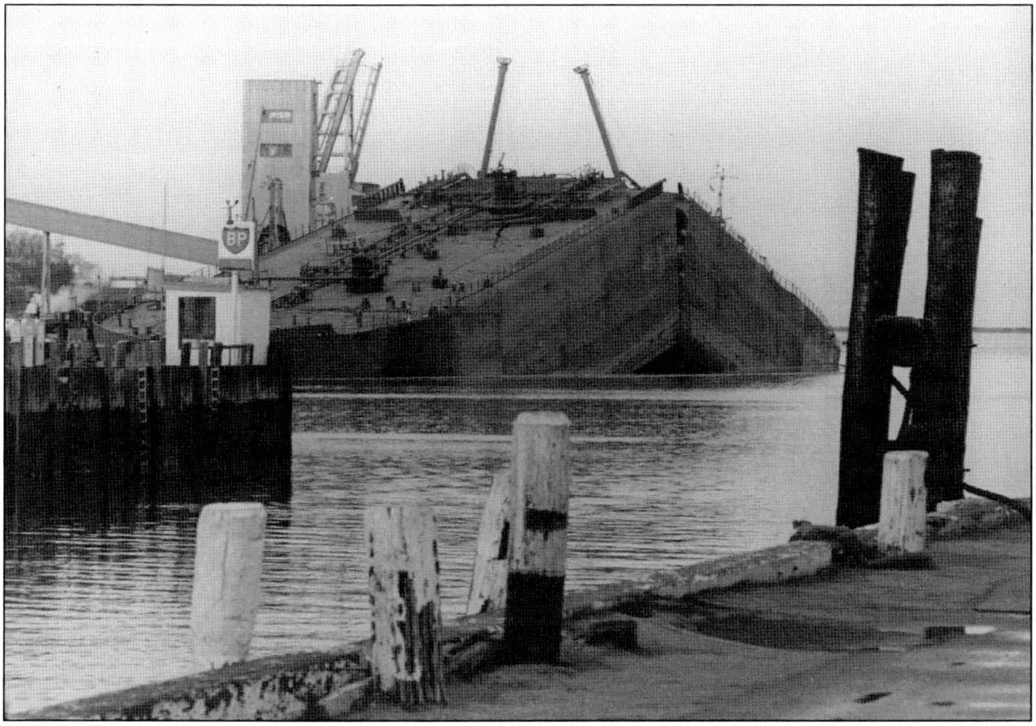

On the morning of January 10, 1972, in one of the most spectacular events in recent Port Jefferson history, the 584-foot, 34,000-ton tank barge *Martha R. Ingram* split in two (pictured) as it was beginning to pull away from the dock. Luckily, it had unloaded its cargo of gasoline and fuel oil. But the accident raised awareness of the potential dangers of oil terminals on the harbor.

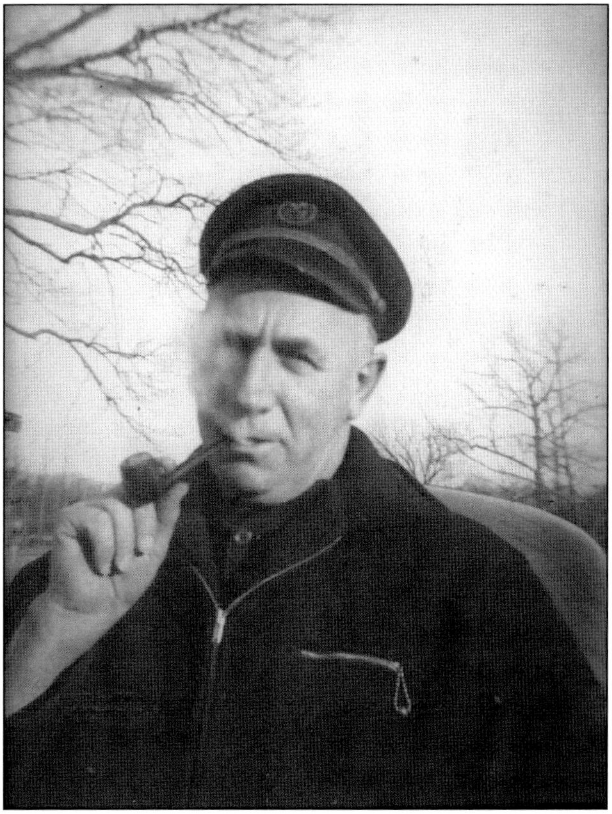

Frederick A. Brown was one of the last of the deepwater ship captains from Port Jefferson. He was a master of four- and five-masted schooners that sailed the world over, even to Antarctica. Brown captained the well-known schooner *Mary Pinchot* on its scientific voyage to the South Seas in 1929. He passed away in 1954.

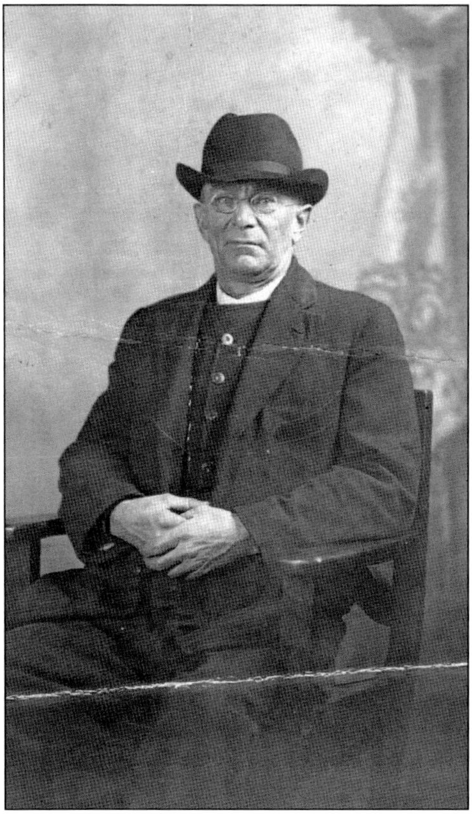

Capt. Selah Darling was born in Northport in 1860 and moved to Port Jefferson in 1886. He sailed on a variety of vessels, including whalers and coastal schooners, and ended his career as a yacht captain. He died in 1941 and is buried in Cedar Hill Cemetery.

Only two whaling ships were ever built in Port Jefferson, the *Horatio* and the *Fleetwing*. Both were launched from the James M. Bayles & Son yard in 1877, and both sailed out of New Bedford, Massachusetts. Capt. Charles Grant of Nantucket, shown here, was in command of the *Horatio* on her four-year-long maiden voyage in pursuit of the sperm whale. The *Horatio* ended her days on a coral reef in the Caroline Islands in 1899.

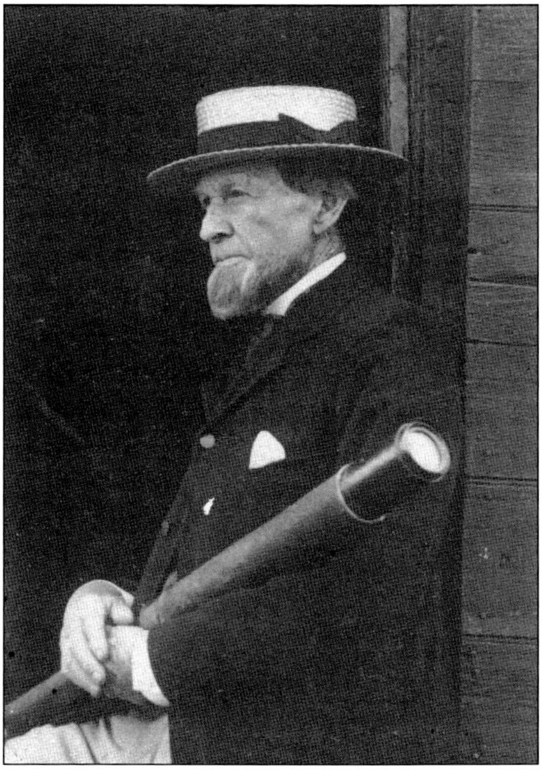

Three

THE BUSINESS OF PORT JEFFERSON

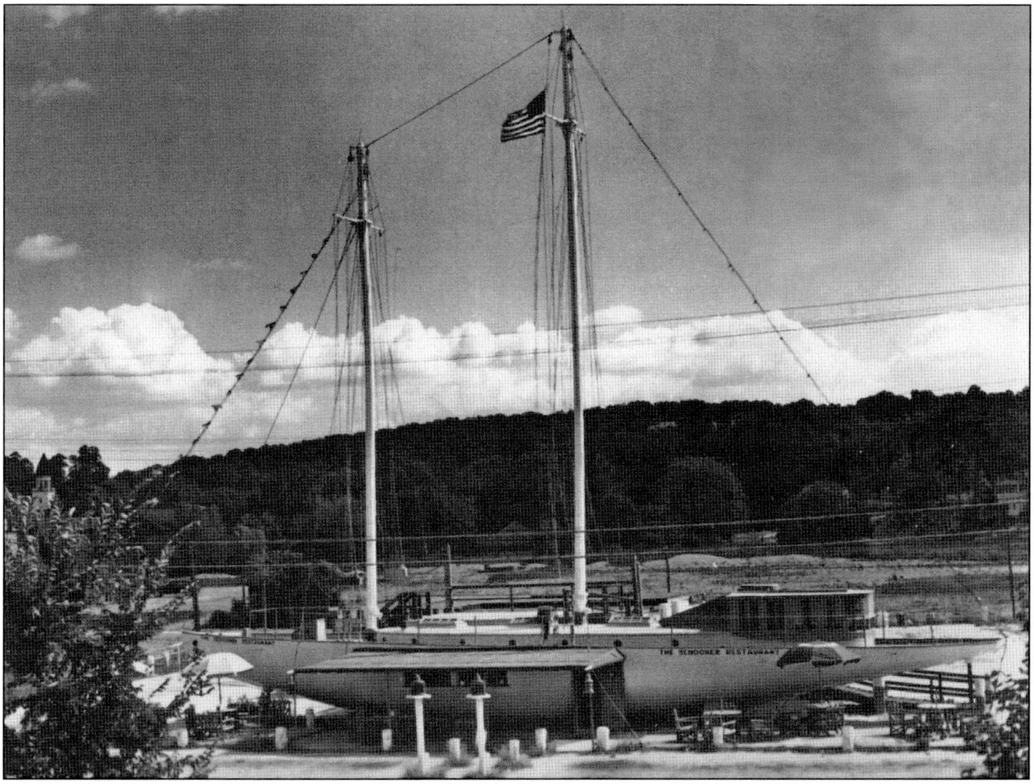

The ship that was to become the Schooner Restaurant was formerly an oceangoing vessel built in Boothbay, Maine, and was once chartered by Alexander Graham Bell. It was located on the south side of West Broadway just east of the present-day Village Hall. The Schooner was run by the Mapp and Ceperano families and, appropriately enough, specialized in seafood. (Courtesy of James McNamara.)

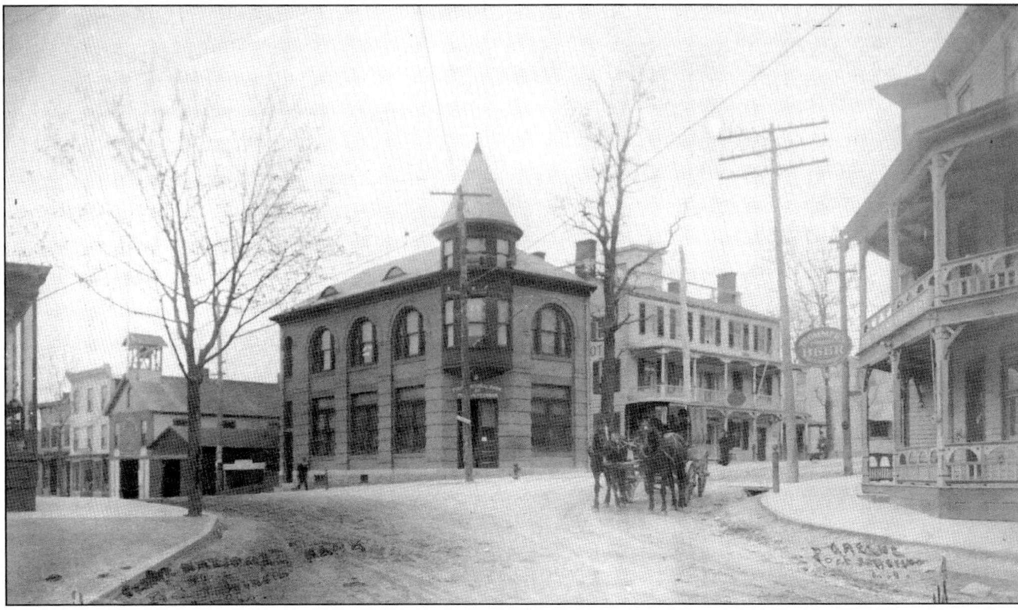

The First National Bank of Port Jefferson, formed in 1898 by a group of prominent businessmen, moved in 1900 into this impressive structure on Hotel Square, which later served as the Brookhaven Town tax office. When the office relocated, the structure was threatened with demolition, but concerned citizens succeeded in having it listed in the National Register of Historic Places. It is now the home of the Long Island Music Hall of Fame.

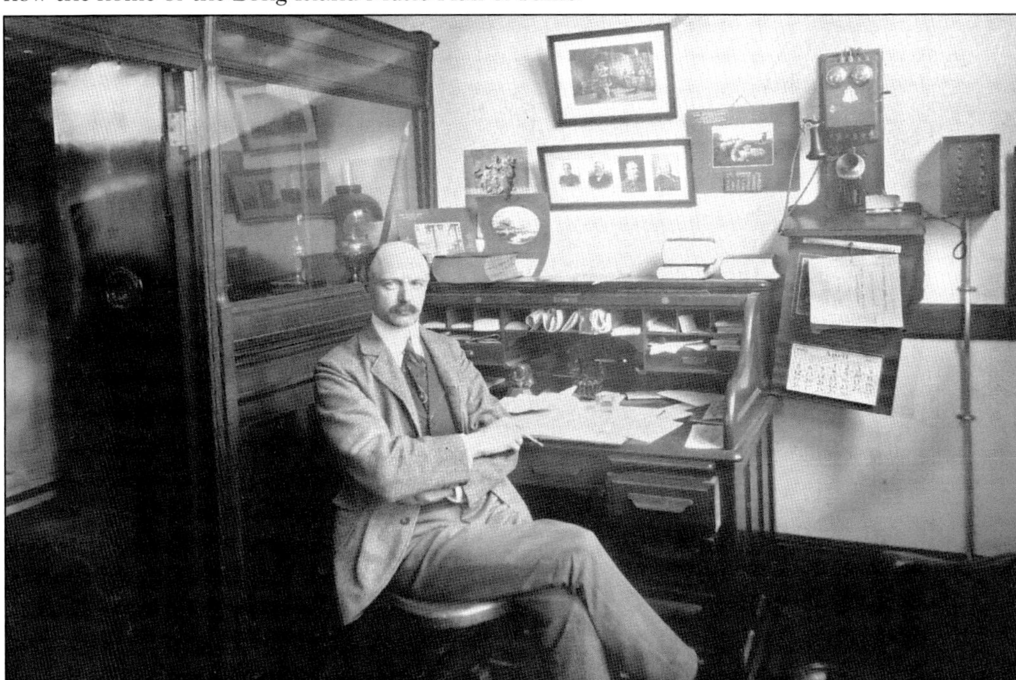

Francis A. Kline, one of the organizers of the First National Bank of Port Jefferson and its cashier for many years, sits in his office in 1903. After the death of Orange T. Fanning in 1927, Kline was elected president of the bank and served in that capacity until he retired in 1944.

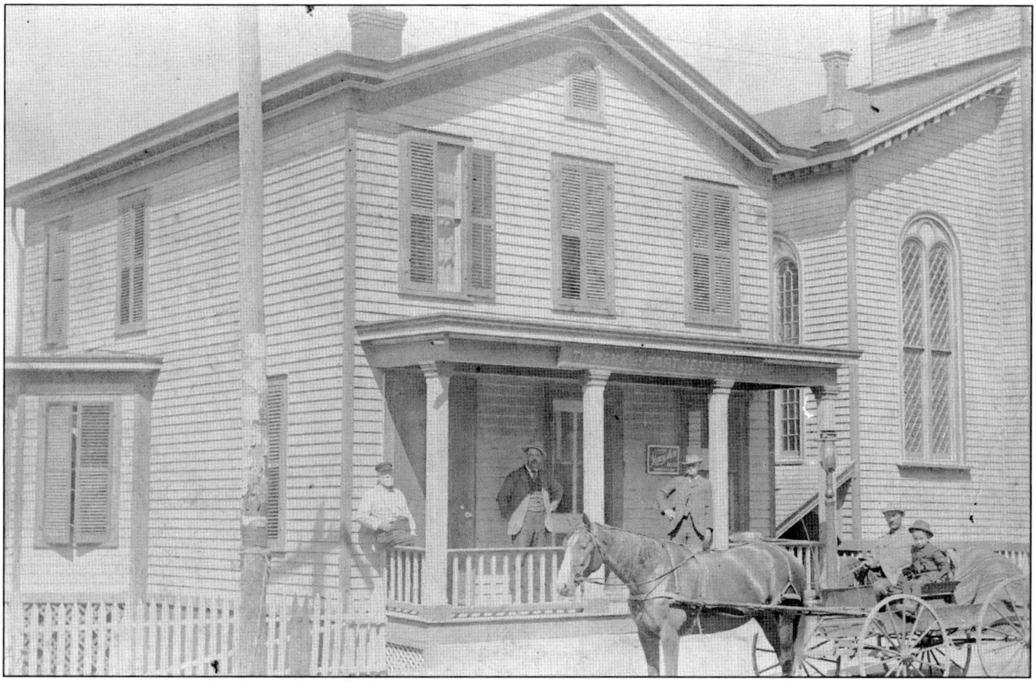

The Bank of Port Jefferson was founded in 1889 by six sea captains. Capt. Henry M. Randall was its first president, and James E. Bayles was the first vice president. The bank occupied this building, which still stands on Main Street, to the left of today's Masonic hall.

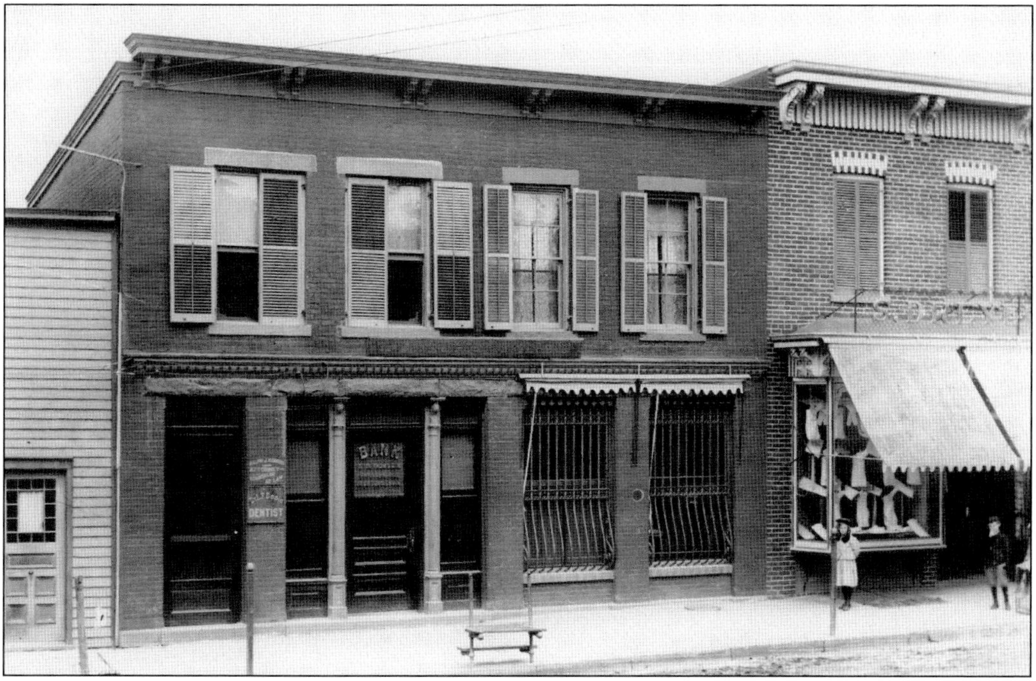

Formerly occupied by the Ryder's Ice Cream Shop, this building on East Main Street near Prospect Street was the home of the Bank of Port Jefferson from 1897 until its merger with the First National Bank of Port Jefferson. A bank has occupied the building for more than 100 years.

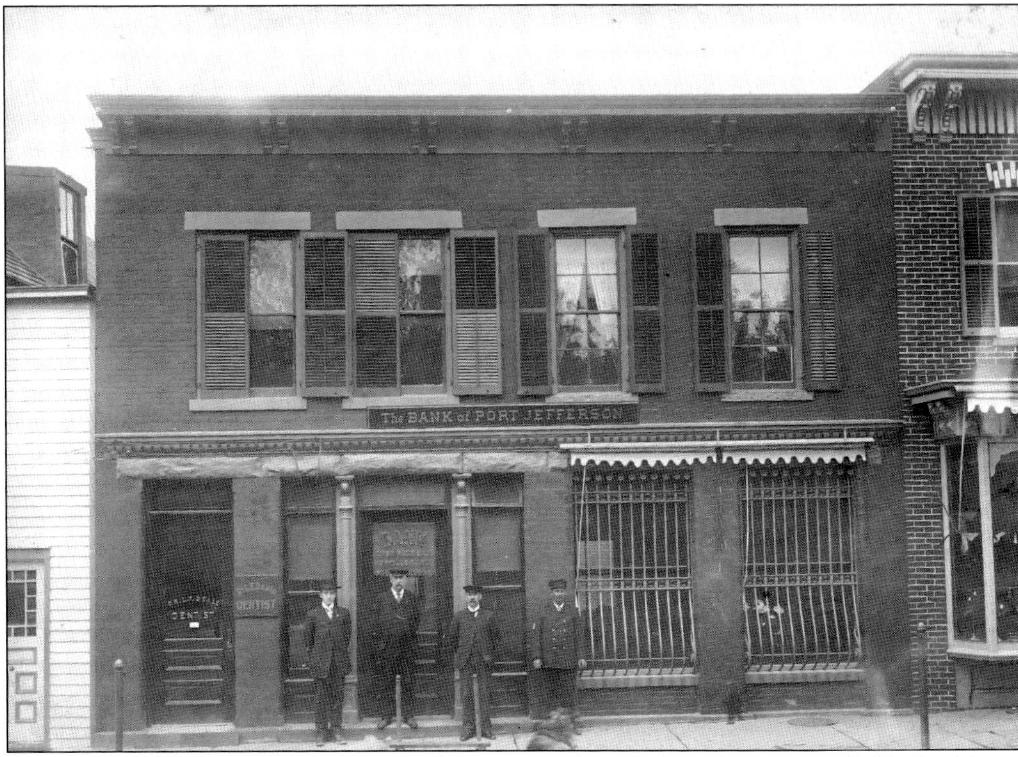

Standing in front of the Bank of Port Jefferson in 1907 are Joshua A. Overton (left), G.M. Davis (center), and Ralph B. Dayton. The office of Leroy Ford Deale, a prominent dentist, was on the second floor. A native of Greenport, Dr. Deale came to Port Jefferson at the turn of the last century and practiced until his death in 1930. He was very active in civic affairs, especially in the fire department.

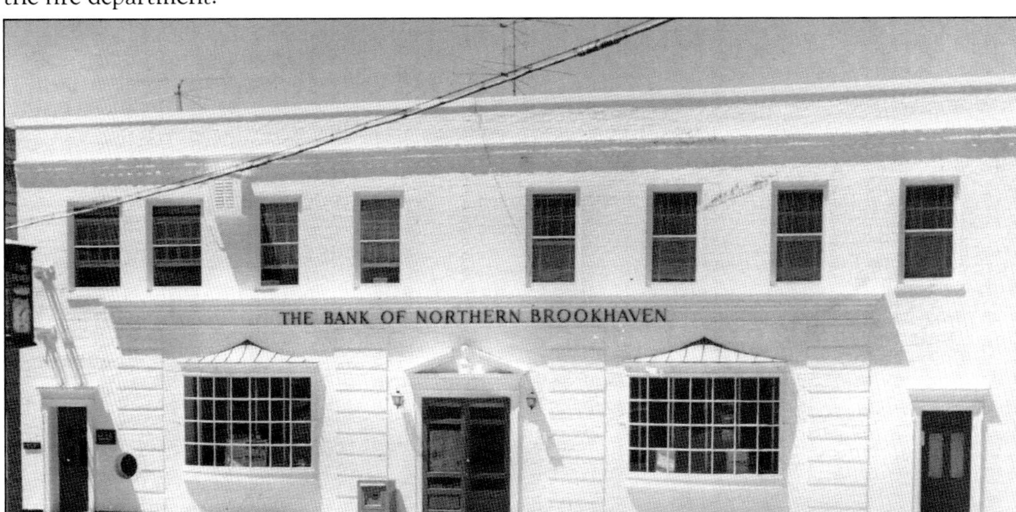

The Bank of Northern Brookhaven was formed in 1947 by the merger of the Bank of Port Jefferson and the First National Bank of Port Jefferson. It occupied the newly enlarged Bank of Port Jefferson building. Through the years, several other banks occupied the site, which is now the home of the Port Jefferson Village branch of the Suffolk County National Bank.

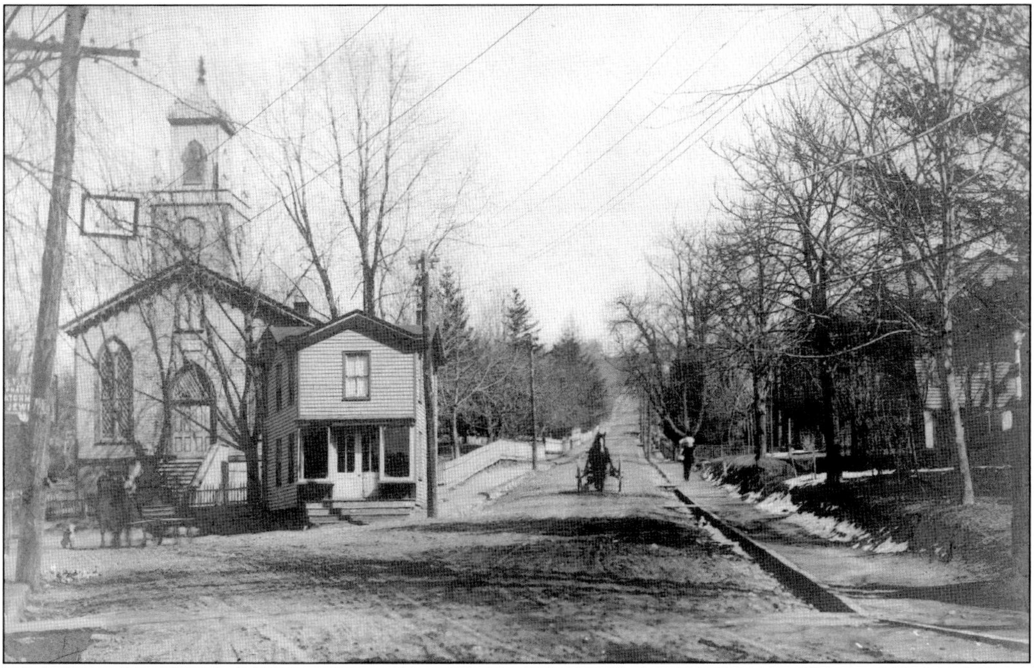

Port Jefferson was named an official port of entry in 1852. As many as 30,000 tons of goods passed through the port yearly. In this photograph from February 1898, the customs house stands in front of the First Baptist Church at the corner of East Main and Prospect Streets shortly before it was moved to Myrtle Avenue to serve as a private residence. The customs office was abolished in 1913.

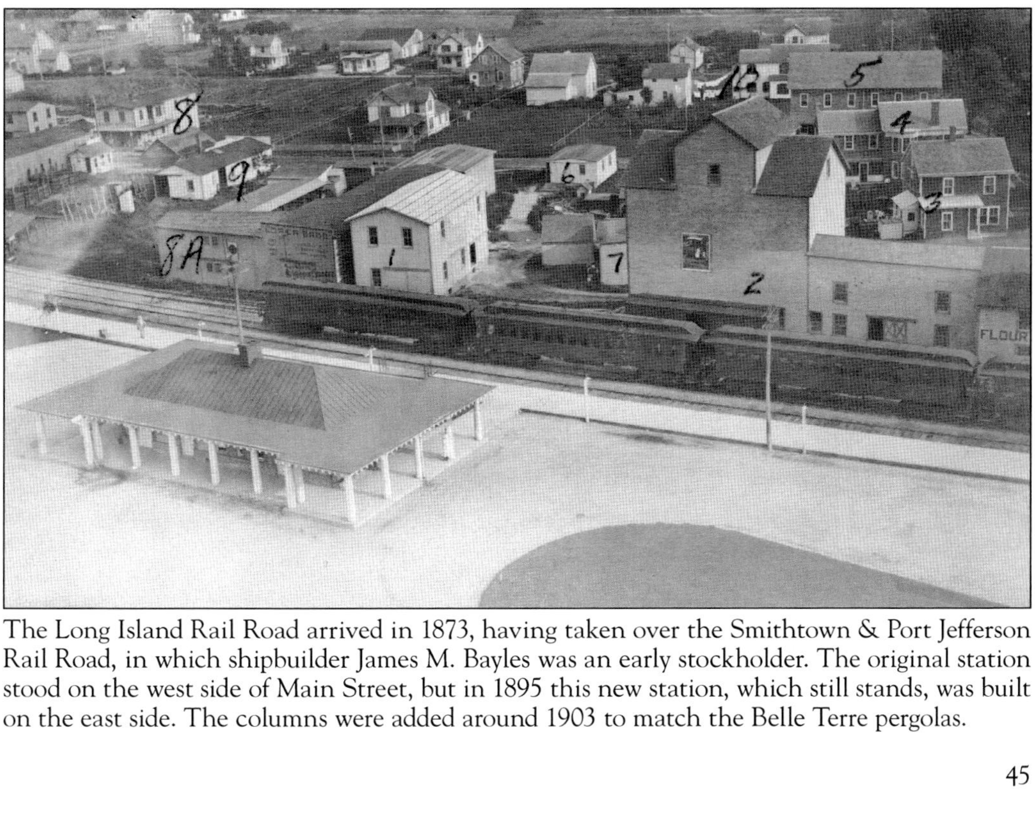

The Long Island Rail Road arrived in 1873, having taken over the Smithtown & Port Jefferson Rail Road, in which shipbuilder James M. Bayles was an early stockholder. The original station stood on the west side of Main Street, but in 1895 this new station, which still stands, was built on the east side. The columns were added around 1903 to match the Belle Terre pergolas.

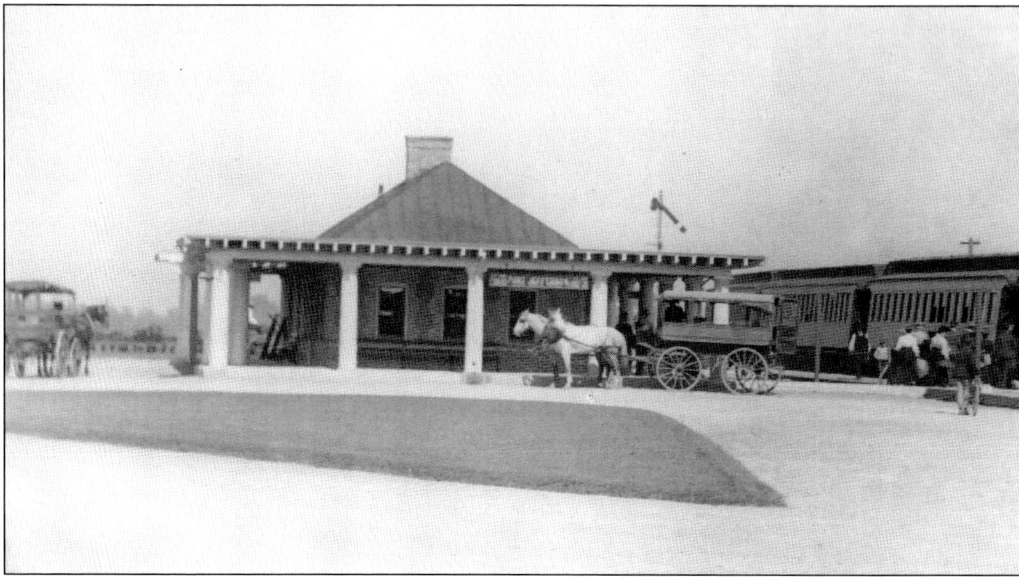

John "Billy" Brown's stagecoach is shown here at the railroad station in the early 1900s. For 50 years, Brown operated this service, first with a horse-drawn coach and then, in 1908, converting to a motorized vehicle. His route ran from Port Jefferson to the train station and then south to Patchogue and back. He kept his horses and carriages behind his house on Prospect Street. (Courtesy of Frances Child.)

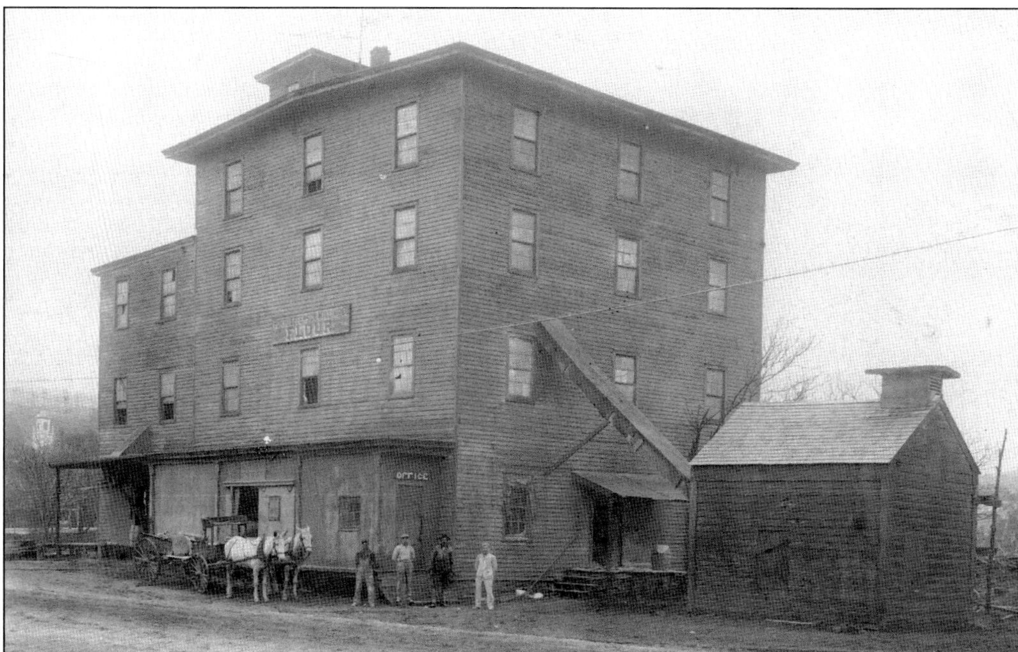

The Port Jefferson Milling Company, shown here in the 1890s, began in 1858 as the Suwassett Steam Flouring Mill. In 1865, a sawmill was added. After fire destroyed the original building in 1877, a new building was erected two years later. At its peak, the mill ran around the clock, producing 100 barrels of flour a day. It was dismantled in 1918. The Port Jefferson Village Hall now sits just west of the site of the mill.

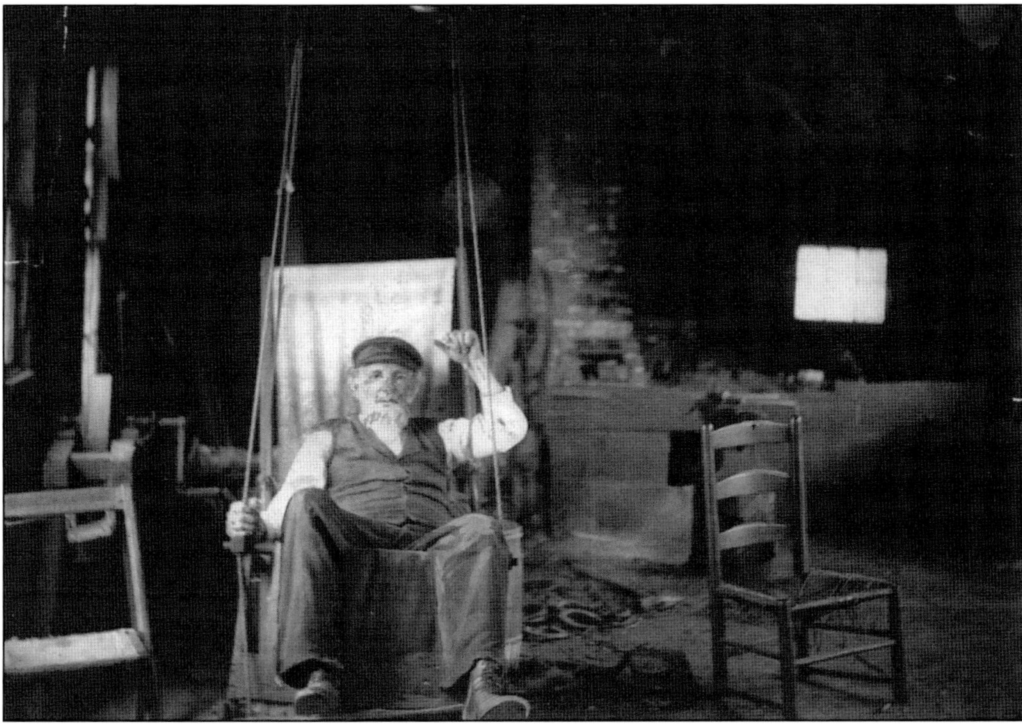

Blacksmith Israel Smith sits in his shop in this portrait from the early 1900s. He served as Port Jefferson's blacksmith for 55 years. In 1898, when he was 74 years old, it was noted that he could shoe as many horses in a day as a man of 50. After his death, the building was demolished.

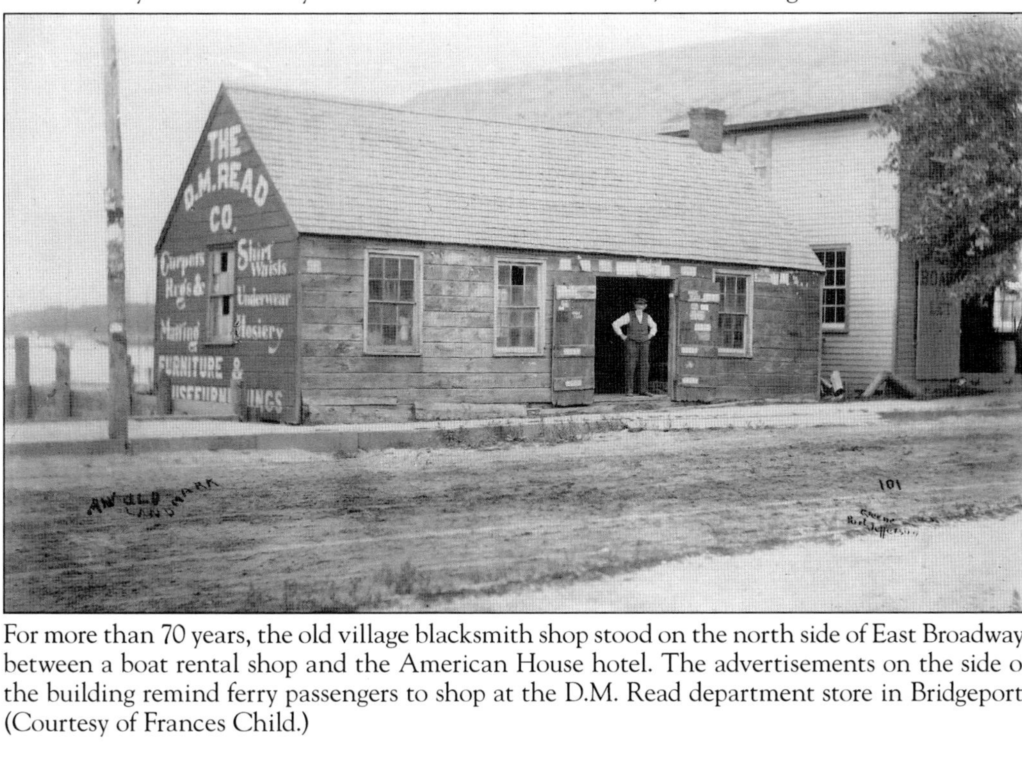

For more than 70 years, the old village blacksmith shop stood on the north side of East Broadway, between a boat rental shop and the American House hotel. The advertisements on the side of the building remind ferry passengers to shop at the D.M. Read department store in Bridgeport. (Courtesy of Frances Child.)

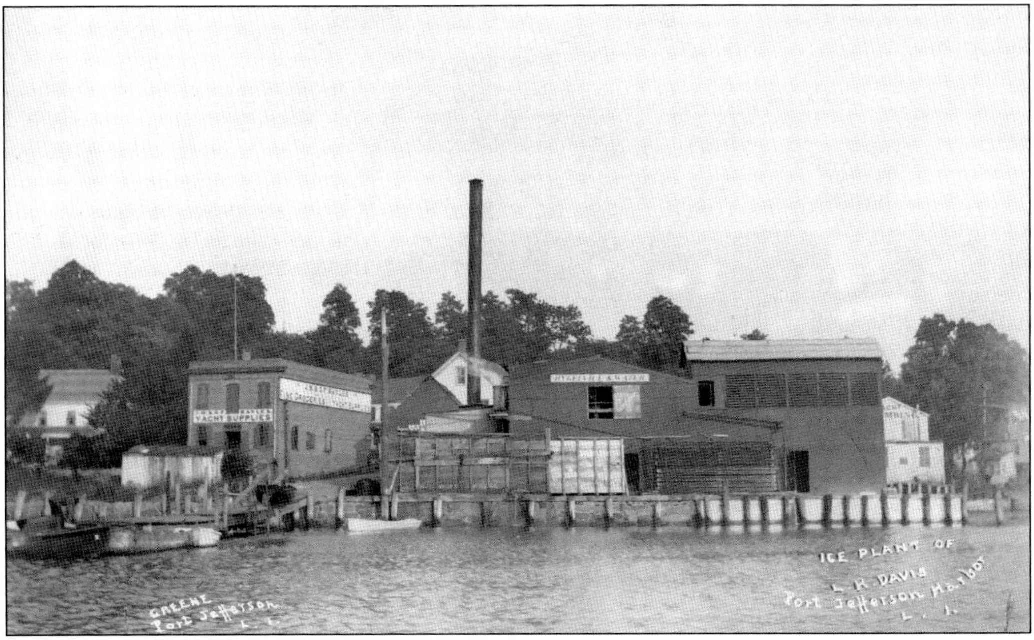

This 1908 photograph, looking south, shows the ice plant of Lester H. Davis on East Broadway. Davis had harvested ice from Parker's Pond and the Setauket Mill Pond before building this ice manufacturing plant in 1900. Among his many civic activities, Davis was the first president of the Business Men's Association, the forerunner of the chamber of commerce.

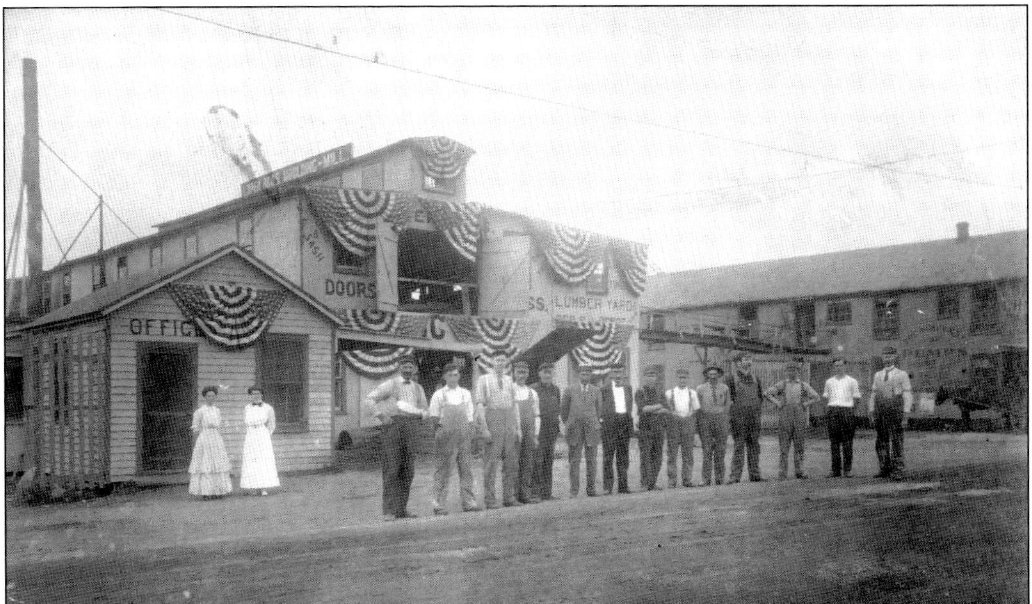

In 1889, the Loper brothers, Gilbert and Arthur, started their lumberyard and milling works on West Broadway. The site is now the location of Port Jefferson Village Hall. They eventually branched out into hardware and contracting and built the current high school, the Methodist church, and a number of private residences. The Lopers owned a lumberyard on the south side of the railroad tracks in Port Jefferson Station as well.

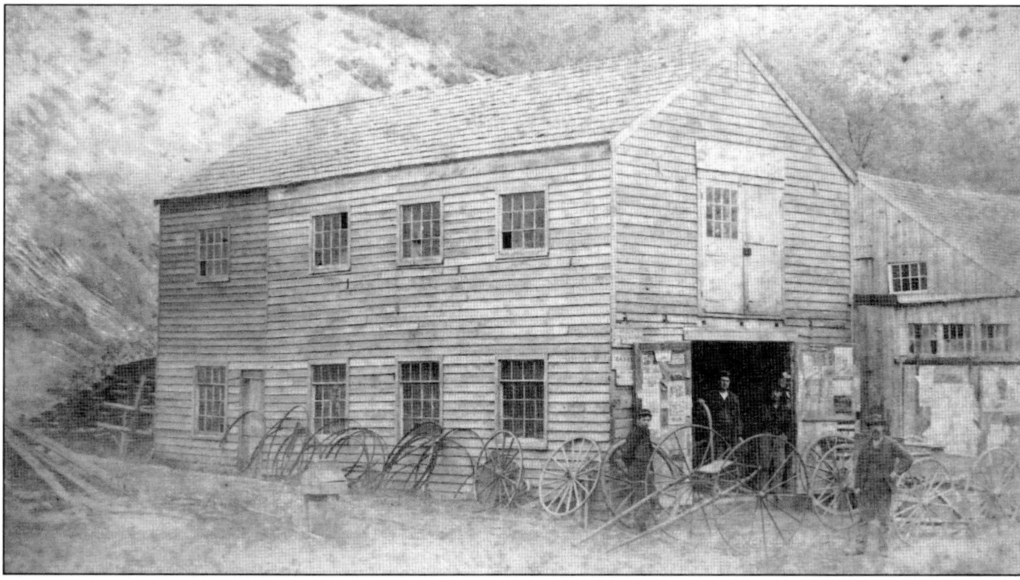

Alanson Overton's carriage shop, shown here in 1875, stood on this piece of property on Main Street opposite Myrtle Avenue. Port Jefferson was widely known for the quality and workmanship of its carriages, starting with the work of Effingham Tuthill, who established the first carriage factory in Port Jefferson in 1856 on the corner of Main Street and Arden Place (where a Starbucks coffee shop now stands).

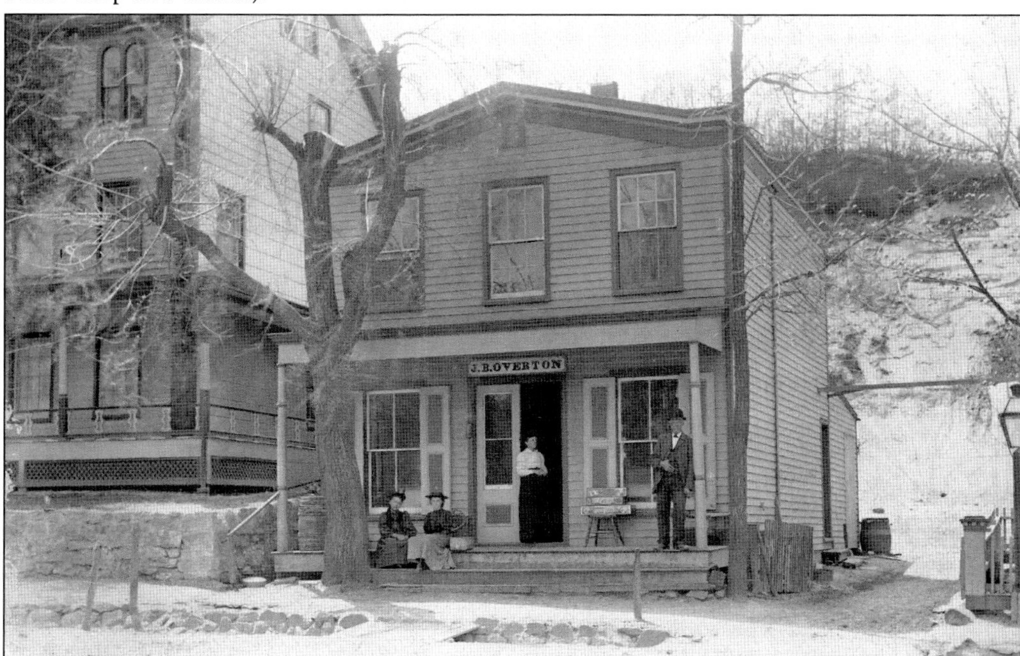

This photograph of Macy's carriage shop, in the same location as the shop mentioned above, dates to around 1898. Alanson Overton sold his business to Charles A. Macy, a former ship's carpenter, in 1875, but Overton retained the right to use the property. The arrangement called for Macy to build the carriages and Overton to sell them. The business remained in the Macy family until his death in 1920.

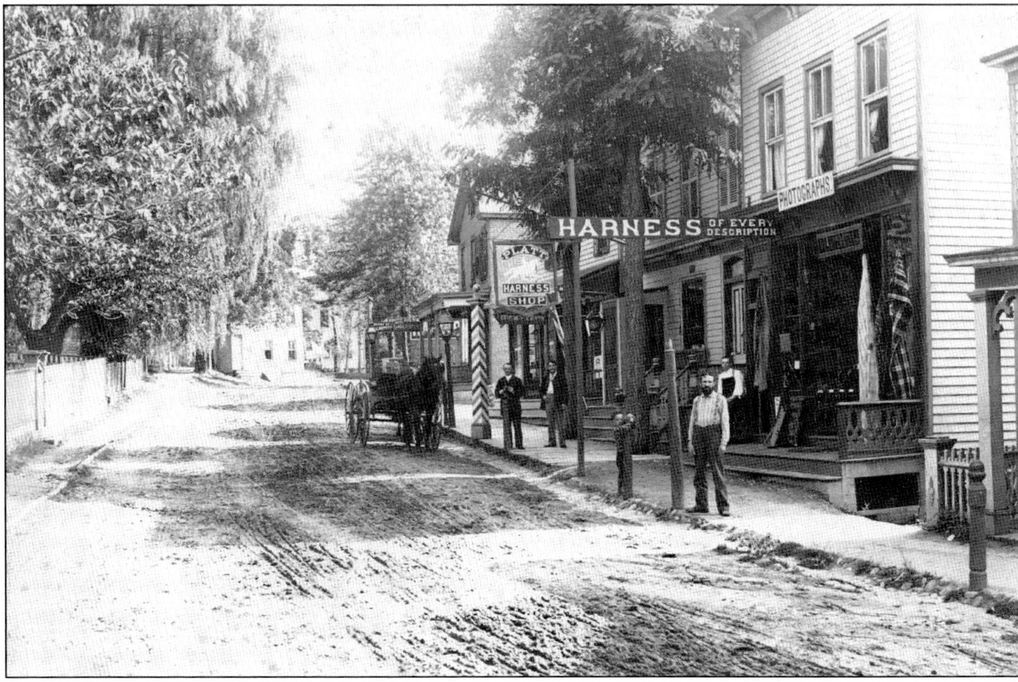

Platt's Harness Shop, seen here in 1894, was located on the west side of East Main Street. In addition to harnesses, the shop offered a "complete assortment of horse blankets, lap robes, heaters, whips and brushes." Augustus Warner's photography studio is on the second floor.

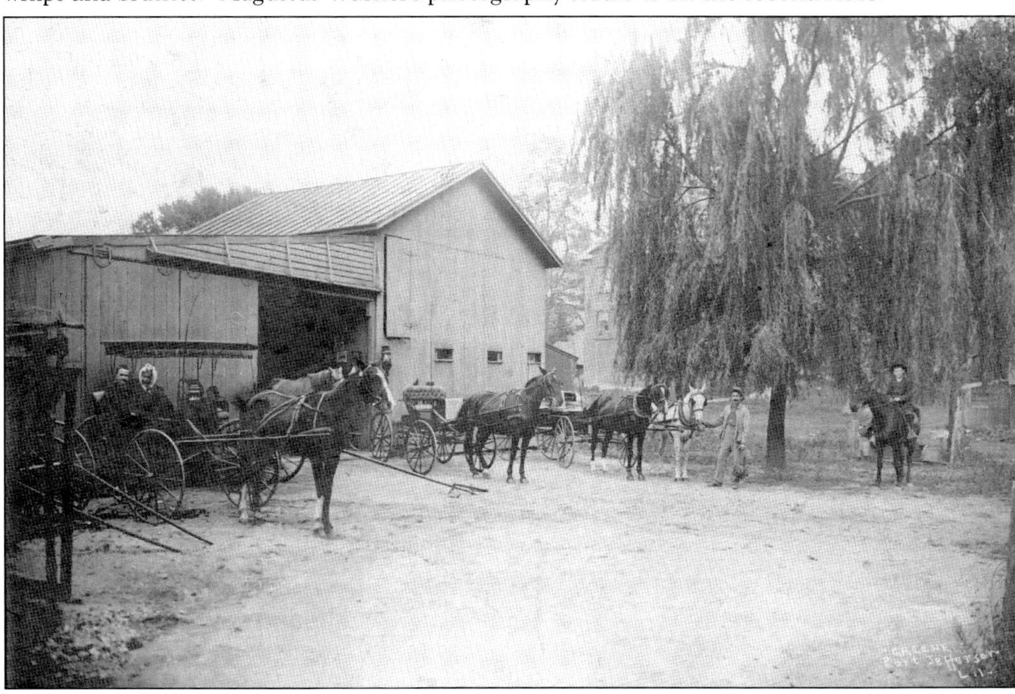

D.W. Phillips Boarding & Livery Stable stood for many years between the old firehouse and the First National Bank of Port Jefferson on Main Street. Proprietor Dave Phillips, who described himself as an "experienced horseman," kept eight horses for hire.

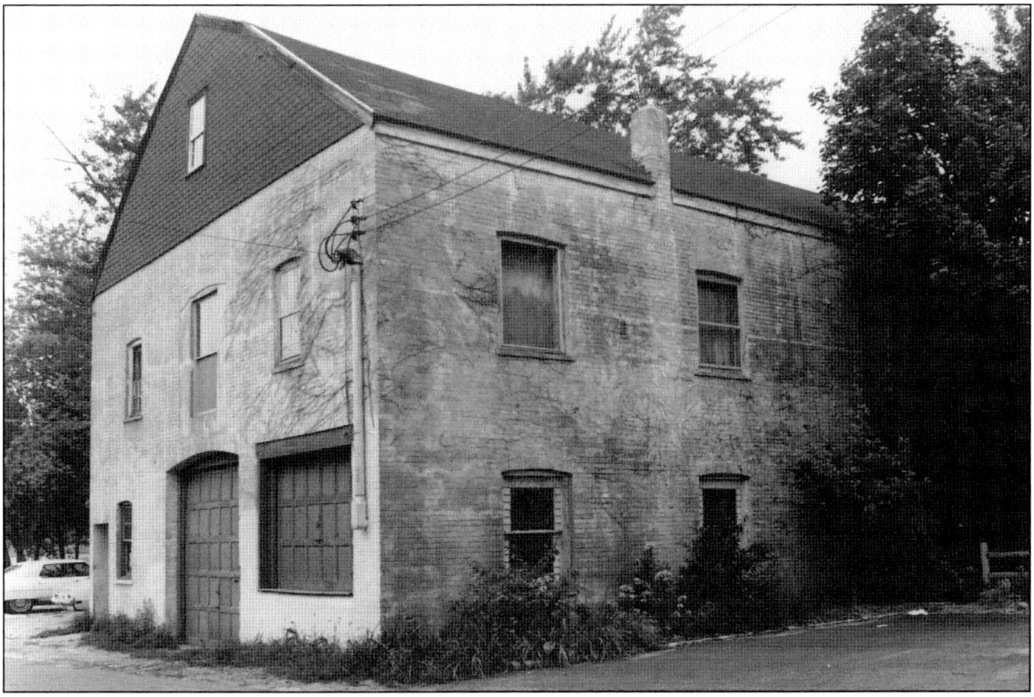

The loft building on Wynne Lane is seen here in the early 1960s. Albert L. Wynne was an African American liveryman who operated a stable on the street for 40 years before converting it to a 20-car automobile garage in 1924. He was born in Georgia in 1856 and probably experienced slavery firsthand. He settled in Port Jefferson in 1872 and lived there until his death in 1942.

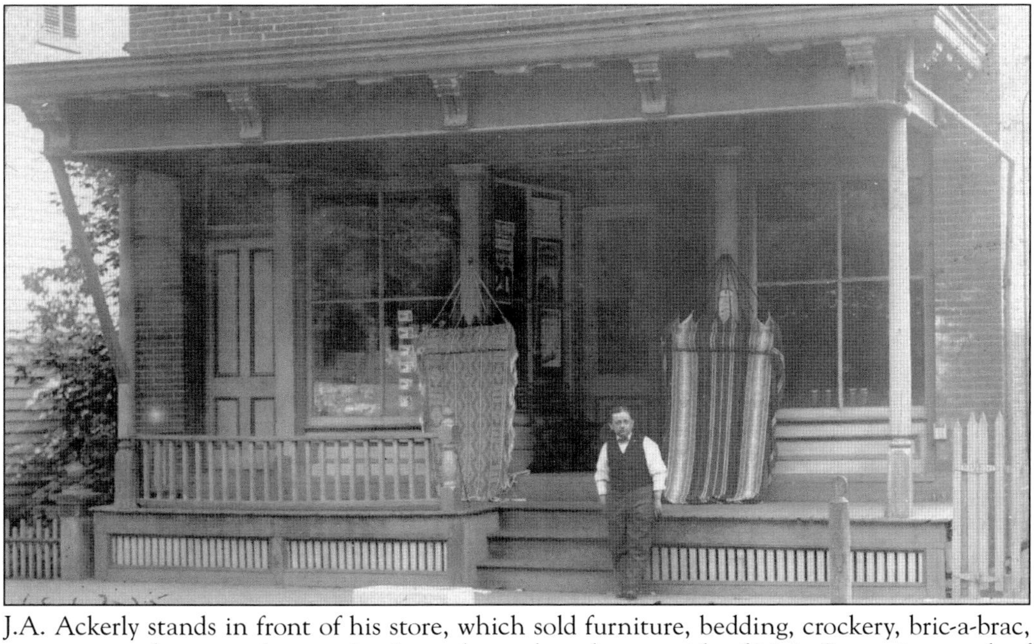

J.A. Ackerly stands in front of his store, which sold furniture, bedding, crockery, bric-a-brac, rugs, carpets, lamps, and souvenirs. It was located on the west side of Main Street, just south of Wynne Lane. In the early 20th century, this building housed Charles B. Tooker's undertaking and furniture businesses.

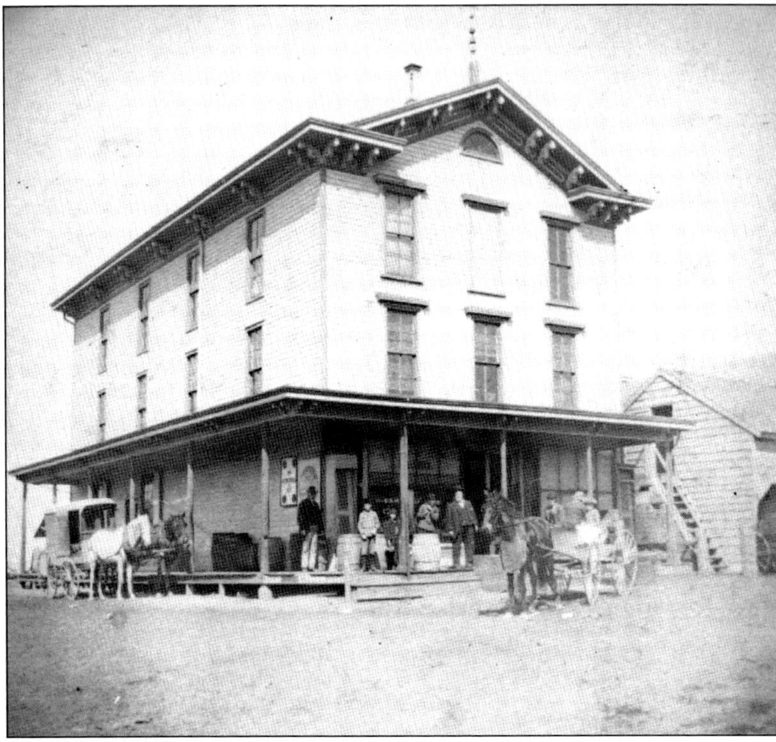

Frederick F. Darling arrived in Port Jefferson in 1852 after clerking in a mercantile house in New York City. He established a small grocery store and then bought the old Jones store on East Broadway. He built this large Italianate store in 1868, and in 1880 he went into partnership with his son as F.F. Darling & Son. After his death in 1896, his son carried on the business.

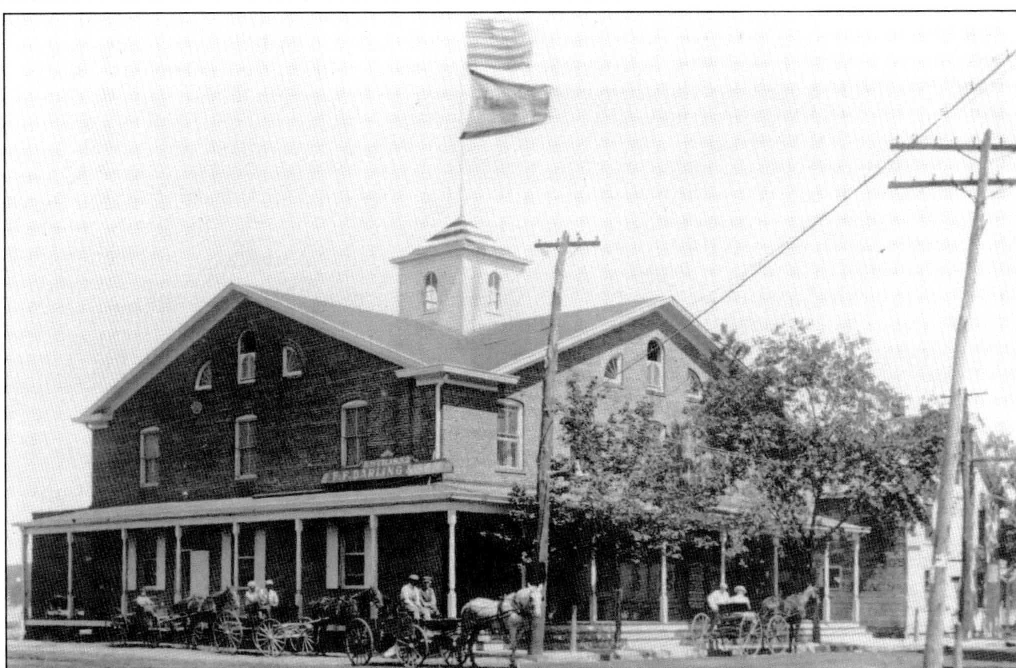

The newer F.F. Darling store, known as one of the most complete in Suffolk County, was located on East Broadway next to the Wilson Sail Loft. The building would later house the Newcomb Brothers Garage and then McAllister Motors before being destroyed by fire in October 1972. The site is now the staging area for the ferry to Bridgeport.

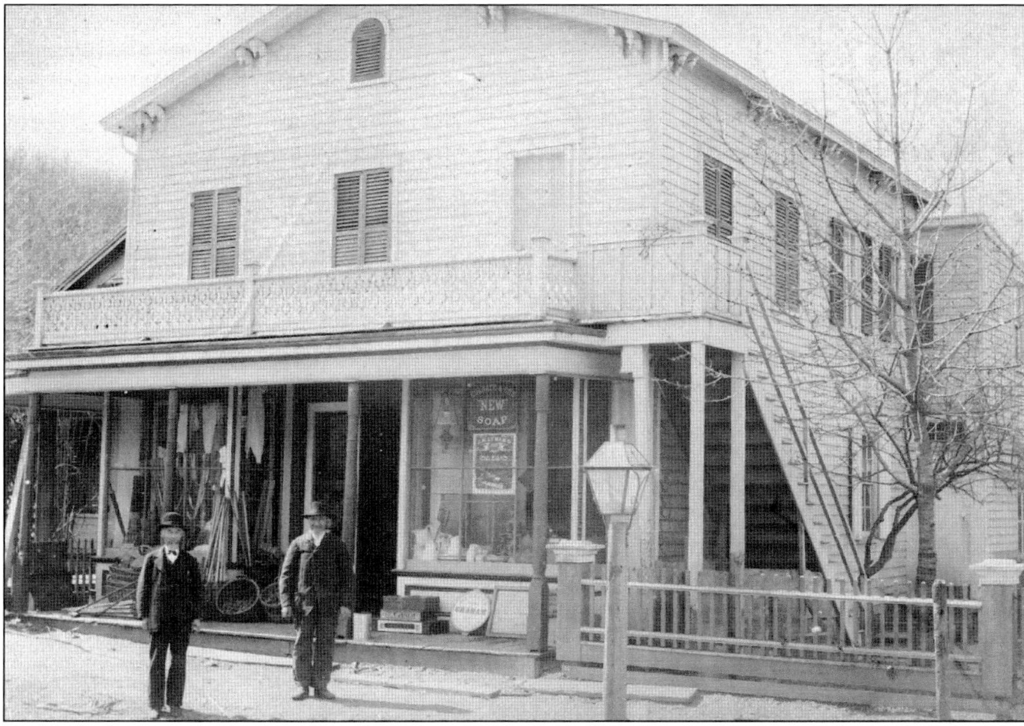

The George Darling store stood on the north corner of Liberty Avenue and Main Street in the late 1800s. The site is now a parking lot. Darling's son, George E., became a prominent lawyer in the village and served as president of the board of education.

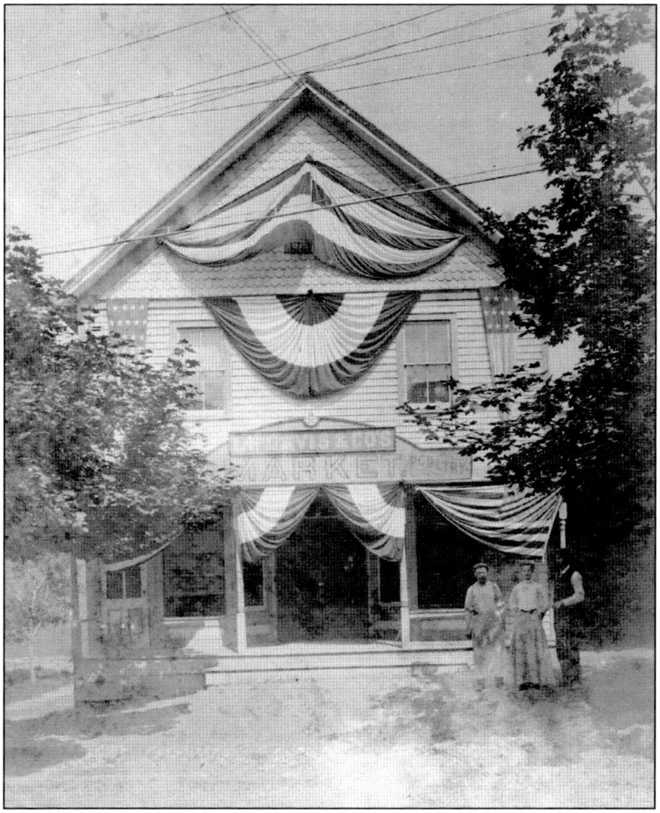

Adjacent to the second Bayles Chandlery on the north side of East Broadway stood the Lester H. Davis Meat Market. It was destroyed in the great waterfront fire in July 1897 and then rebuilt. Joseph Vandall kept a meat market in the same building before opening up a store directly across the street.

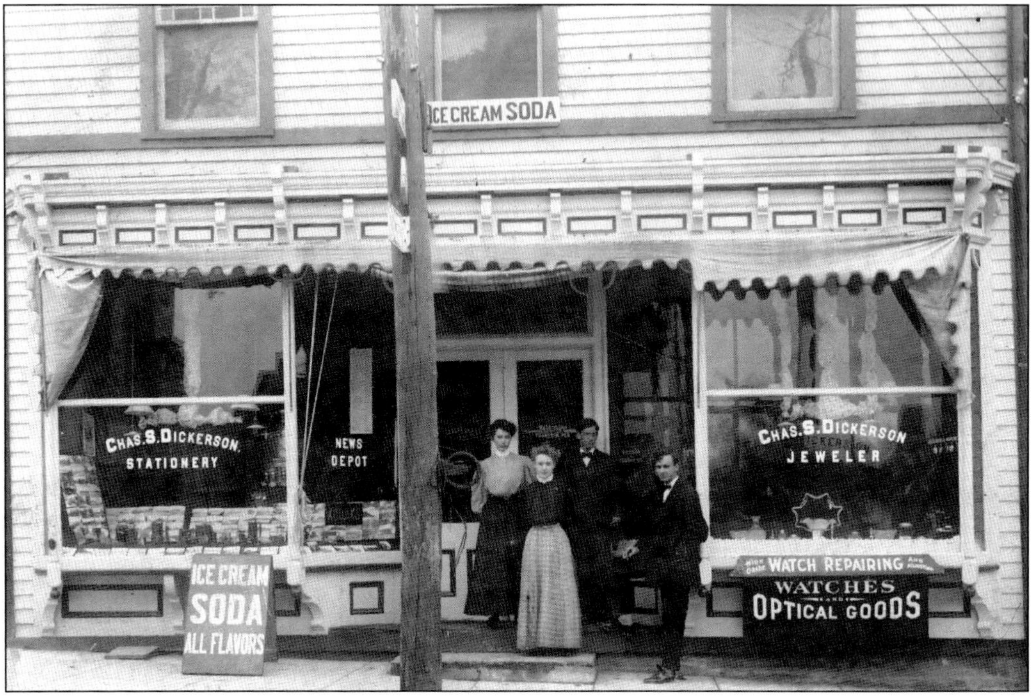

Pictured here in 1905, the Charles S. Dickerson store was located on Hotel Square next to the Townsend House. It sold stationery, jewelry, and cameras. On the second floor, the Independent Order of Odd Fellows, Lodge No. 627, held its meetings. The Odd Fellows, a fraternal and charitable organization, had been established in the United States in 1819. Many prominent Port Jefferson men and women were members.

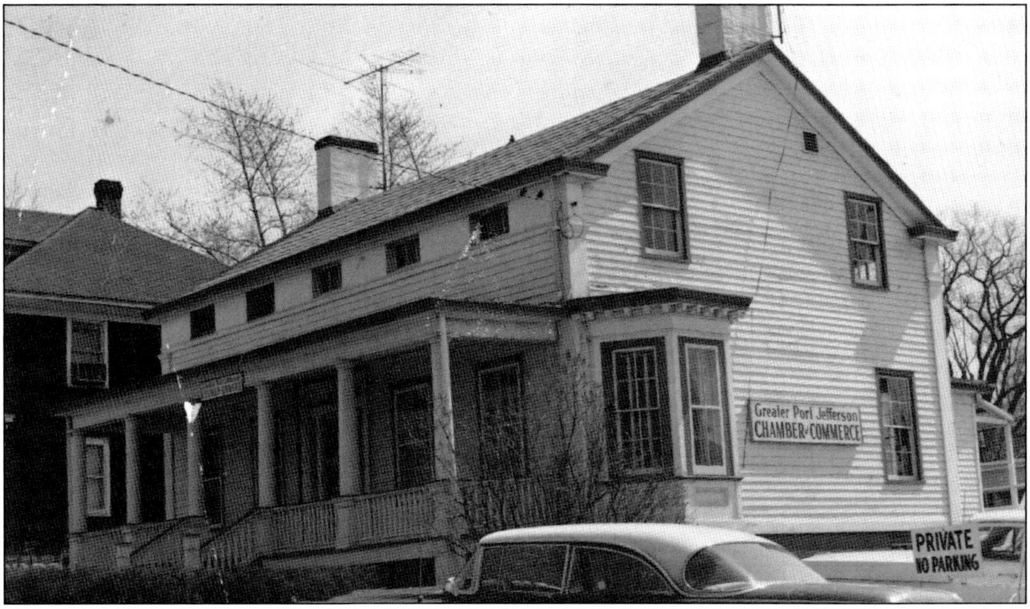

This handsome building on East Main Street was the home of Dominick Dondero. In the early years of the 20th century, he operated a fruit market across the street from his home, next to the Port Jefferson Hotel. The house was later torn down to make way for the present post office.

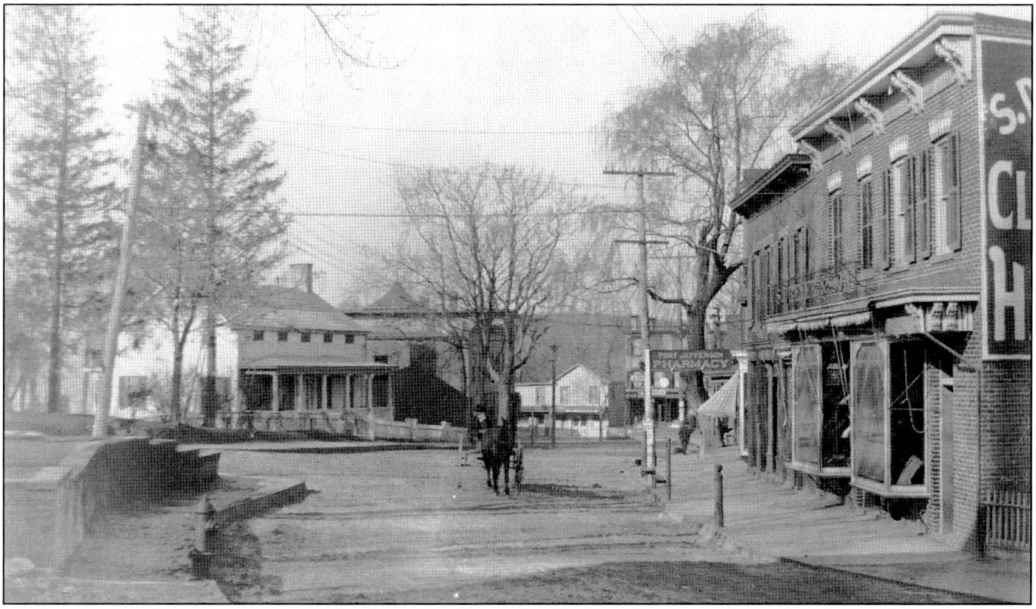

This view of East Main Street, dating from the early 1900s, looks west from the corner of Prospect Street. S. Dreyer & Sons men's furnishings store is on the right, and the Bank of Port Jefferson is beyond it. In the left foreground, the base of the Biddle Fountain can be seen.

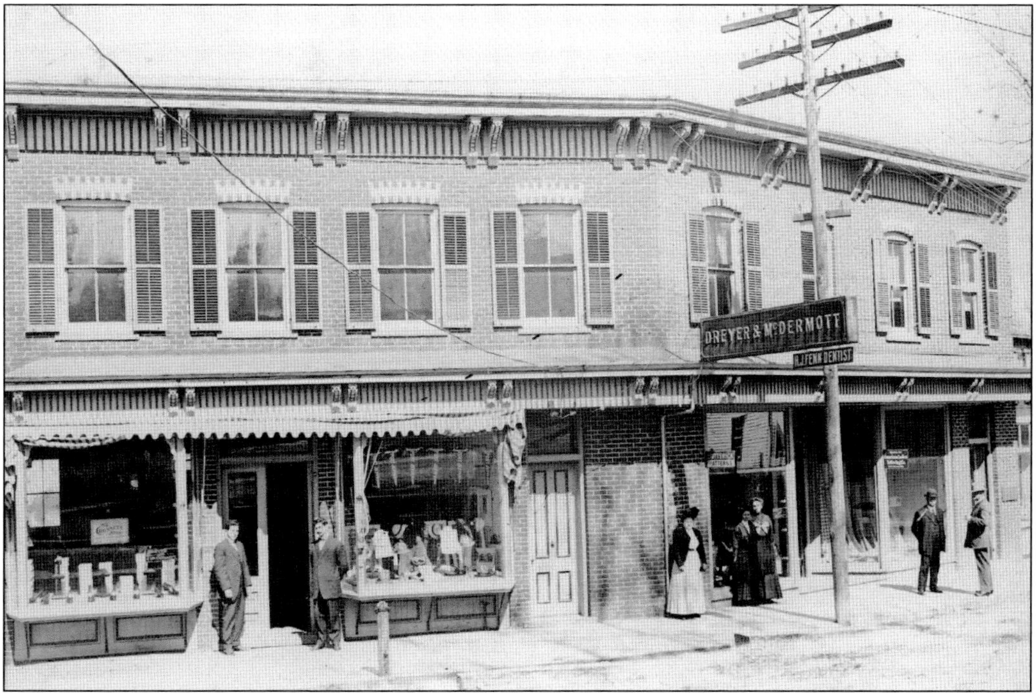

After 1909, the S. Dreyer & Sons shop was known as Dreyer & McDermott. The principal partners, Jacob S. Dreyer and Donald McDermott, headed a corporation composed of many of the leading men of the community. The store sold clothing for the whole family, in the hope that the shop would carry such an extensive line of merchandise that the people of Port Jefferson would have no need to shop elsewhere.

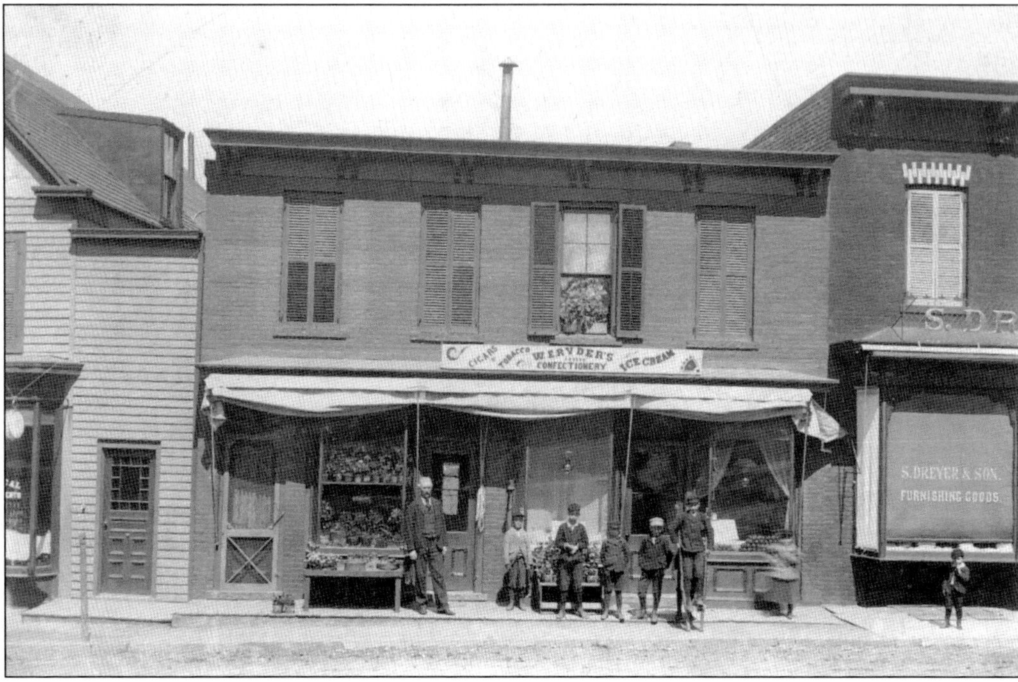

East of Hotel Square on East Main Street stood W.E. Ryder's restaurant and confectionery, shown here in 1895. The store also sold oysters, fruits, and vegetables. The building stood next to S. Dreyer & Sons men's furnishings and was later the home of the Bank of Port Jefferson.

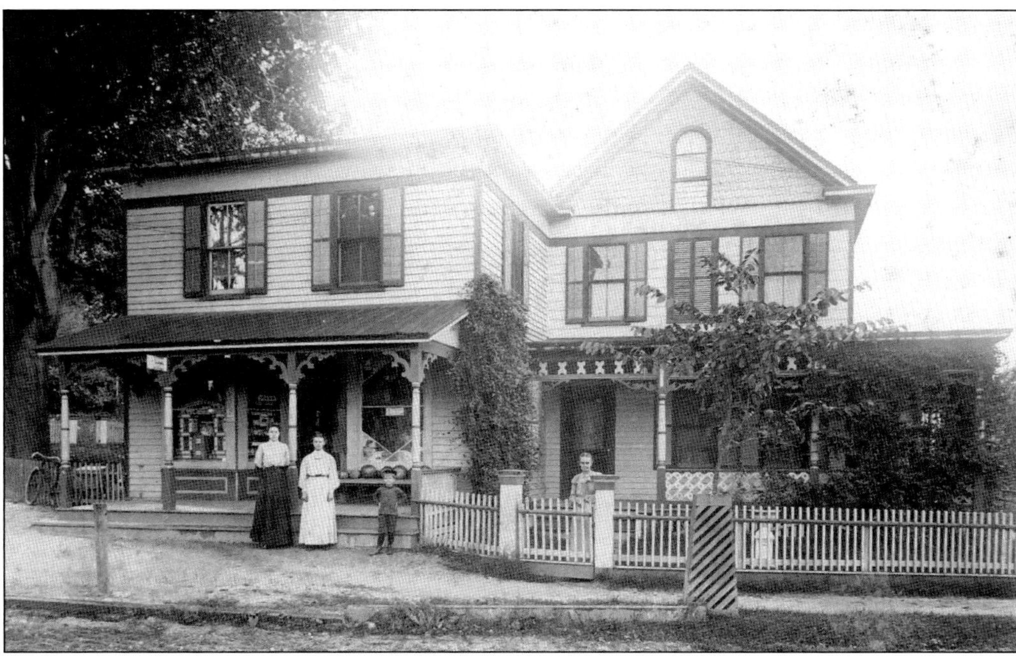

A store had stood on the corner of Beach Street and West Broadway for 60 years when Annie Odell took it over in 1936. The family lived in the 17-room house next door, which had also served as a boardinghouse for summer visitors. Until the 1970s, Odell's Country Grocery and Meat Market supplied the children of Port Jefferson with penny candy.

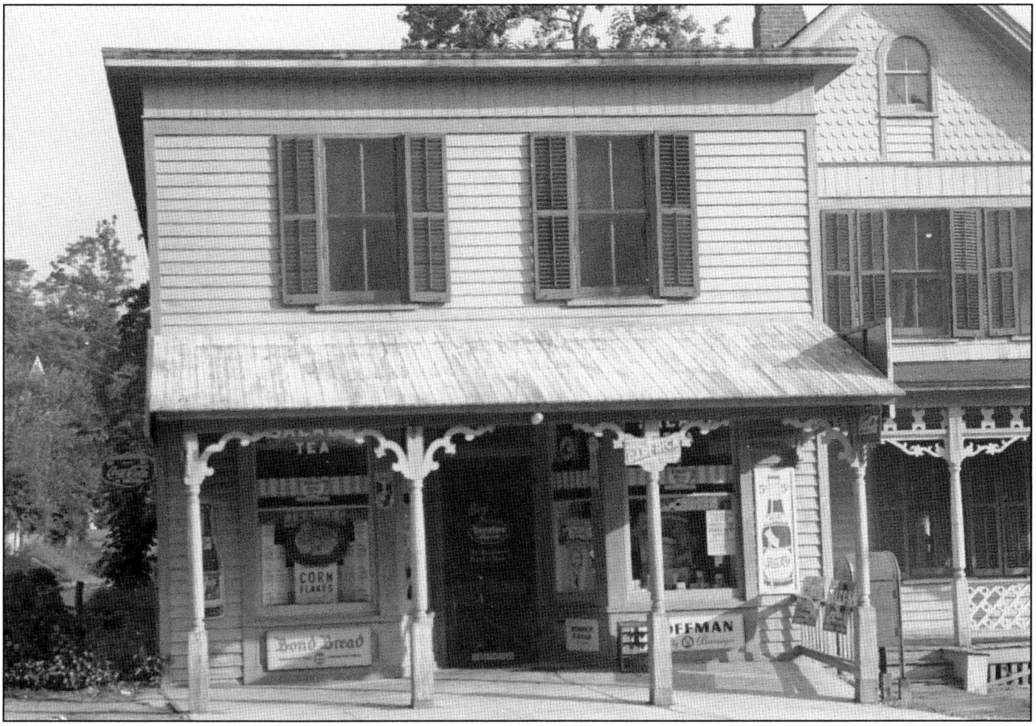

Later, Annie's son George and his wife, Janet, ran the store. During World War II, they would order three to five crates of pies baked by Frisbes in Bridgeport, to be delivered by the ferry every day. When the Long Island Lighting Company plant was being built in 1948, the store opened at 4:00 a.m. to make 400 cups of coffee by 9:00 a.m. for the morning shift of construction workers.

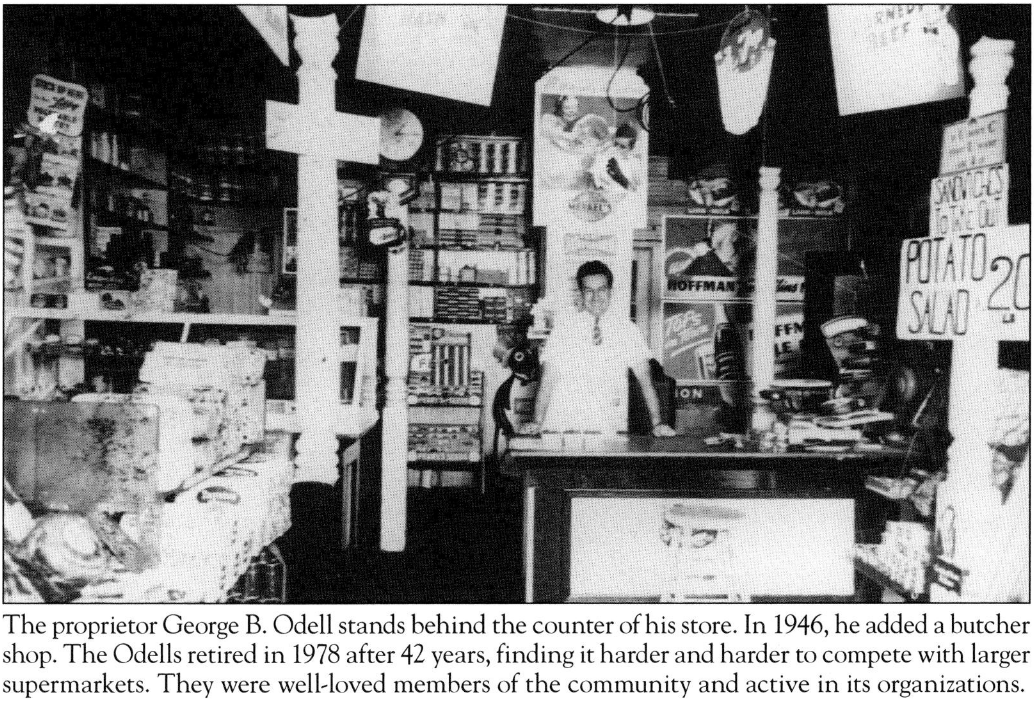

The proprietor George B. Odell stands behind the counter of his store. In 1946, he added a butcher shop. The Odells retired in 1978 after 42 years, finding it harder and harder to compete with larger supermarkets. They were well-loved members of the community and active in its organizations.

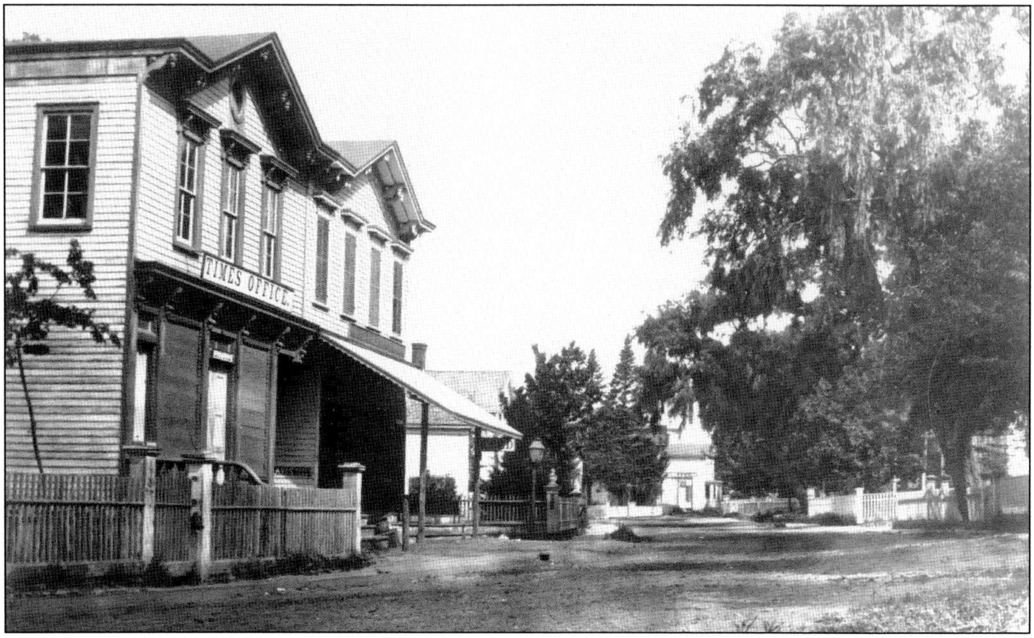

This 1870s photograph shows Petty's Confectionery sharing a building on the west side of Main Street with the offices of the local newspaper. Originally founded in 1873 as the *Long Island Leader,* the paper's name was changed to *Port Jefferson Times* in 1878. It merged with the *Port Jefferson Echo* in 1931, and continued to publish until 1966.

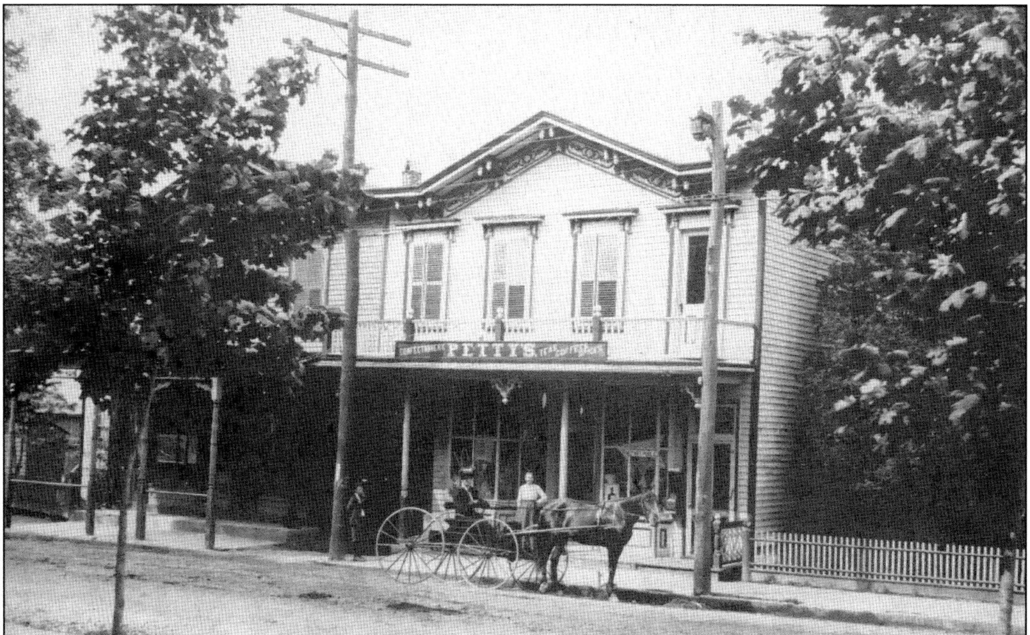

It is now some 20 years later, and Petty's is still satisfying the sweet tooth of many Port Jefferson residents. The store advertised mixed candy, raisins, nuts, and fruits, in addition to New Orleans molasses and syrups, Colgate's perfumes and soaps, and "a nice line of crockery." This is a view of the shop across Main Street from the grounds of the Methodist church.

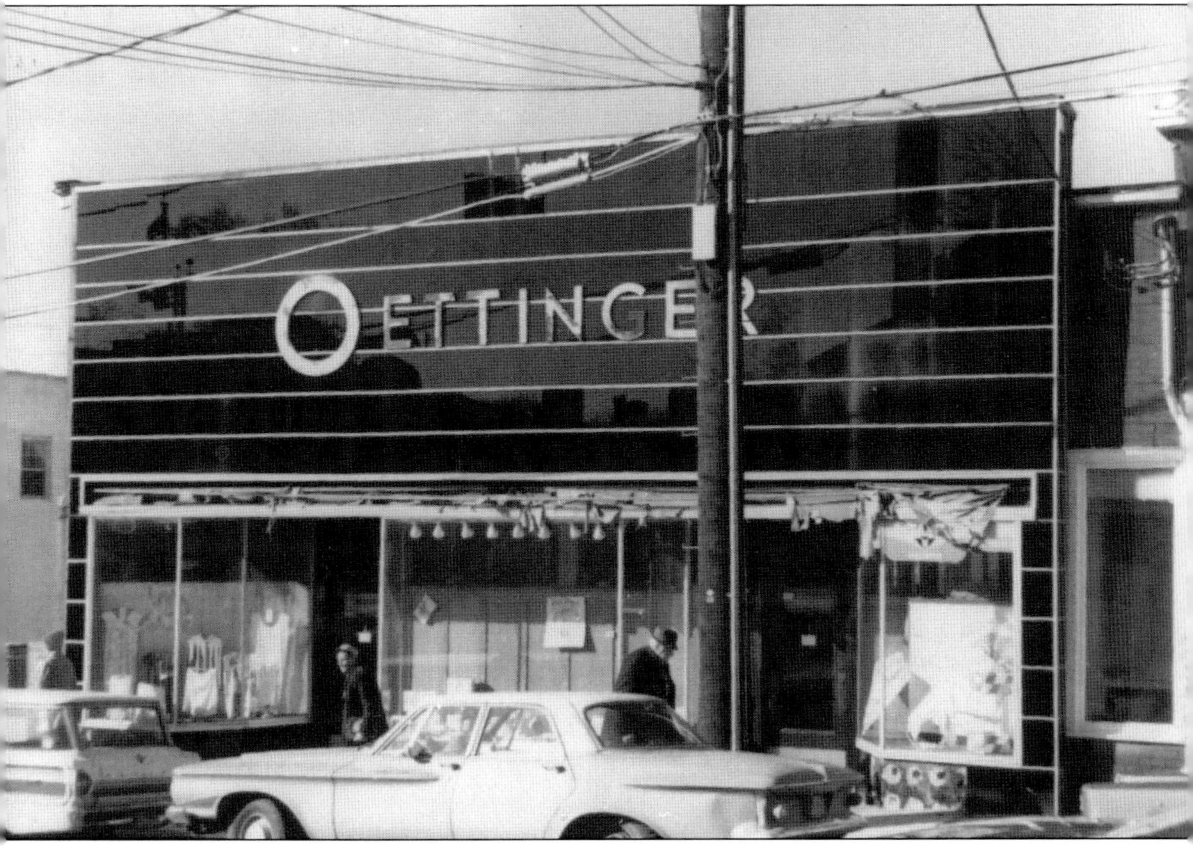

Thaddeus Oettinger moved his variety store to East Main Street in 1916 and expanded to two floors in 1936. Oettinger's was a true hometown variety store, selling everything from the smallest everyday items to stoves and heaters. In a local newspaper story about the store, Oettinger's policy is stated simply as wanting to leave the customer "pleased and satisfied." In the 1950s and 1960s, it was "The Store" in town. Oettinger's turned out to be the last of a dying breed of mom-and-pop downtown department stores whose days were numbered with the advent of the indoor shopping mall. These new "Main Streets" were a magnet for shoppers drawn by the variety of stores and the free and abundant parking. Most malls were anchored by large department store chains such as Macy's, A&S, and Sears Roebuck. Oettinger himself was an active member of the community throughout his life. The store stood just to the right of the present-day iron stairs leading to the Trader's Cove parking lot.

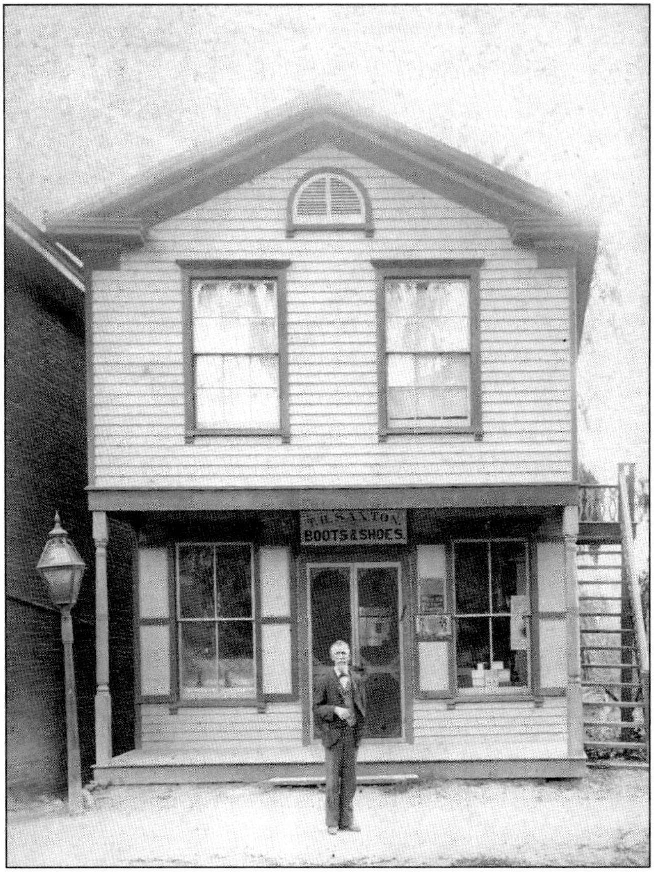

In the late 1800s, Thomas H. Saxton kept a shoe store on the west side of East Main Street, opposite the present-day library, where the stairs to the parking lot are now located. He also served as the surveyor of customs in Port Jefferson for four years in the 1890s.

The substantial building below stood on the south side of East Broadway, just west of the Harborview Hotel. Shown here in 1925, it housed, from left to right, the Lerch Music Shop, Azenaro's Fruits and Vegetables, and the Vandall food market. Joseph Vandall had previously worked for Lester H. Davis in his market across the street.

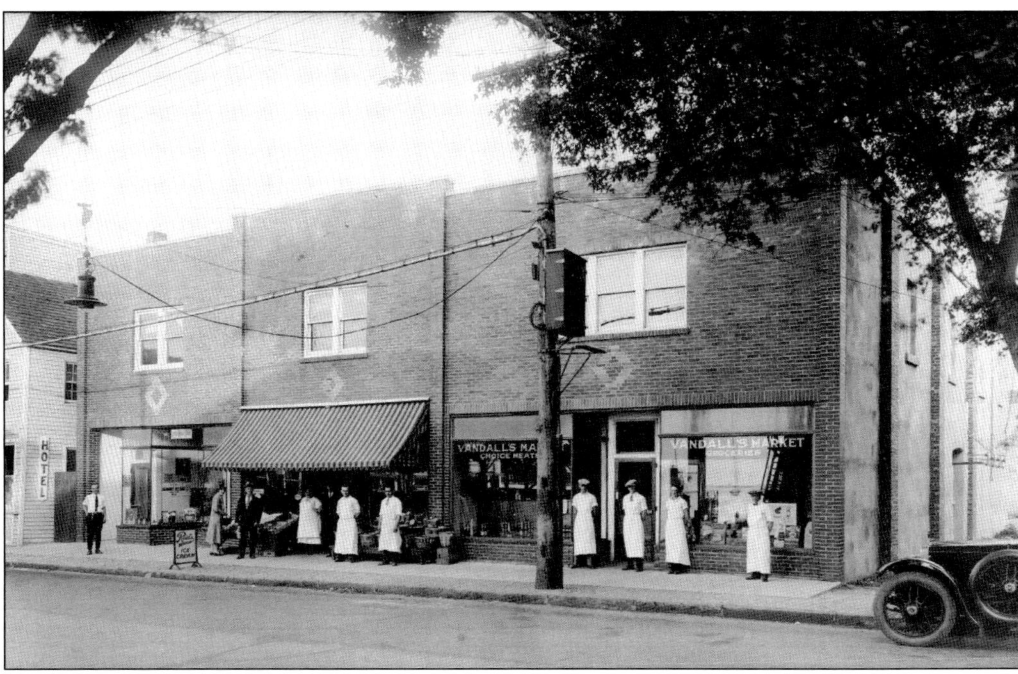

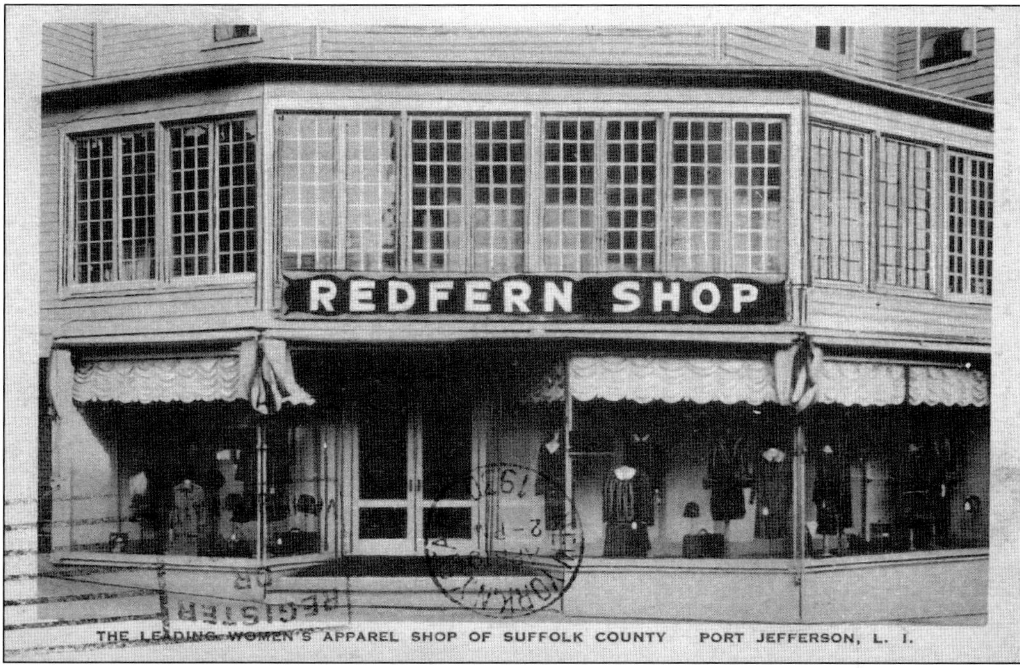

The Redfern Shop opened in the Townsend House building around 1919. At the time of this photograph, taken in the 1930s, it was known as "the leading women's apparel shop of Suffolk County." It moved to Port Jefferson Station in 1964, where it remained in business into the 1980s.

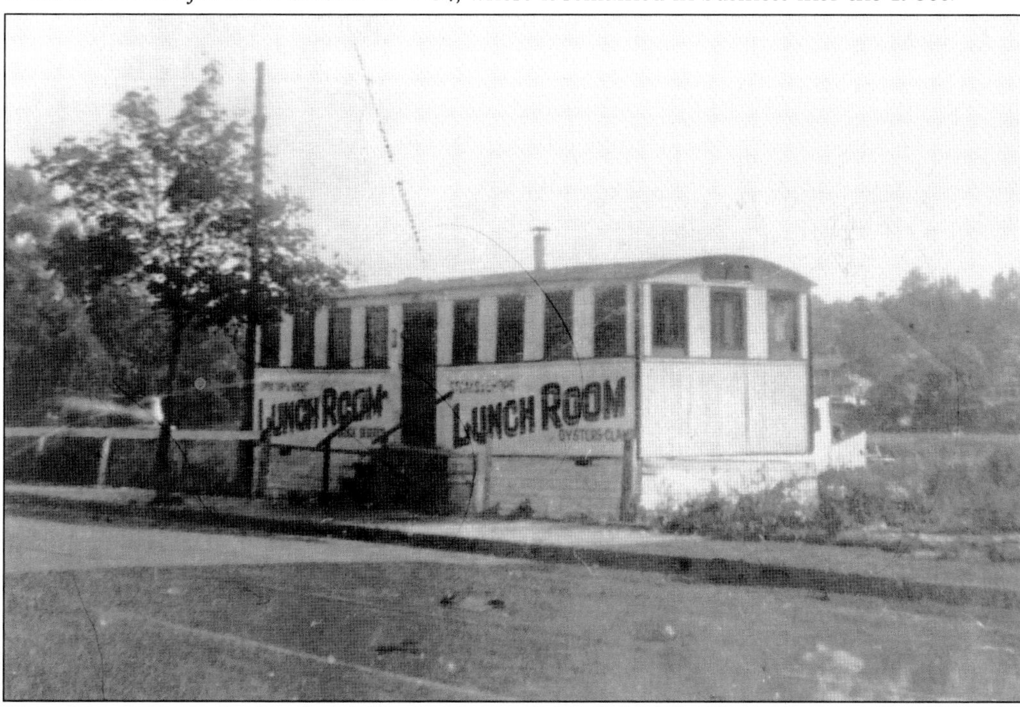

Popular with workers from the Bayles Shipyard until it was moved in the late 1920s, the Lunch Room diner, shown here in 1918, stood on the west side of Main Street. Note that even at this late date, the west side of the street was largely undeveloped.

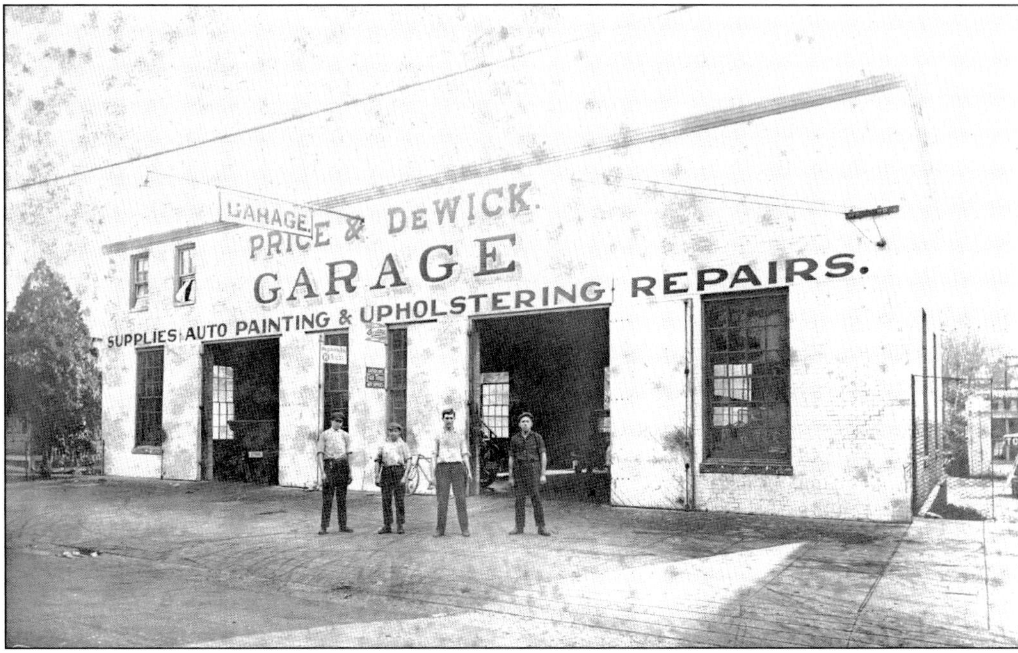

Frederick C. Griswold built this garage in 1910, shortly after purchasing the property and the adjacent Athena Hall on Main Street. As owner of the theater, he was prompted to invent a better system for splicing film. The resulting Griswold Film Splicer was used in movie studios and theaters throughout the world. After numerous owners and uses, the building was torn down in 1987 to make way for the current Plaza 414 offices.

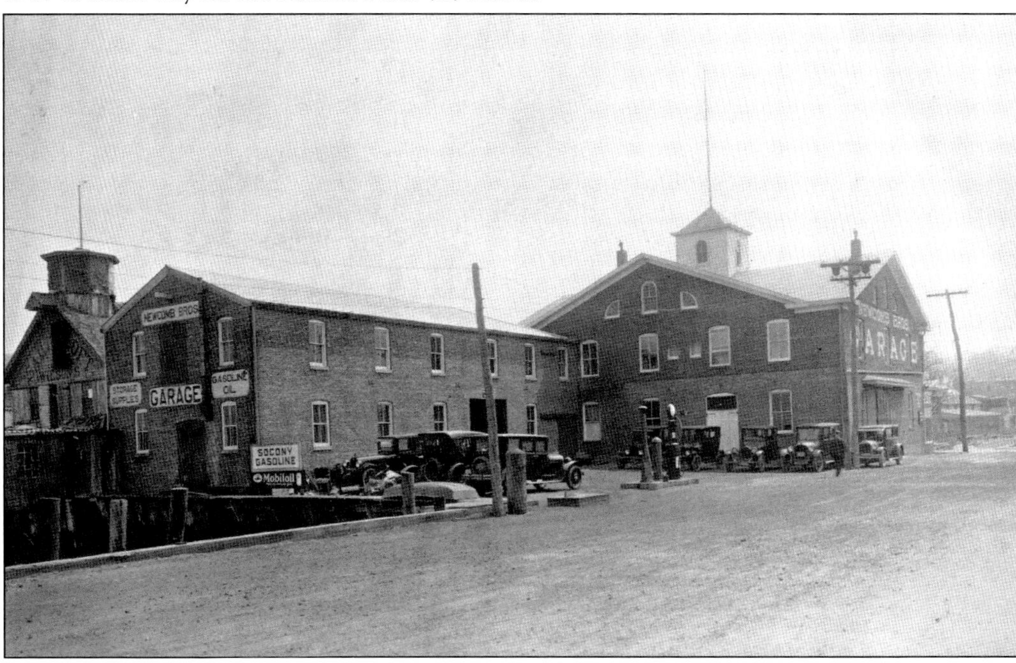

The Newcomb brothers, Seward and Andrew, opened their automobile sales and repair business in the old F.F. Darling store on the north side of East Broadway in 1919. They sold Nash and Dodge cars and Graham Brothers trucks. Shown here is the garage as it appeared in 1926.

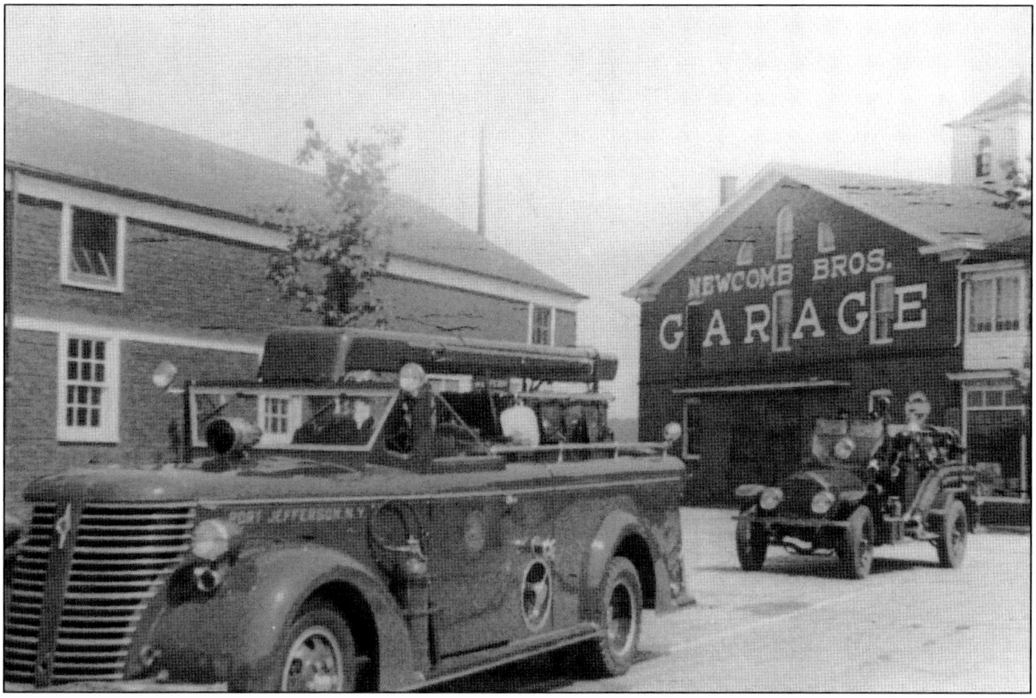

Port Jefferson Fire Department trucks from 1939 and 1922 are shown in front of the Newcomb Brothers Garage. In later years, the building was the home of McAllister Motors, dealing in Dodge automobiles. The building was destroyed by fire in 1972, and McAllister Motors moved across the street to what is now Chandler Square.

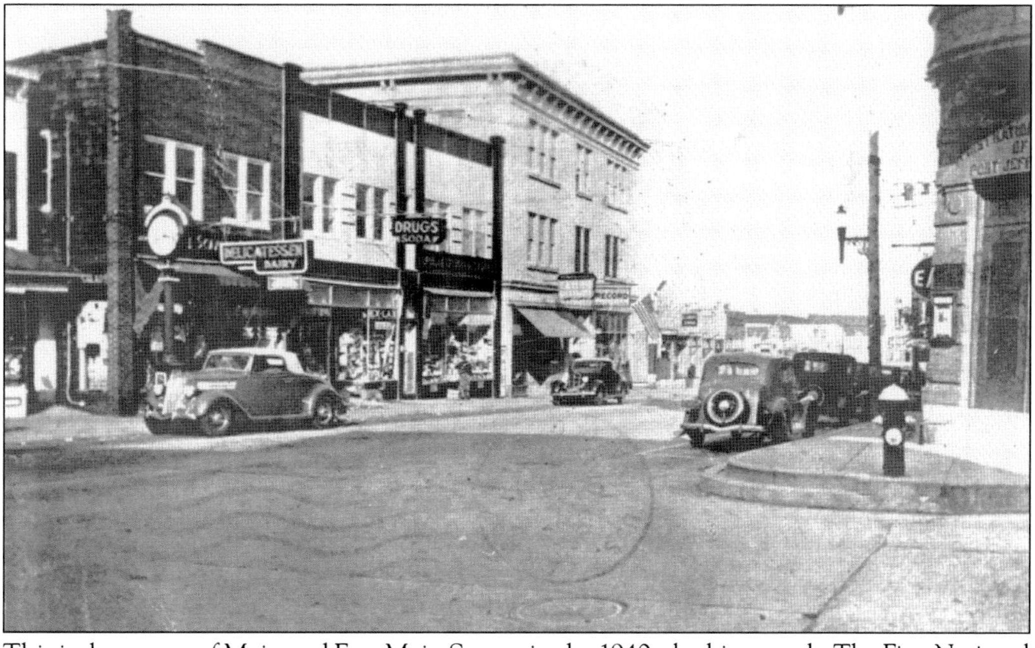

This is the corner of Main and East Main Streets in the 1940s, looking north. The First National Bank is on the right. The post office (with flag) and the offices of the *Port Jefferson Record* newspaper are in the Dyett Brick building on the left, as are Feldman and Glaser, tailors.

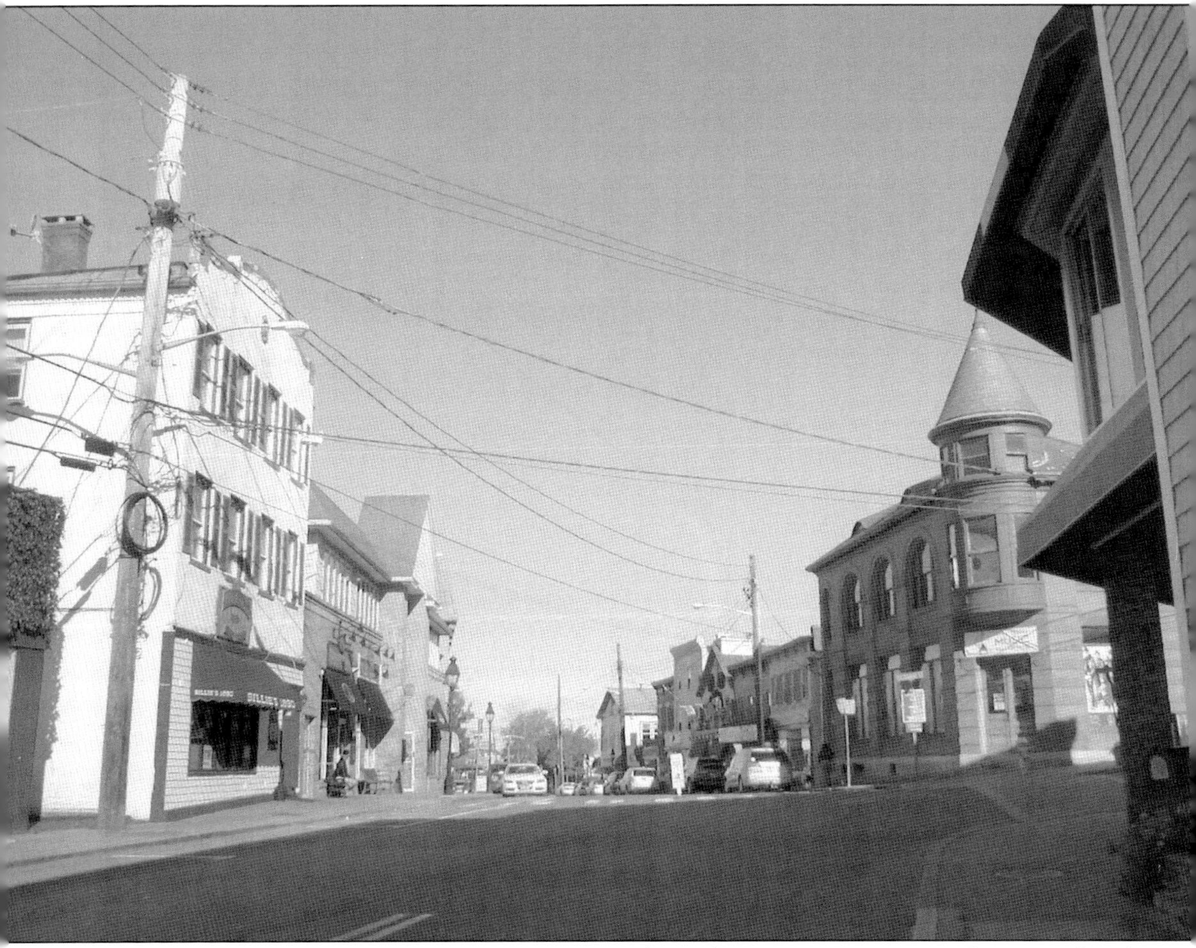

This is Port Jefferson's Main Street as it appears today. Where at one time or another it was lined with hotels, a livery stable, the fire department, various automobile dealerships, a sweet shop, and the post office building, the present incarnation is comprised principally of a combination of retail shops and dining establishments, the majority of them locally owned. The village remains an attractive destination for a number of reasons. Be it browsing the many stores, dining in its myriad restaurants, attending a production at Theatre Three, or taking a historical walking tour, Port Jefferson's allure is undeniable. Local government and civic associations continually strive to promote the village by cosponsoring events, such as Greenfest, the American Music Festival, Harvestfest, and the Dickens Festival. The Port Jefferson Business Improvement District organization aims to improve the overall appearance of downtown through architectural upgrades, enhanced landscaping and decoration, and attractive signage and improved cleanliness. These goals reflect the civic aspirations of groups of more than a century ago, such as the Village Improvement Society and the Port Jefferson Business Men's Association. (Courtesy of the Port Jefferson Free Library.)

Four

PLENTY OF ROOM IN PORT

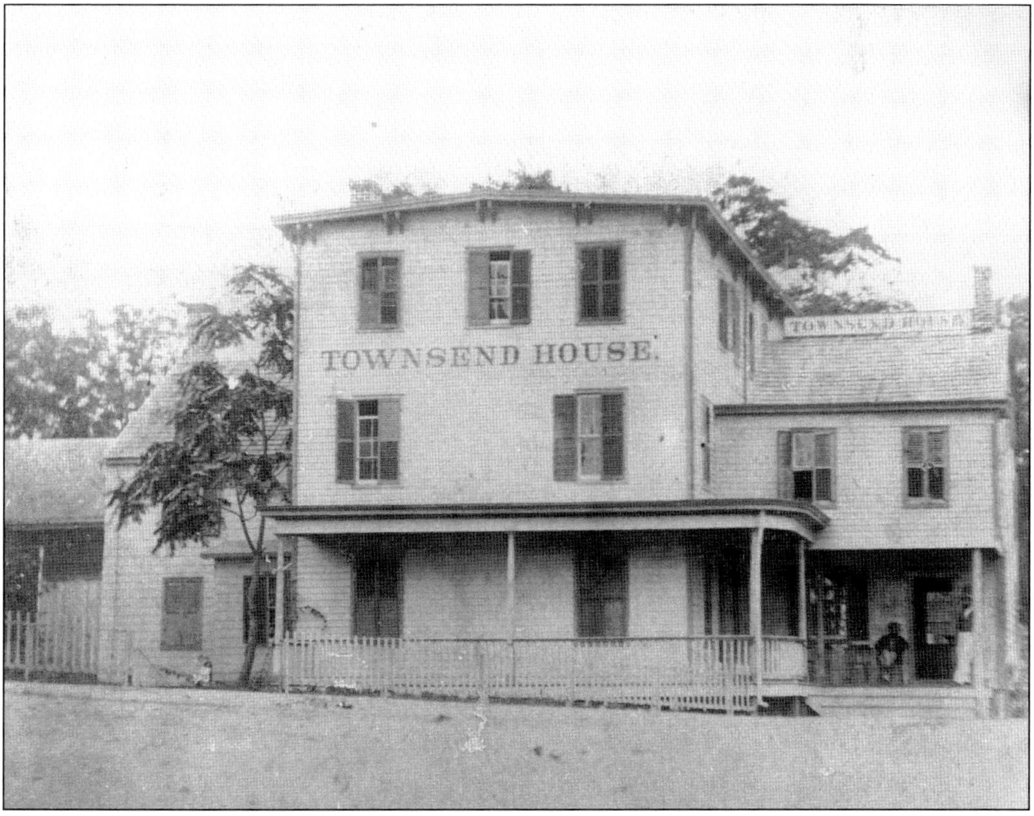

The old John Roe House (1682) became the Townsend House hotel when it was acquired by Henry K. Townsend in 1840. The intersection of Main and East Main Streets was known for years as Hotel Square. Port Jefferson's first permanent post office was established there around 1855, with Townsend as the first postmaster.

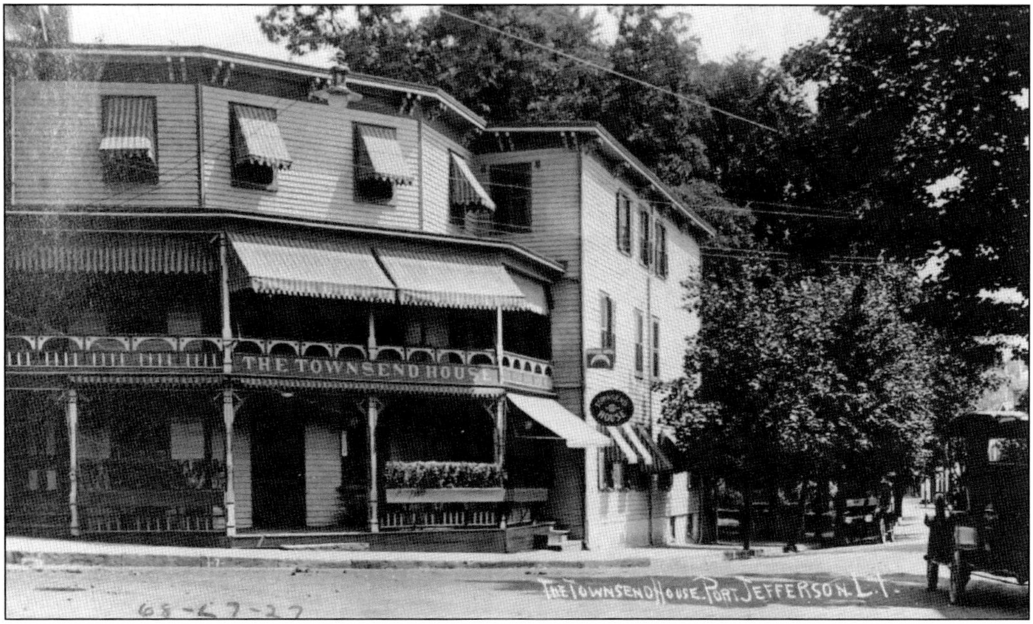

After Caleb Davis bought the Townsend House in 1868, he enlarged it by inserting a three-story middle section between the two original halves of the house. The west wing was removed in 1893, and with the new curved appearance, welcoming verandas and awnings were added.

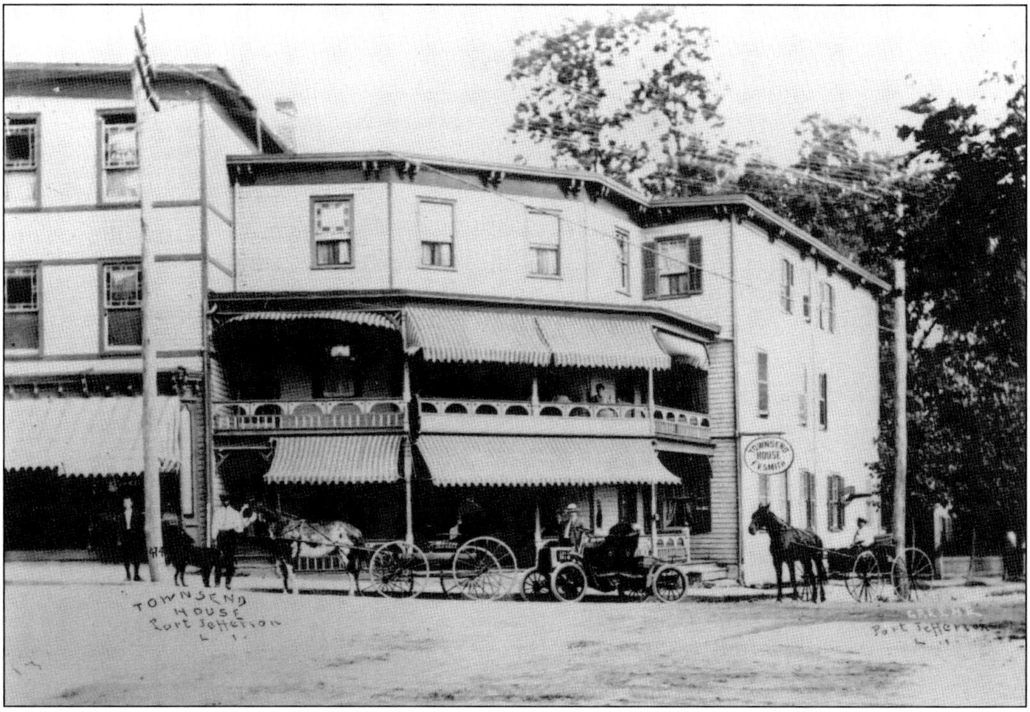

The Townsend House remained popular with travelers and residents for dinners and meetings into the 20th century. It advertised "First class board with airy rooms." In this 1905 photograph, livery and stage drivers are waiting for passengers, perhaps to take them to the Long Island Rail Road station.

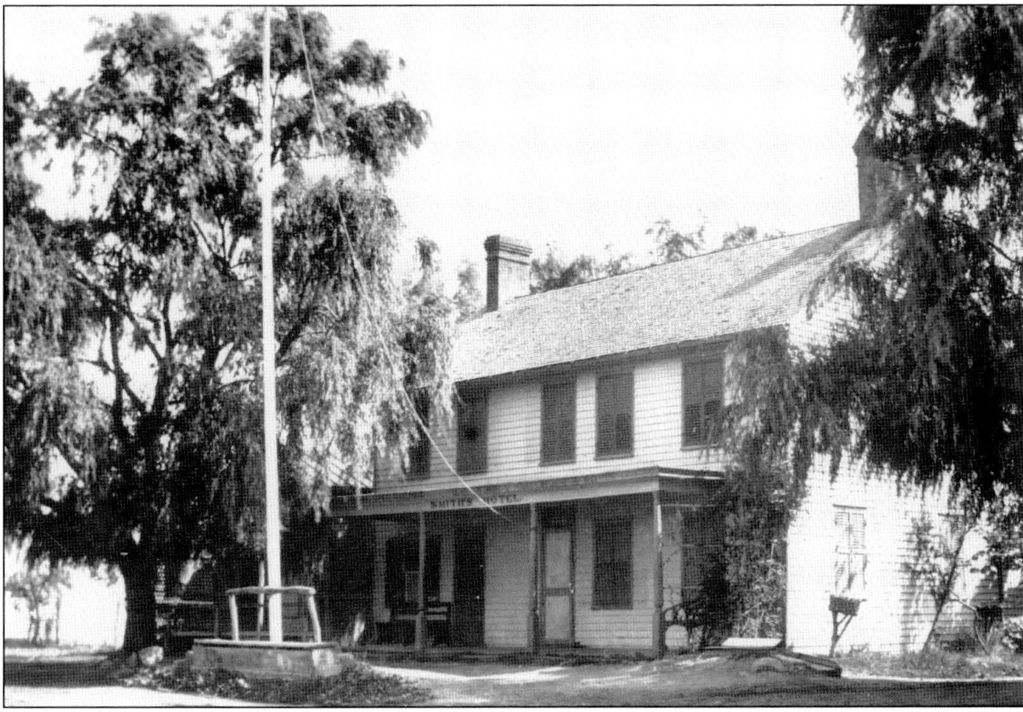

Thomas Smith erected this two-and-a-half-story hotel on what is now the northeast corner of Main Street and Arden Place in 1870. His daughter Lizzie enlarged it and made it into one of the most popular hotels in the village. Around 1908, Lizzie Smith's Hotel was purchased by William Thompson, who greatly enlarged it and renamed it the Ardencraig Inn.

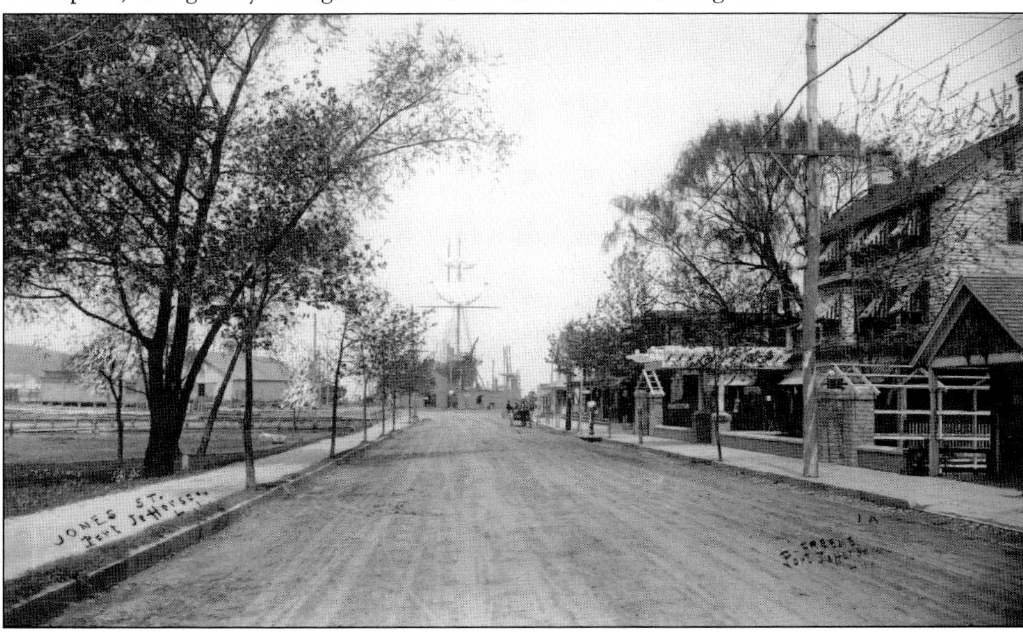

The Ardencraig Inn is on the right in this north-facing view of Main Street. Known for its excellent cuisine and accommodations, the inn was particularly popular with visiting yachtsmen. (Courtesy of Frances Child.)

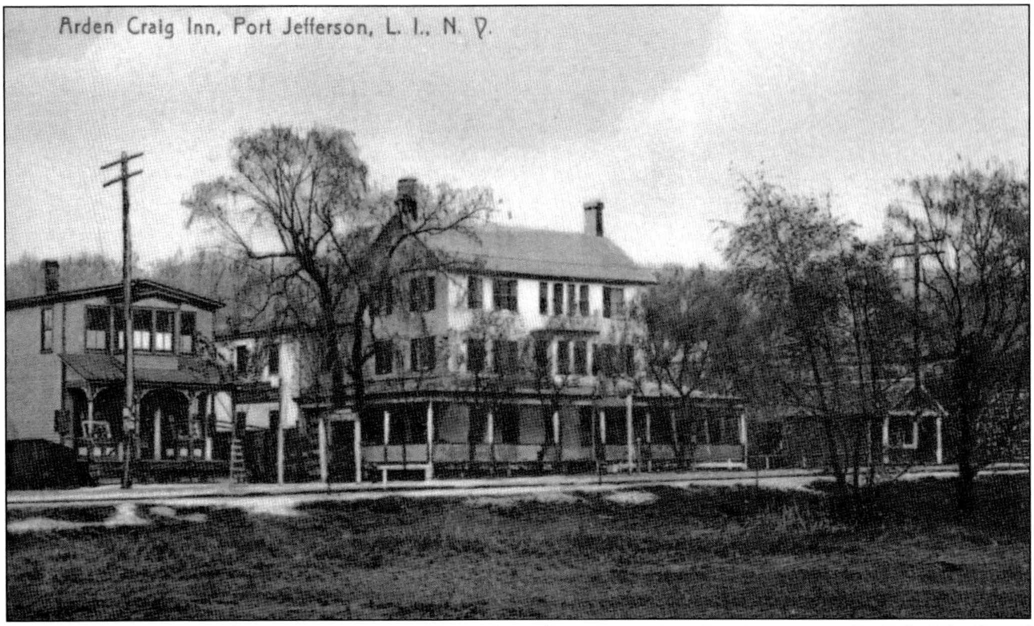

In this view of the Ardencraig Inn, Russell's Café and Summer Garden is seen on the left. The hotel was destroyed by fire in 1920 and replaced by a bowling alley and billiard parlor. Later, a car dealership, a supermarket, and now a Gap store have occupied the corner. (Courtesy of Frances Child.)

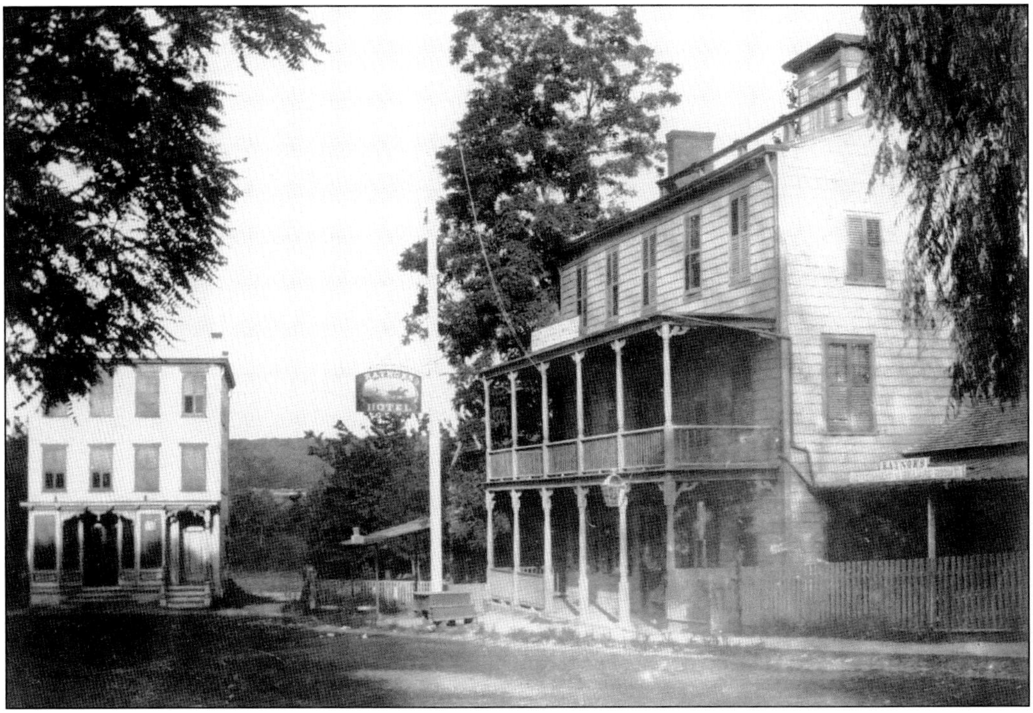

Raynor's Hotel, also known as the Port Jefferson Hotel, was built in 1879 on the corner of Main and East Main Streets, across Hotel Square from the Townsend House. It stood until 1949, when it was razed to build the town police station, later the Brookhaven tax office annex. To the left is the building now housing Billie's 1890 Saloon.

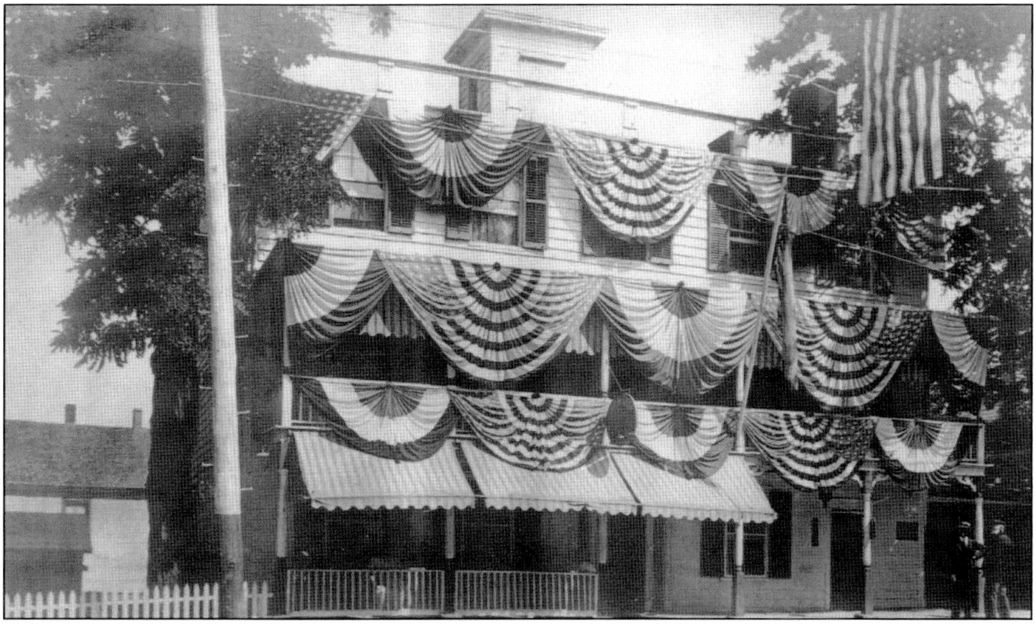

Originally known as the Mansion House and distinguished by the cupola on its roof, the Port Jefferson Hotel is shown here decorated for Old Home Week, probably in 1908. Albert Walker, a Civil War veteran, became manager in 1889. The cupola was a magnet for mischievous youngsters, who were known to attempt to fly kites from it.

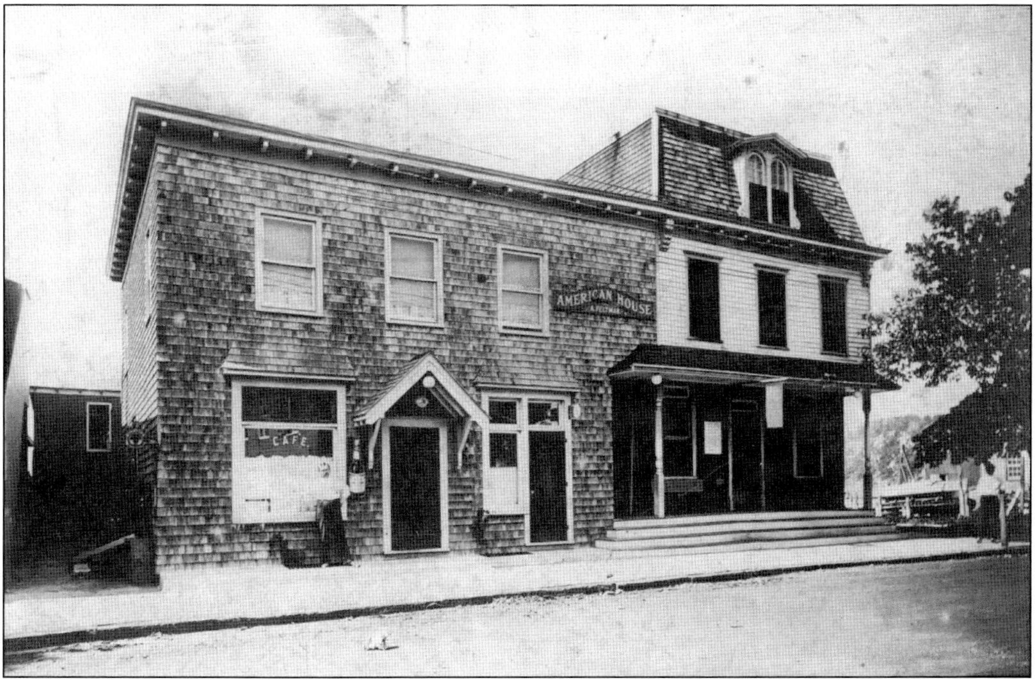

Pictured in the early 1900s, the American House hotel, owned by Arthur Feltman, was located on the north side of East Broadway. In 1913, it was enlarged and remodeled to include 22 sleeping rooms, two dining rooms, a party room, a café, and a large porch "directly on the water." The property was purchased for use as a sand and gravel yard in 1929.

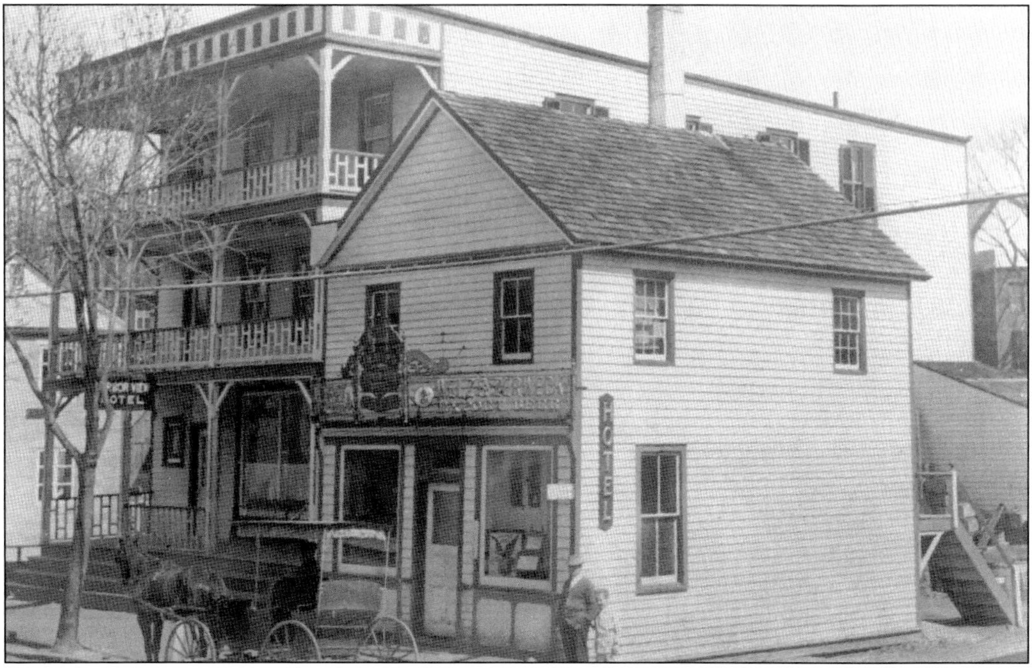

The Harborview Hotel was built around the turn of the last century on the south side of East Broadway. As its name implies, it offered a panoramic view of the harbor from its elegant porches. It was a popular venue for meetings and for a time served as headquarters for the Port Jefferson Yacht Club. It was declared unsafe and torn down in 1969.

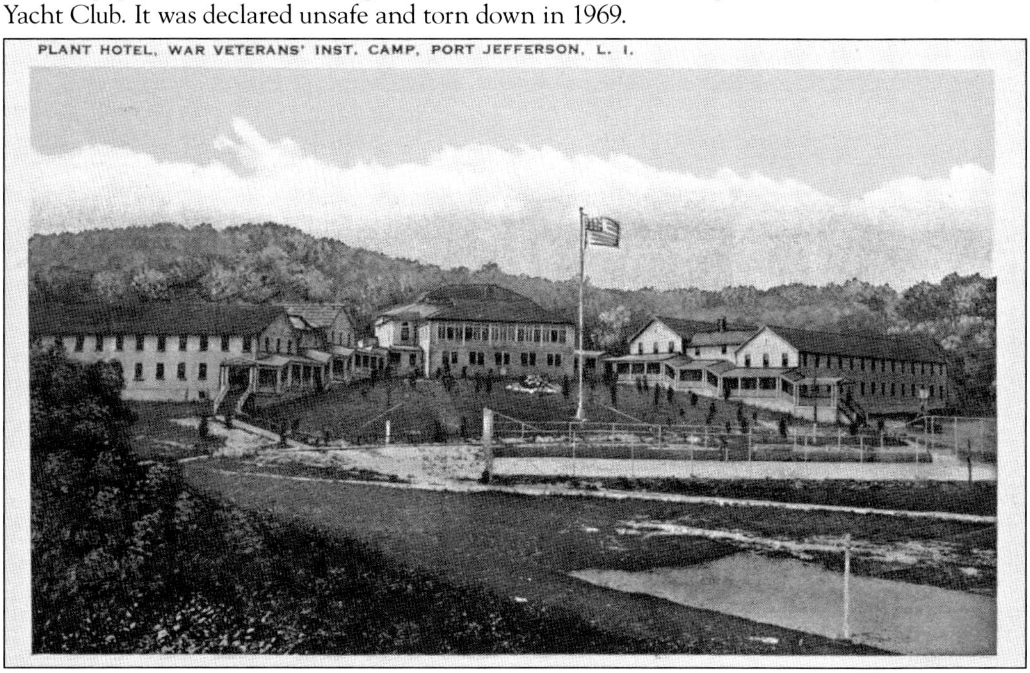

The Plant Hotel was built in 1918 to accommodate some of the 1,100 workers hired by the Bayles Shipyard. After the New York Harbor & Dry Dock Company dismissed almost all of the workers on December 24, 1920, the building became a training school for disabled veterans before being demolished in 1934 to build the present-day high school.

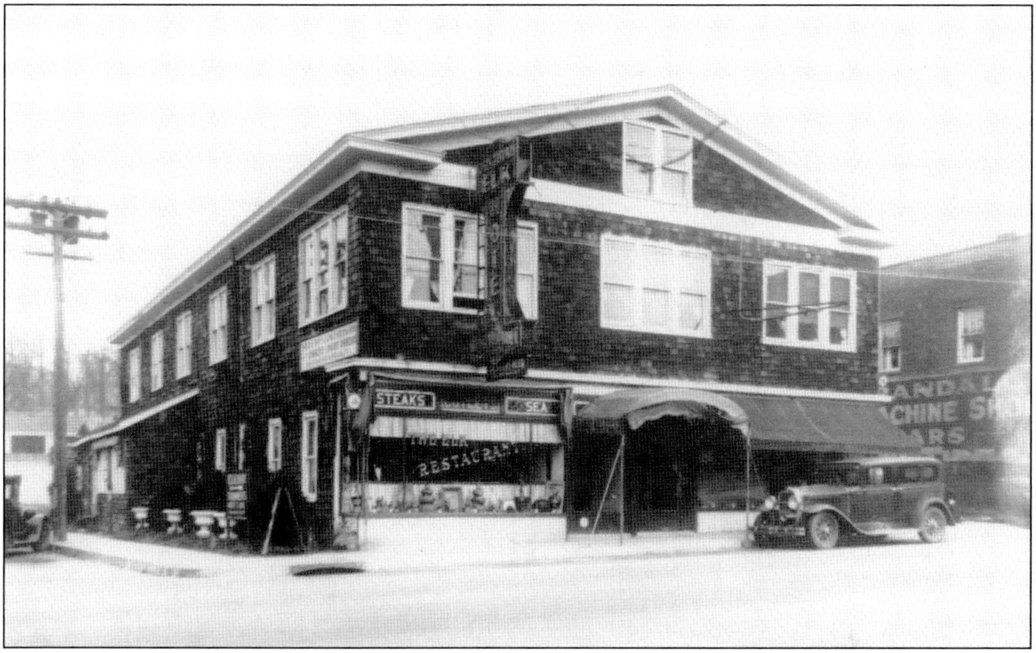

Shown here in 1933, the Elk Hotel and Restaurant was built in the 1920s on the site of the Effingham Tuthill Carriage Manufactory, on the southeast corner of Main Street and Arden Place. Owned by the Koutrakos family for almost 80 years, it was a popular meeting place for residents and visitors alike.

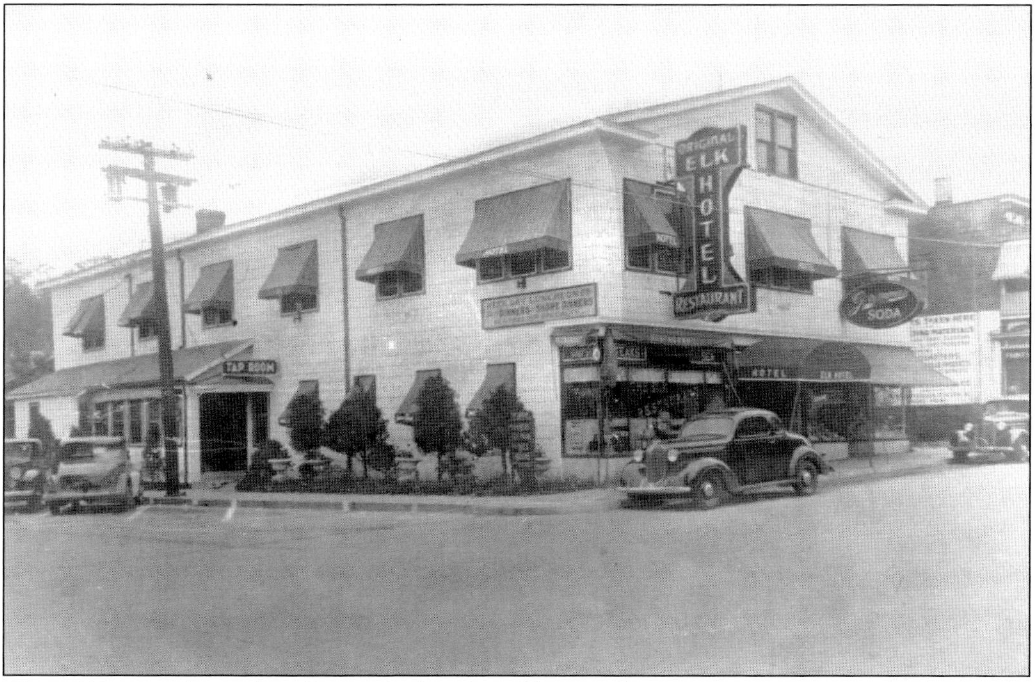

This 1937 view shows the Elk Hotel after the addition of a taproom entrance in the back. The building also housed Grammas's soda fountain before it moved a block south and to the opposite side of the street. The building still houses a restaurant as well as a Starbucks coffee shop.

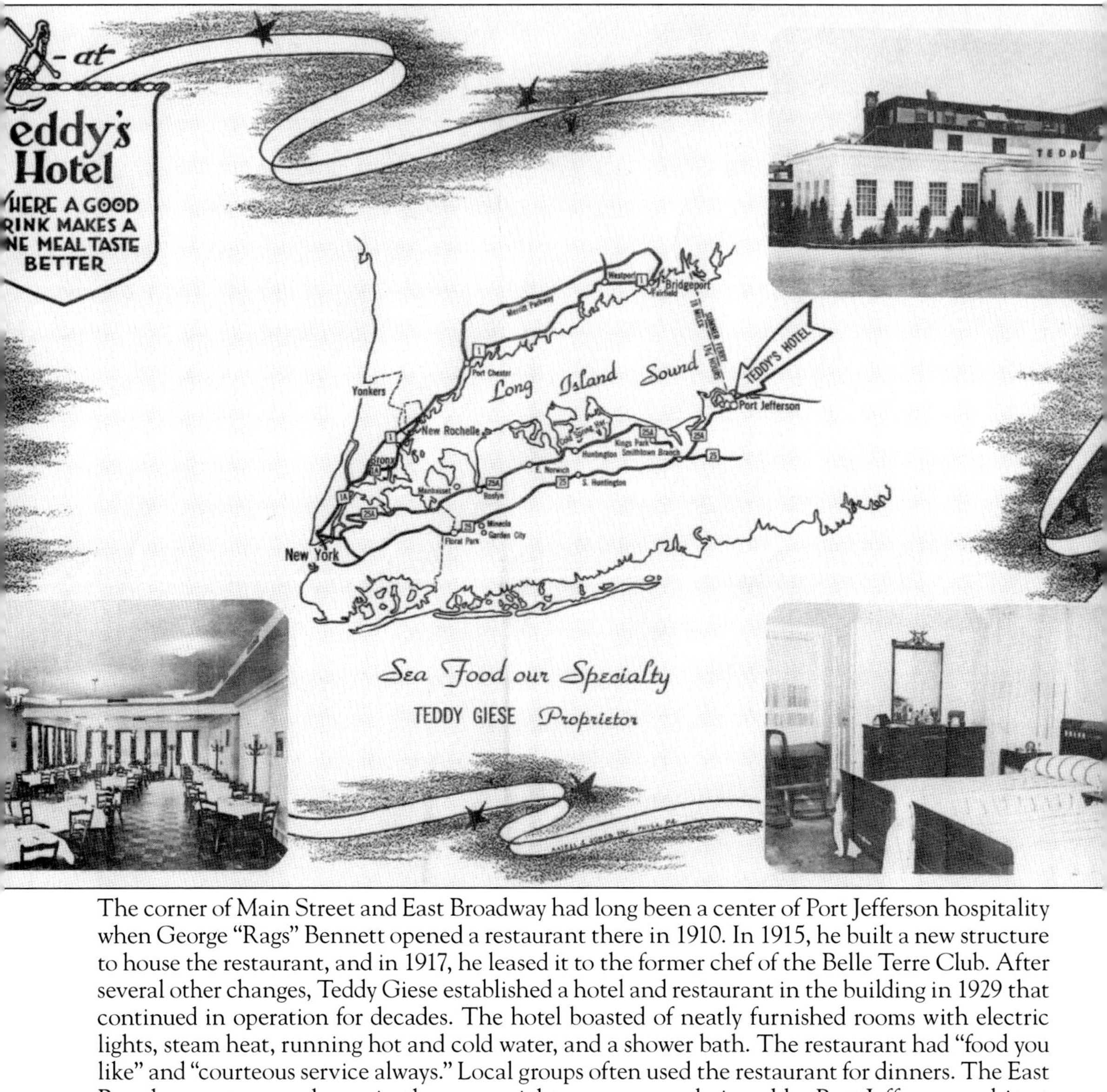

The corner of Main Street and East Broadway had long been a center of Port Jefferson hospitality when George "Rags" Bennett opened a restaurant there in 1910. In 1915, he built a new structure to house the restaurant, and in 1917, he leased it to the former chef of the Belle Terre Club. After several other changes, Teddy Giese established a hotel and restaurant in the building in 1929 that continued in operation for decades. The hotel boasted of neatly furnished rooms with electric lights, steam heat, running hot and cold water, and a shower bath. The restaurant had "food you like" and "courteous service always." Local groups often used the restaurant for dinners. The East Broadway entrance, shown in the upper right corner, was designed by Port Jefferson architect Daniel Perry. Later known as the Whaler's Inn, the building was demolished in 1967.

Five

SERVING THE COMMUNITY

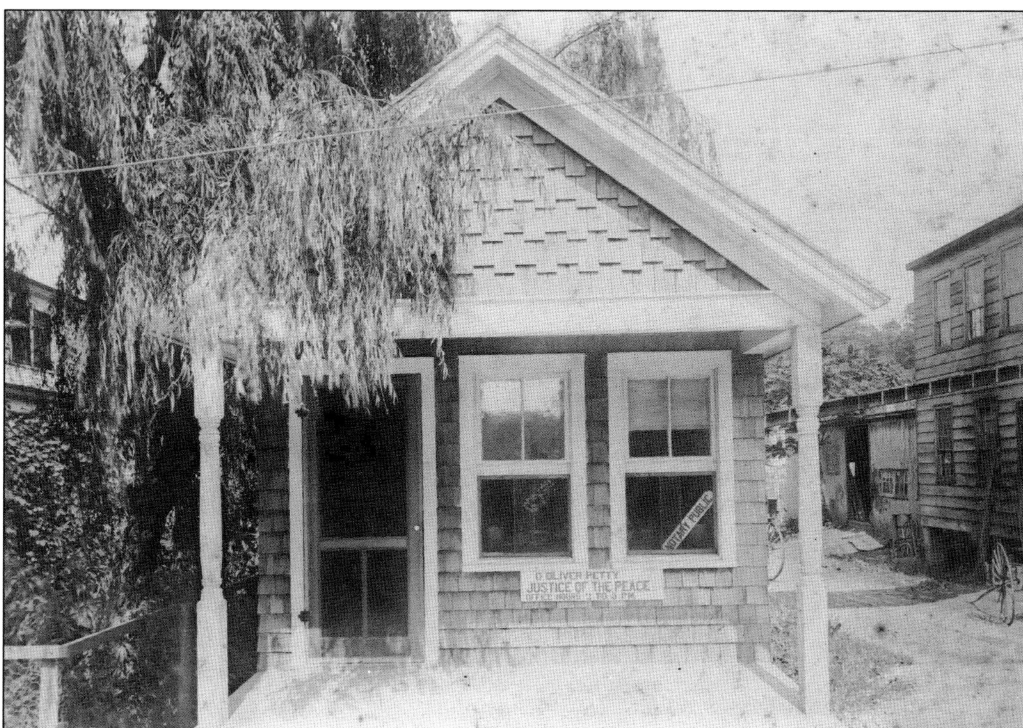

The offices of Justice of the Peace D. Oliver Petty were located on Main Street and Arden Place. Petty was a Republican elected to office in 1907 after having been appointed to an unexpired term in 1906. He later operated a variety store in Brooklyn until his death in 1920.

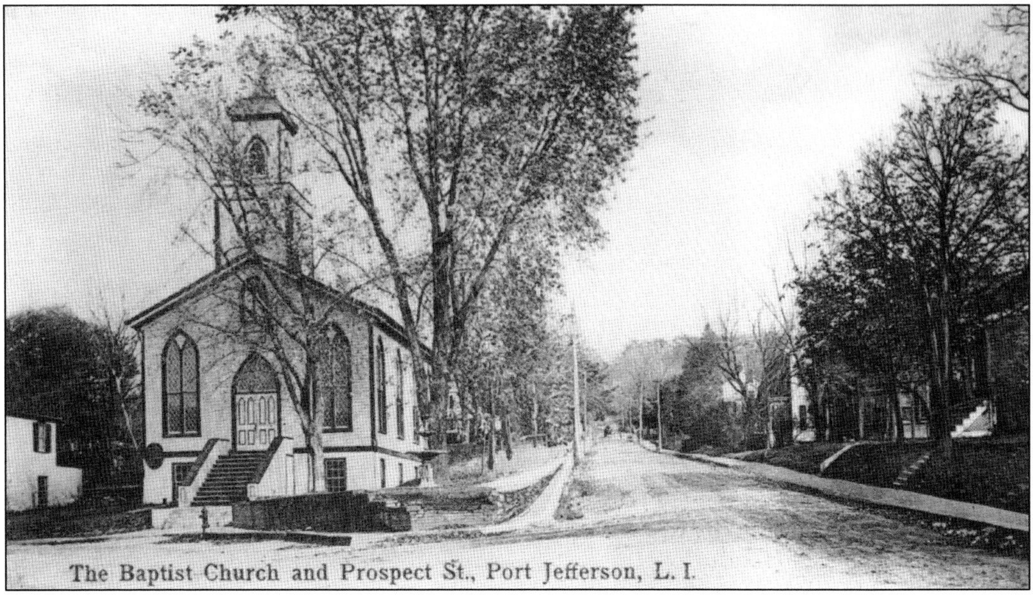

The First Baptist Church building was originally a place of worship for the Congregationalists. Unable to sustain their number, they sold the church to the Baptists in 1861. Its location on the corner of East Main and Prospect Streets made it a popular gathering place for the community. The Biddle Fountain stood in front of the church for a number of years. Today, the church is the Island Christian Church.

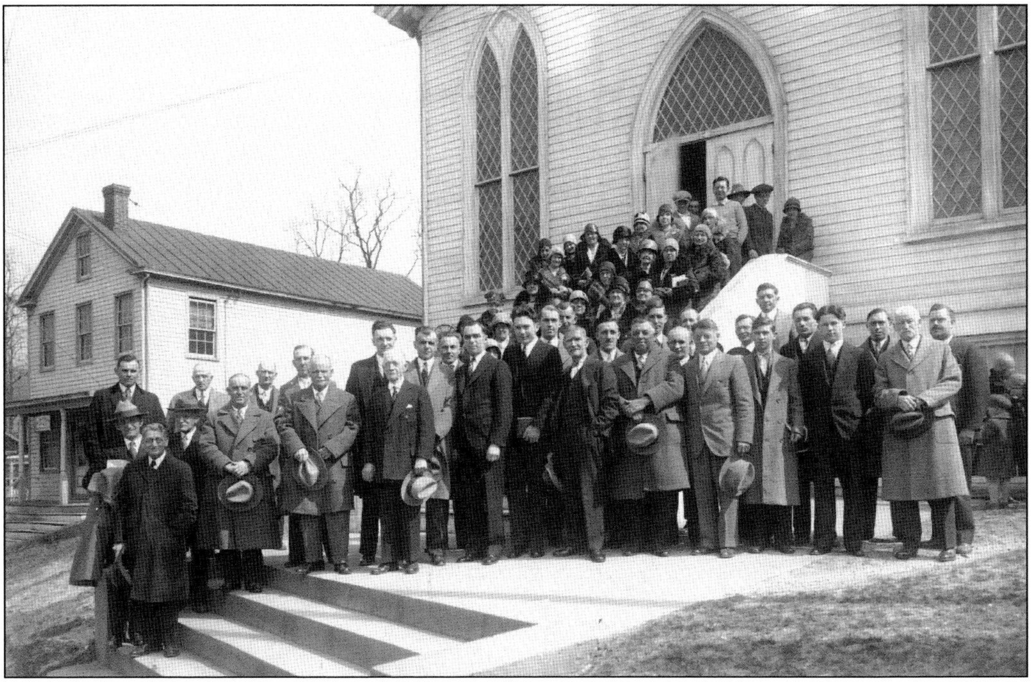

This c. 1930 photograph shows a gathering of the Baptist congregation outside the church. Madeline Randall Woodard, the congregation's organist, was transported to the fleet anchored off Port Jefferson to play for Sunday services during World War I. The headquarters of the Wilson Ritch Post of the American Legion is on the left, in what had been the library building.

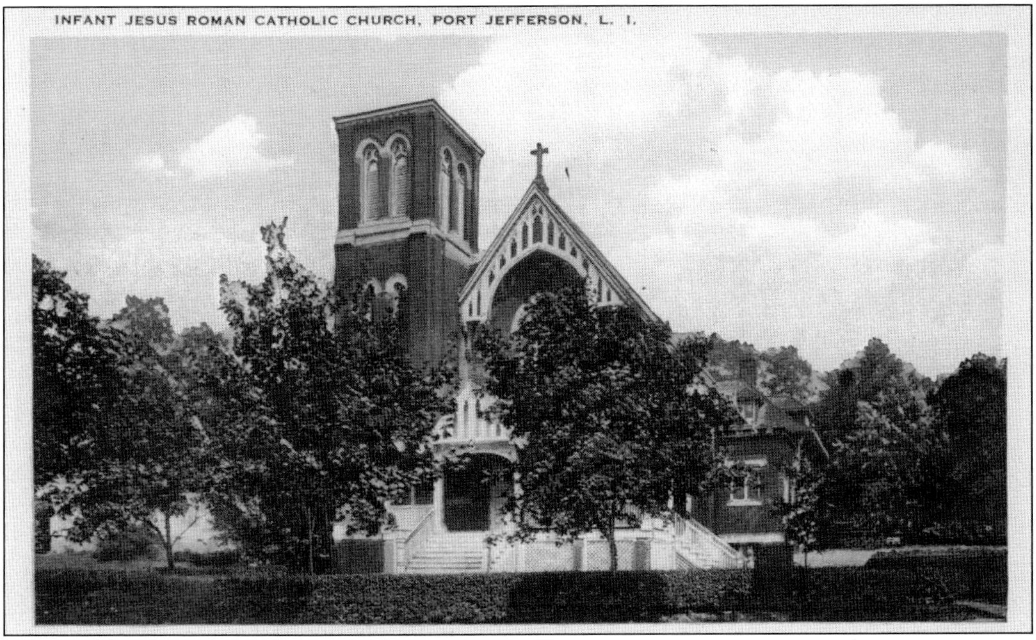

After meeting in the Bayles Chandlery hall and then in the home of Franklin Hawkins at the corner of Main Street and Myrtle Avenue, the Roman Catholic congregation of Infant Jesus purchased Hawkins's property and built a church on it. The building, dedicated on June 30, 1912, had a seating capacity of 500 and cost $25,000 to construct. It is still serving the Catholic community of Port Jefferson.

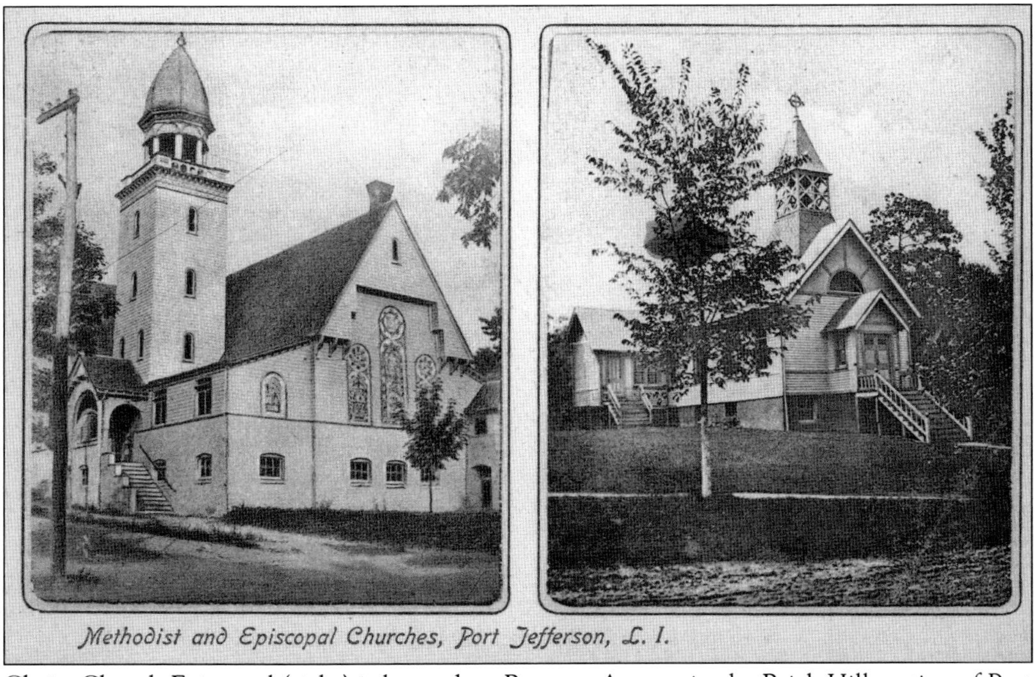

Christ Church Episcopal (right) is located on Barnum Avenue in the Brick Hill section of Port Jefferson. The land was worth $400 in 1879, but P.T. Barnum sold it for the discounted price of $150 in recognition of the plan to build a church on it. The first services were held in June 1888.

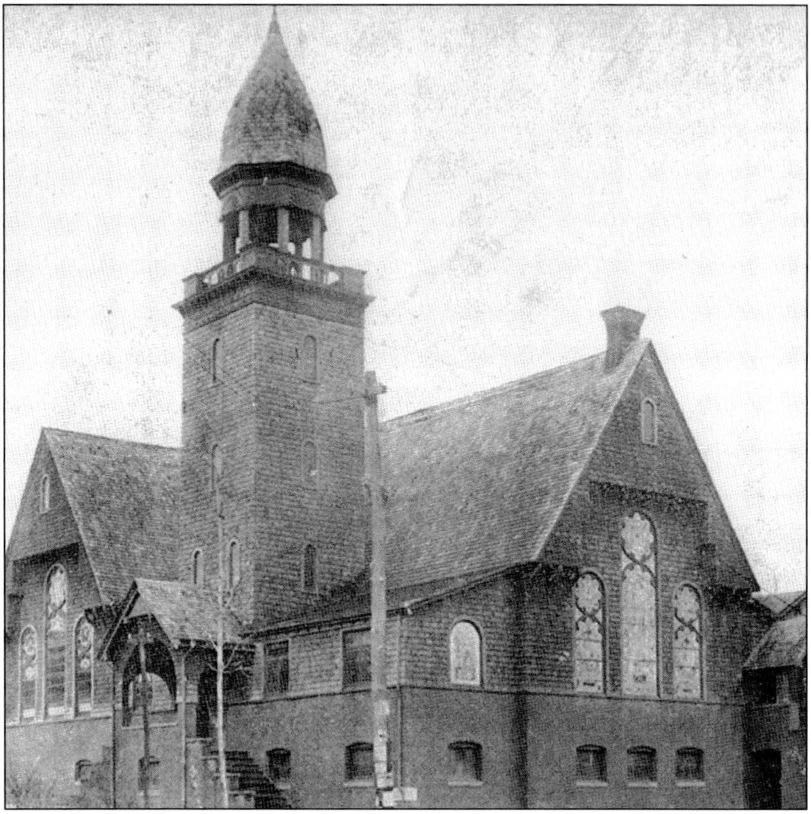

The first formal Methodist house of worship was built on Thompson Street in 1838. In 1873, the chapel was moved to the corner of Main and Spring Streets. After that structure was no longer adequate, the current church, shown here, was erected by the Loper brothers in 1894.

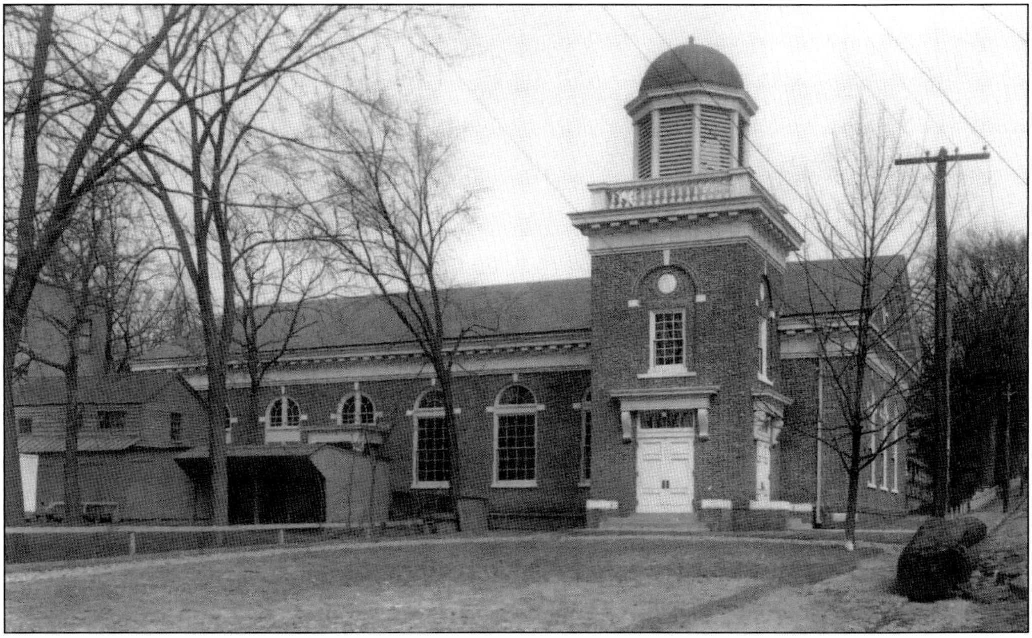

In 1854, Port Jefferson Presbyterians built their first church on the west side of Main Street, now used as the Masonic hall. They moved across the way to the corner of Main and Spring Streets, where the current church, shown here shortly after its dedication in 1912, still stands.

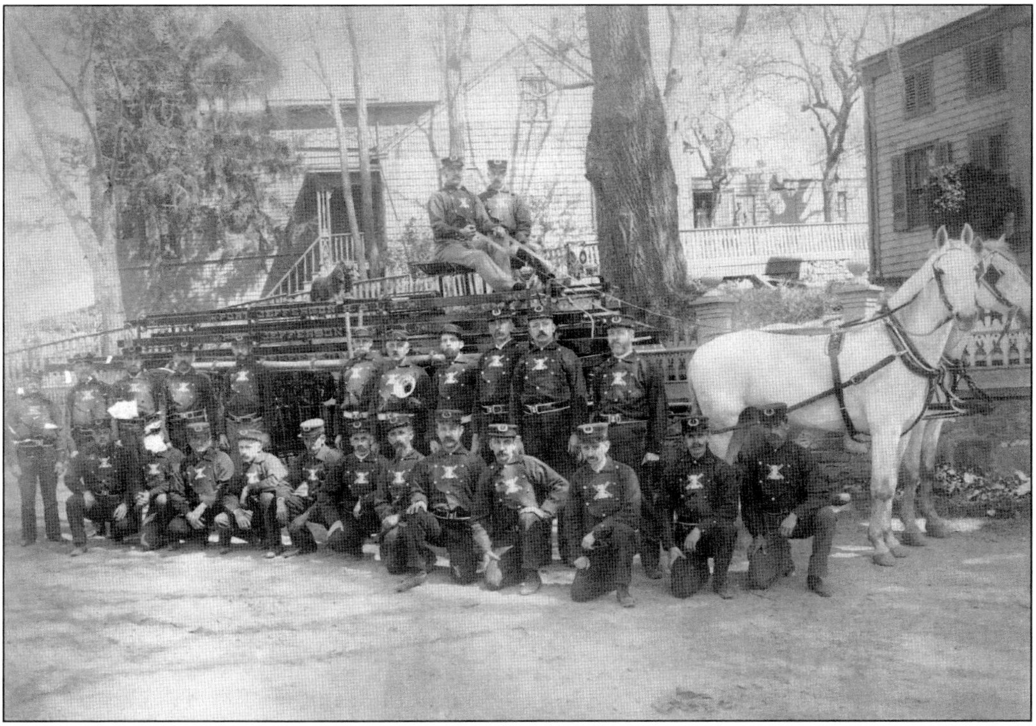

Hook and Ladder Company No. 1, the forerunner of the Port Jefferson Fire Department, was formed in 1887. Here, the members of the newly formed group pose with their horse-drawn fire engine near the corner of East Main and Thompson Streets, the site of the present library.

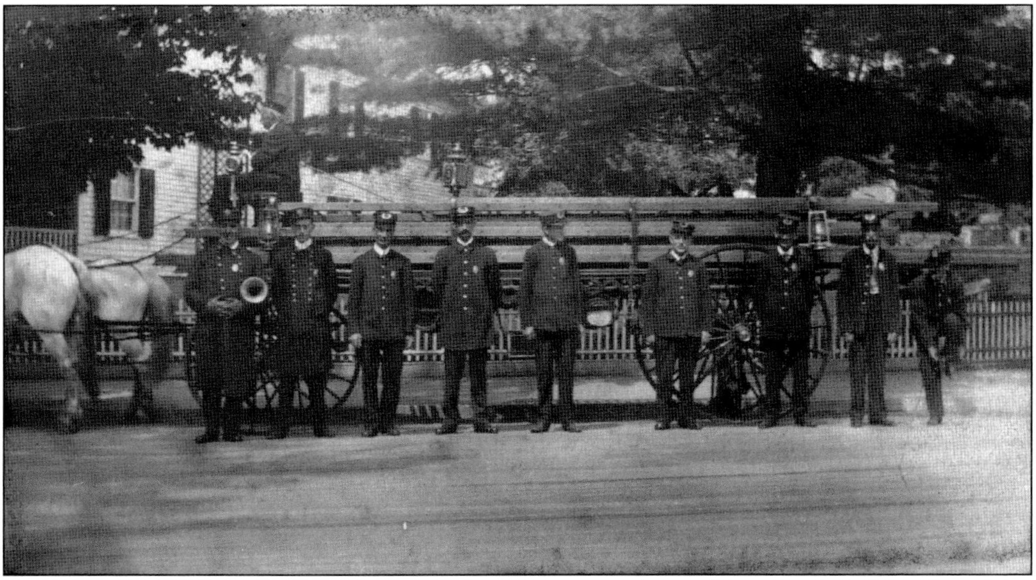

The Hook and Ladder Company changed its name to the Port Jefferson Fire Department in 1890. The firefighters are shown in front of the Raynor house on the east side of Main Street in that year. In spite of the firemen's best efforts, the lack of a pressurized water system hindered their ability to fight fires. After the disastrous waterfront fire of 1897, the men got the pressurized water they needed.

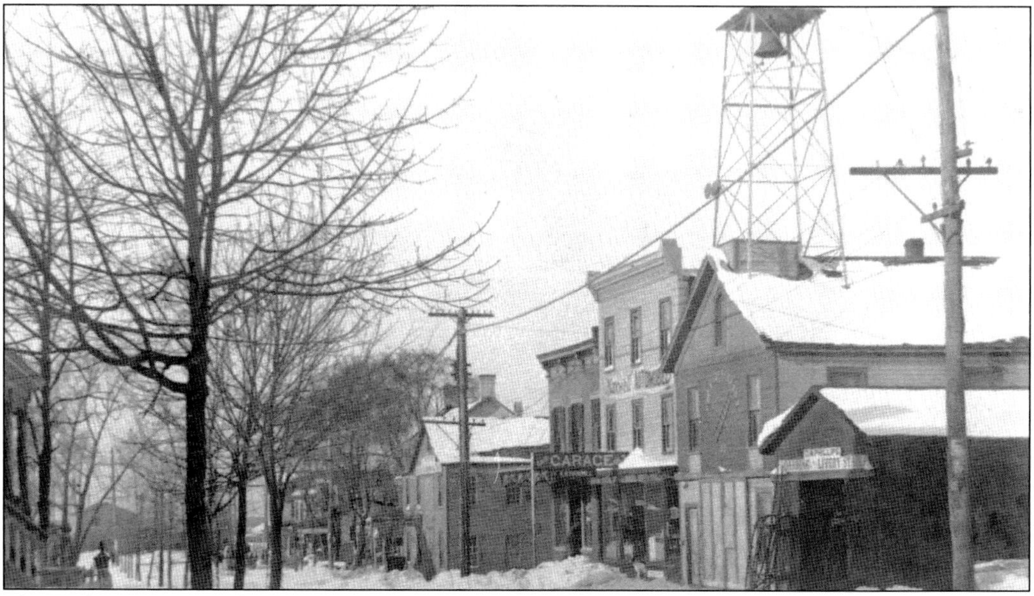

Shown here in 1925, the old firehouse, the second building from the right, stood in the middle of the block on the east side of Main Street. The tower on the roof supports the alarm bell, which had formerly been a mechanics' bell in the Mather Shipyard. North of the firehouse is A.N. Randall's Garage and Maxwell Auto Sales. To the south is D.W. Phillips Boarding & Livery Stables, indicating that the switch to automobiles was not yet complete.

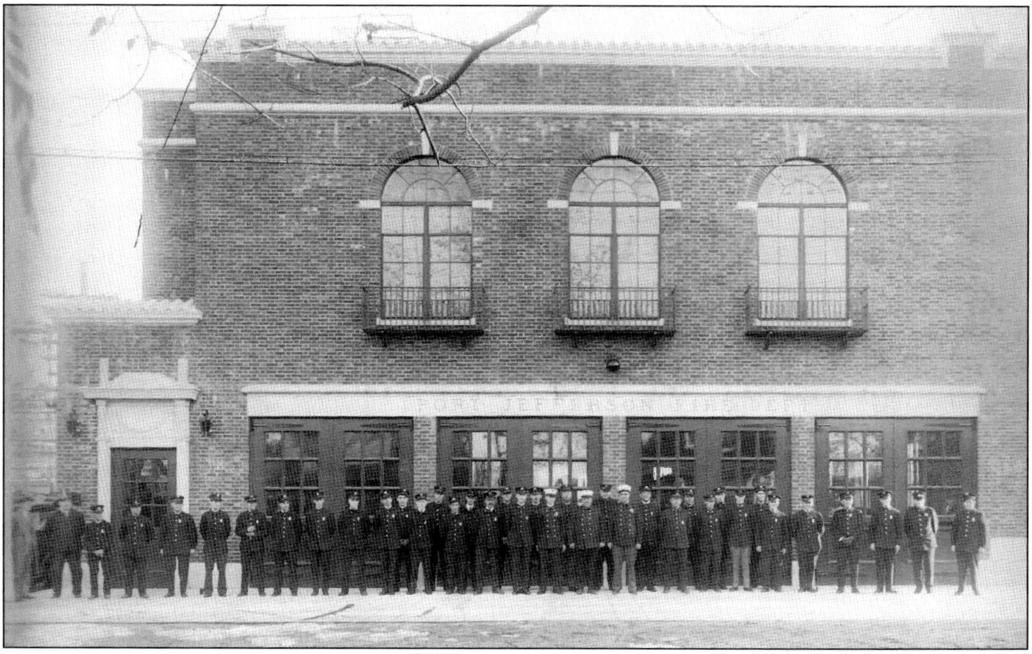

It is 1932, and the members of the Port Jefferson Fire Department proudly stand in front of the new firehouse on Maple Avenue, near the former site of Parker's Pond. The cornerstone had been laid by James E. Bayles, a charter member and the oldest member of the fire department, on September 3, 1927. The fire bell and siren tower from the old firehouse on Main Street were moved to the new building, which is still in use today.

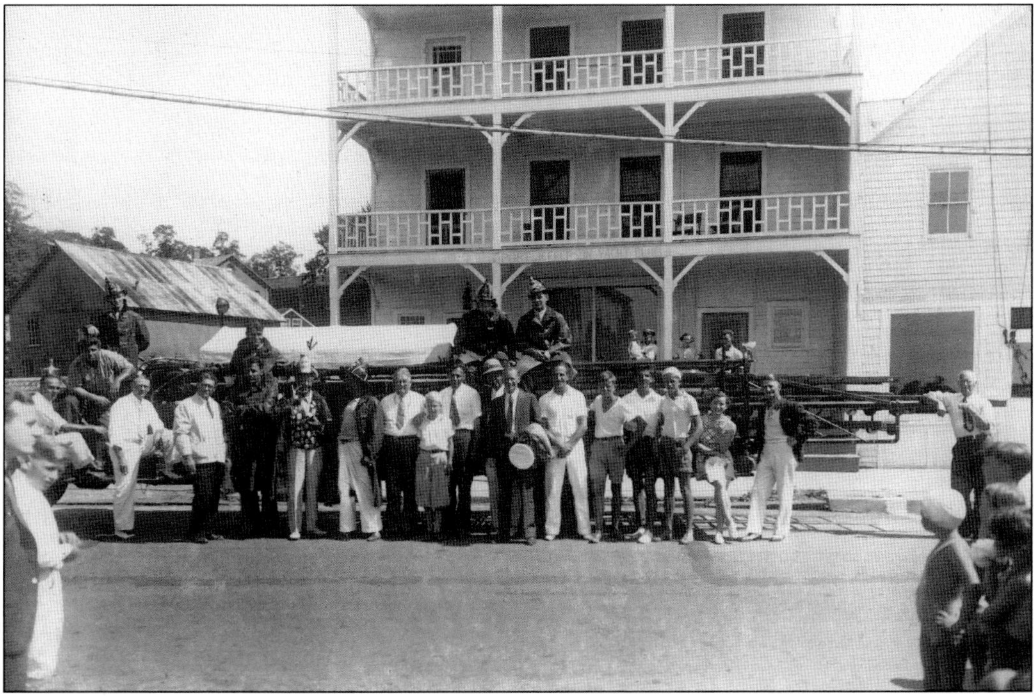

Well-known actor and comedian Ed Wynn (indicated by the arrow) poses as an honorary fire chief in front of the Harborview Hotel in August 1935. He was hosting a popular radio show at the time called *The Fire Chief*, sponsored by Texaco. Wynn plays the same character in the 1933 movie *The Chief*.

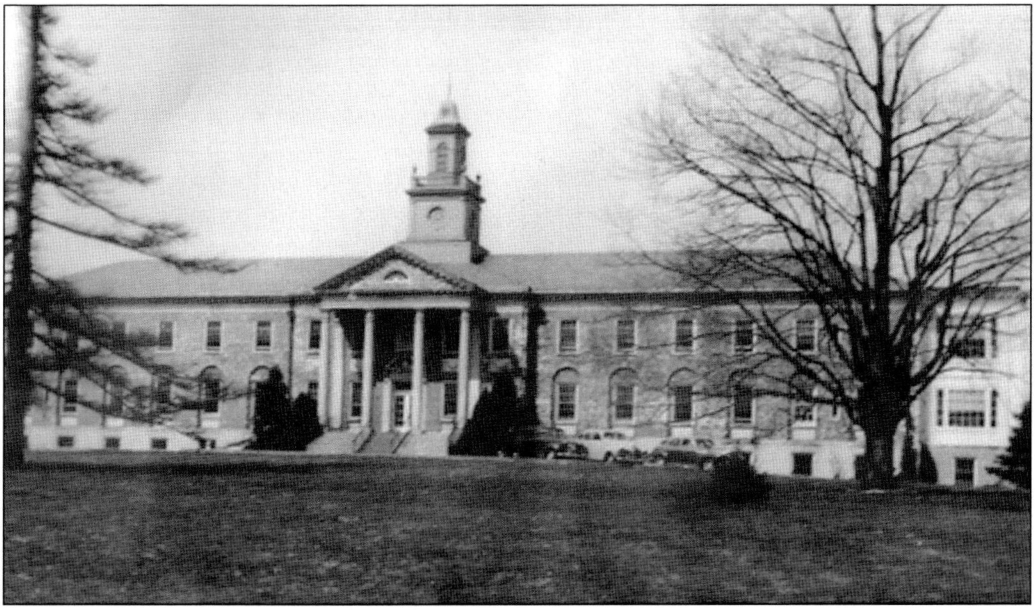

John T. Mather Memorial Hospital opened in December 1929, just at the start of the Great Depression. Mather stipulated in his will that a "non-sectarian charitable hospital" be built within a year of his death, and he left close to a million dollars to assure his wishes would be fulfilled. This original facade is still visible in the hospital's courtyard.

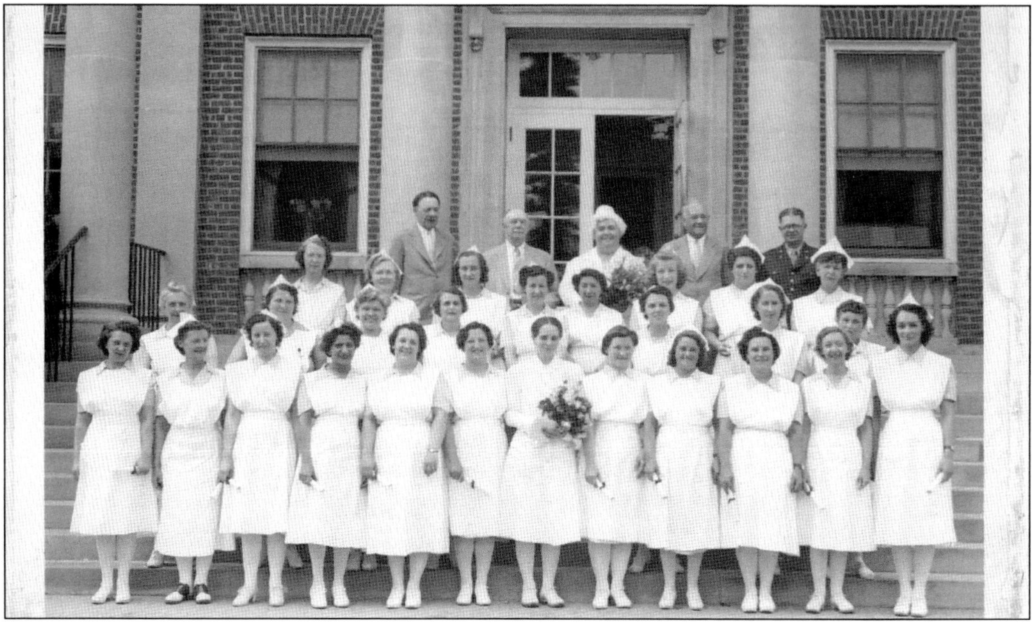

A class of graduating nurses poses with staff in front of Mather Memorial Hospital. In the fourth row are, from left to right, Dr. F.L. McCrea, Forrest Raynor, Myrtle DeYoung, Dr. Frank S. Child, and a Dr. Campbell. DeYoung, the first executive nurse, had previously been in charge of the Cottage Hospital in Port Jefferson. Dr. Child was the first physician at St. Charles Hospital as well. (Courtesy of Frances Child.)

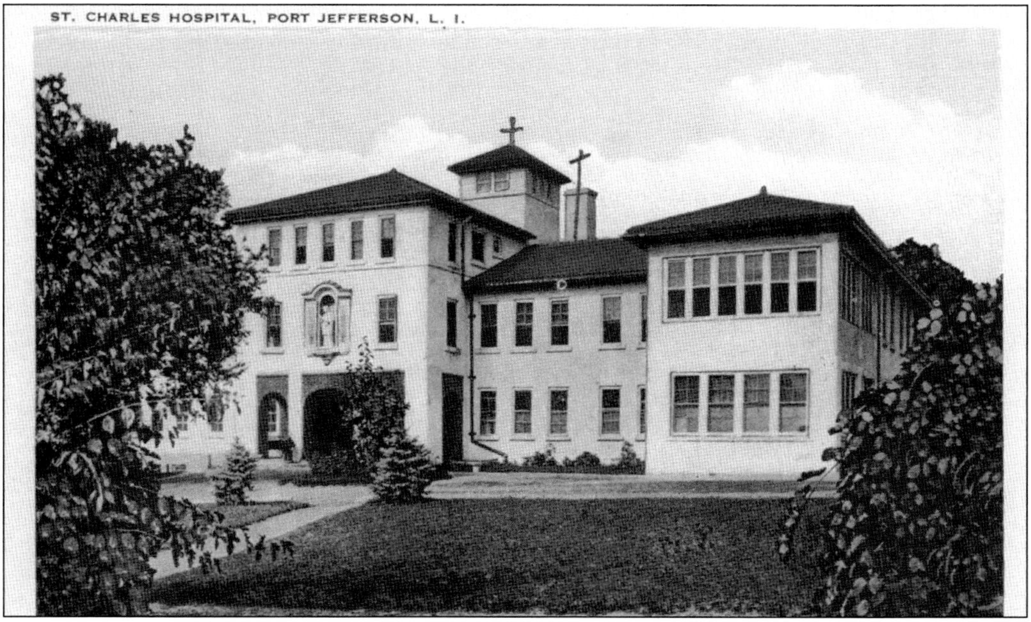

St. Charles Hospital began in 1907 as a haven for homeless and disabled children from New York City. Staffed by Sisters from the Order of the Daughters of Wisdom, the facility expanded until, in 1910, a larger building was constructed and dedicated as St. Charles Hospital. Its innovative treatments, including the use of swimming pool therapy for victims of polio, gained national attention. Franklin D. Roosevelt and his wife, Eleanor, visited the hospital in 1929.

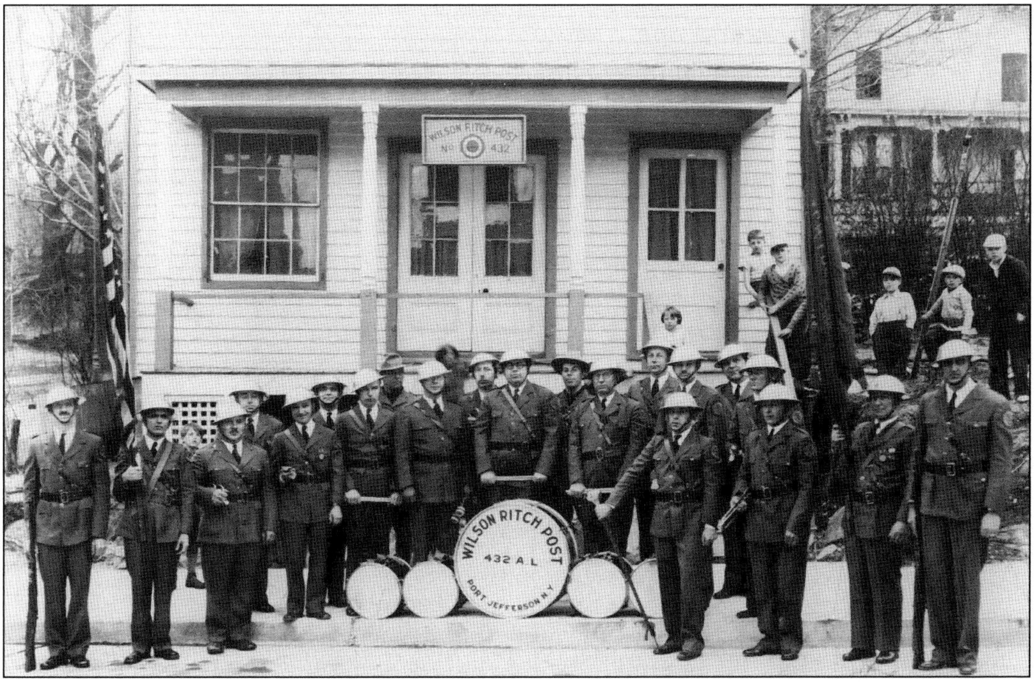

American Legion Post 432 was formed in September 1919 and named the Wilson Ritch Post in honor of Port Jefferson's first World War I casualty. The post rented meeting space from the library in the Good Templars Hall, but then bought and renovated the building when the library moved out in 1925. This photograph of the post probably dates from that time. The building still stands next to the Island Christian Church.

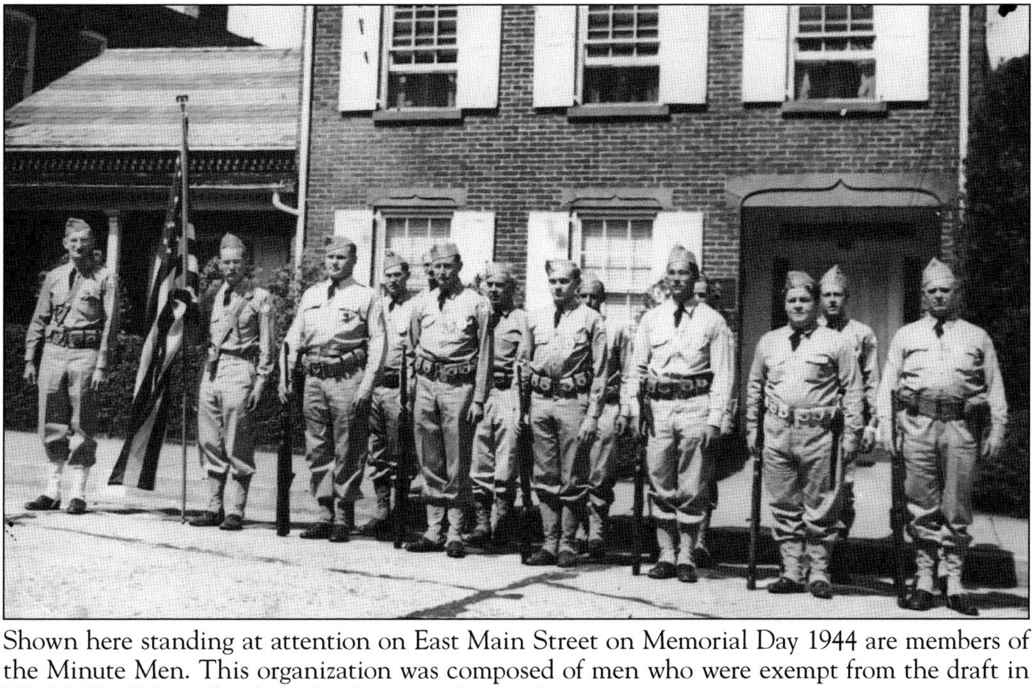

Shown here standing at attention on East Main Street on Memorial Day 1944 are members of the Minute Men. This organization was composed of men who were exempt from the draft in World War II but who drilled to be in readiness if needed.

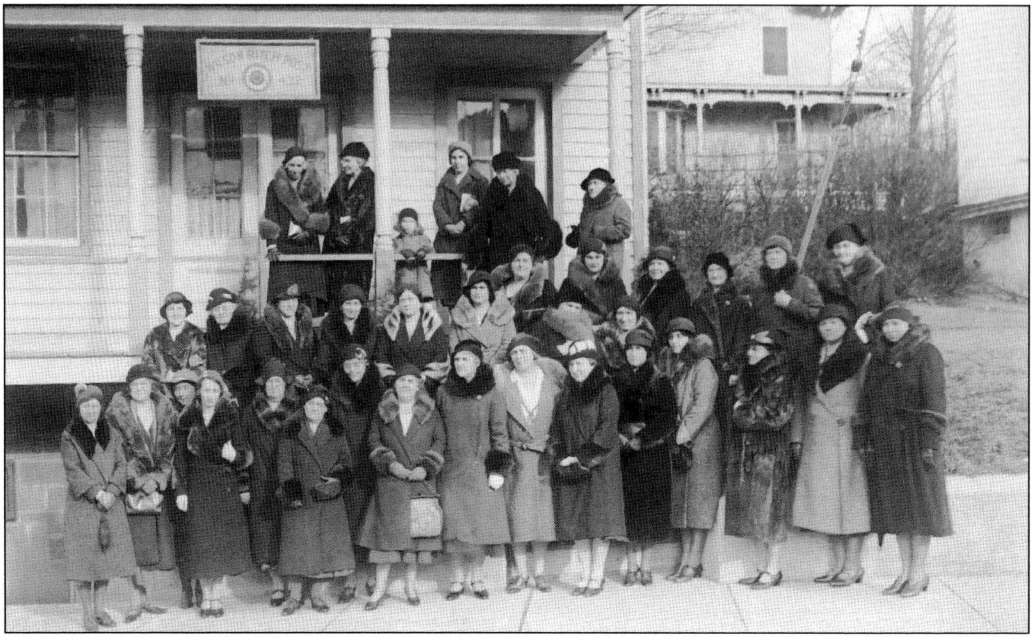

The Suwassett Garden Club was organized in 1912, disbanded during World War I, and was revived in 1929. Among its varied roles, the club was responsible for beautifying village public spaces through colorful horticultural displays. It protested against the encroachment of billboard advertisements and advocated roadside beautification. The club is still very active in carrying out its mission today. Here, club members stand before the Wilson Ritch Post on East Main Street in 1932.

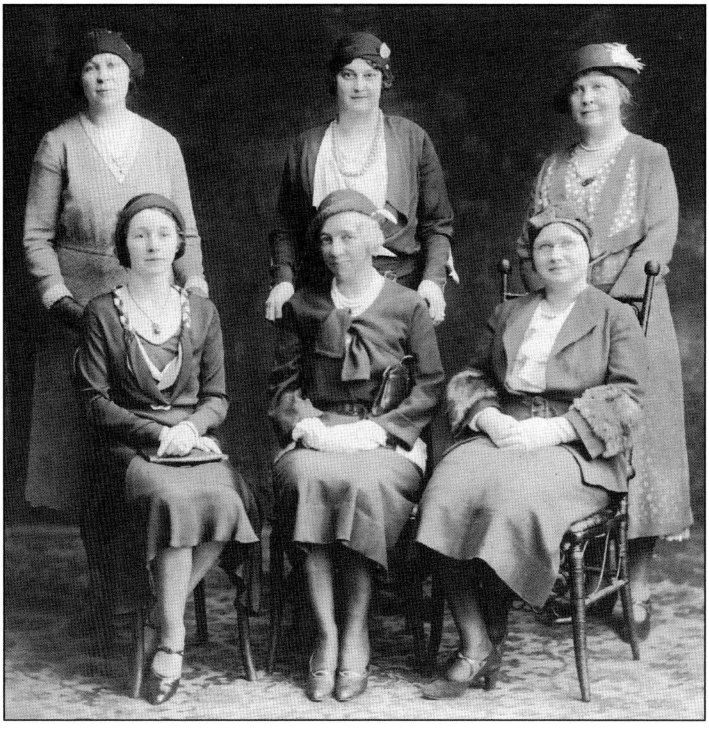

Suwassett Garden Club officers of the 1930s included some of the leading women of the community. Shown here are, from left to right, (first row) Ella Reeve, recording secretary; Helen Bayles Child, first vice president; and Florence C. Chamberlain, corresponding secretary; (second row) Mrs. Leigh Robartes, treasurer; Catherine R. Ritch, president; and Mrs. Frank Potter, second vice president. (Courtesy of Frances Child.)

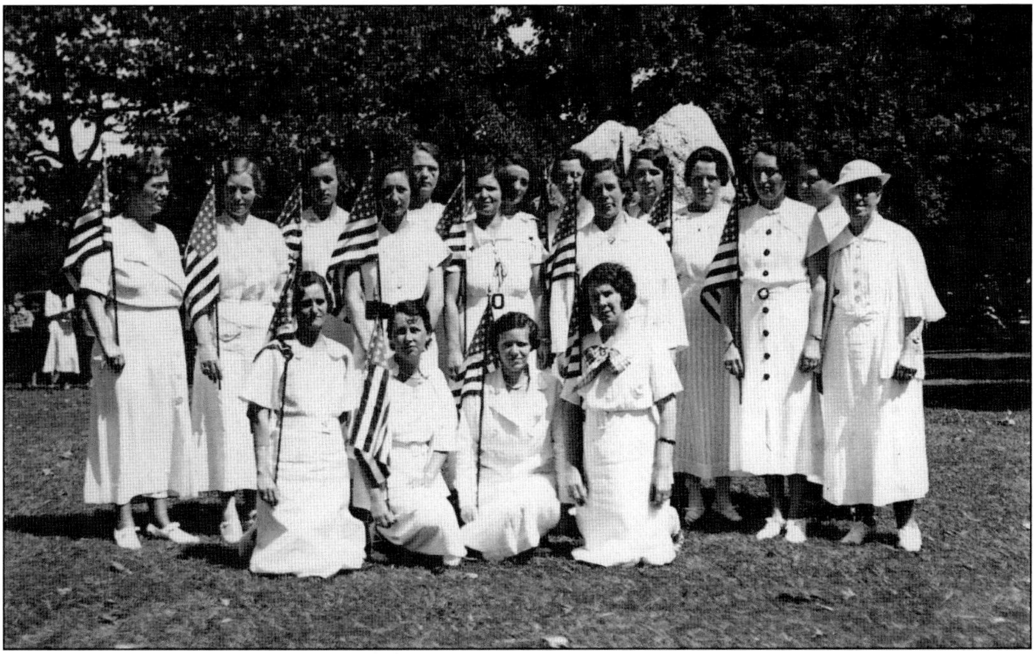

The Suwassett chapter of the Order of the Eastern Star, a fraternal organization for the close female relatives of Master Masons, was organized on June 19, 1907. Above, members attend the unveiling of a monument to Revolutionary War hero Abraham Woodhull at Setauket Cemetery on June 25, 1936.

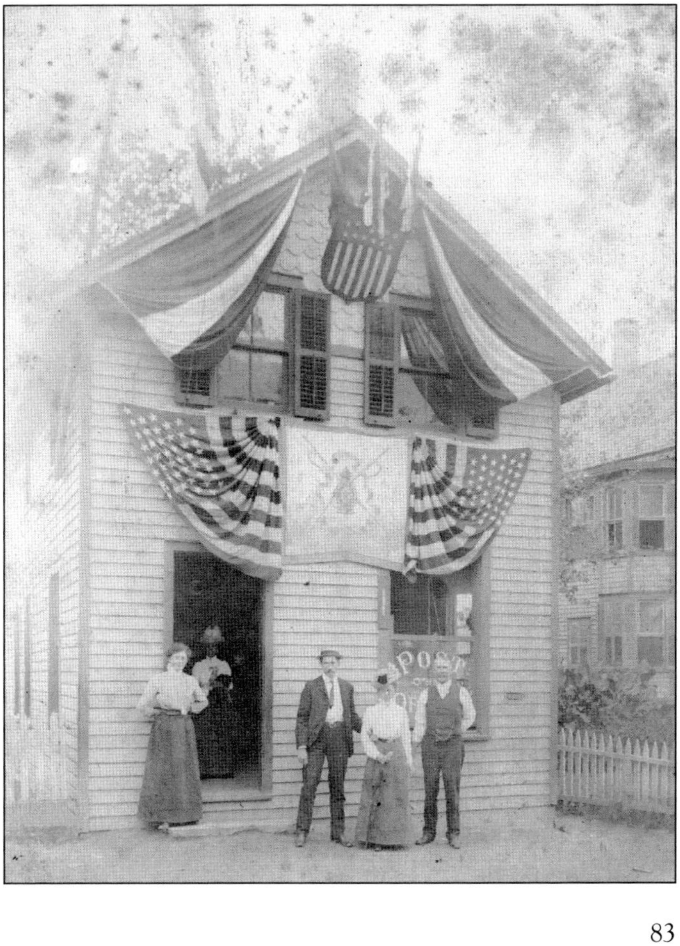

The post office building on Main Street is decorated for Old Home Week in 1908. This building, originally former postmaster George W. Kinner's house, succeeded the first permanent post office, in the Townsend House. Postmaster John M. Brown is on the right.

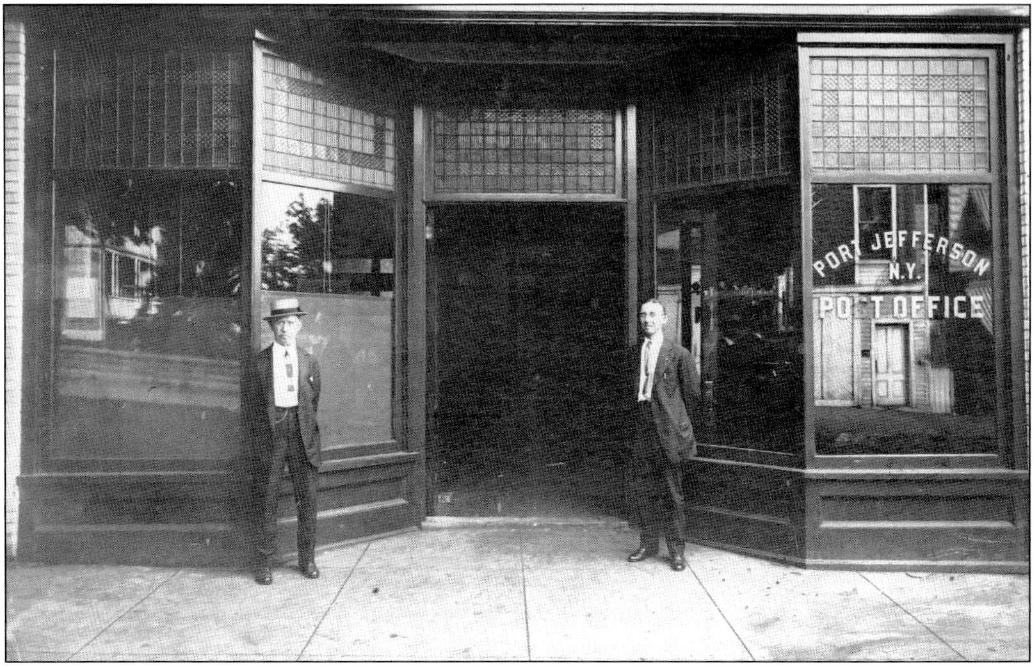

A few years later, John M. Brown (left) poses with his successor, L.O. Davis, in front of a new post office, also on the west side of Main Street, opposite the firehouse. Port Jefferson residents began to have mail delivered to their homes in 1920.

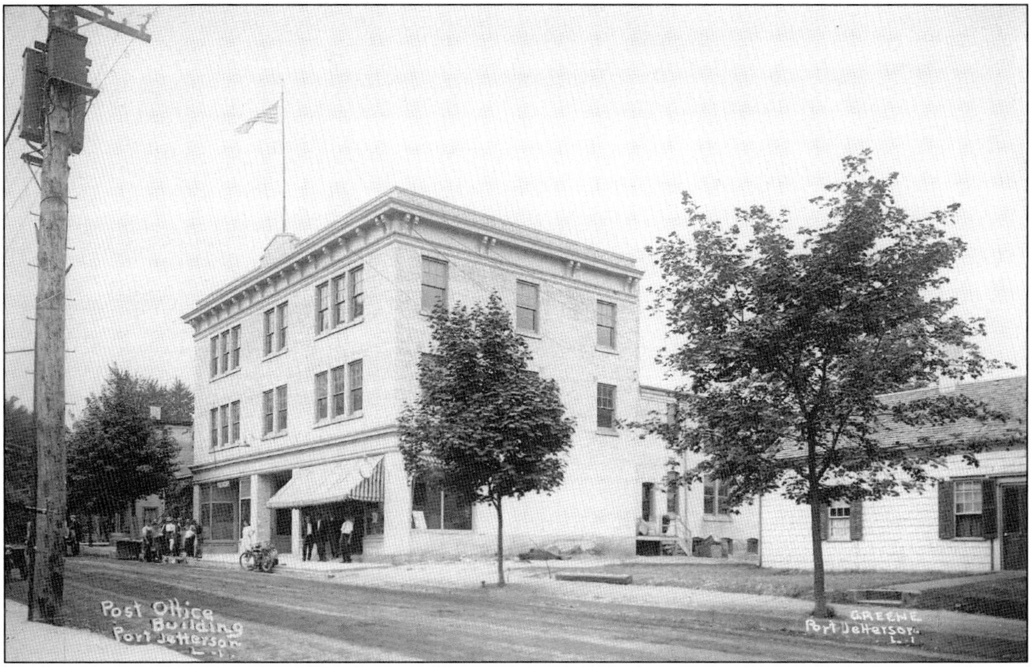

For many years, the Port Jefferson Post Office was located in the white building on the right. It was constructed of bricks made by the Dyett Sand-Lime Brick Company, whose facility was on the site of the California Grove pavilion. This view, looking south on Main Street, is from the early 20th century.

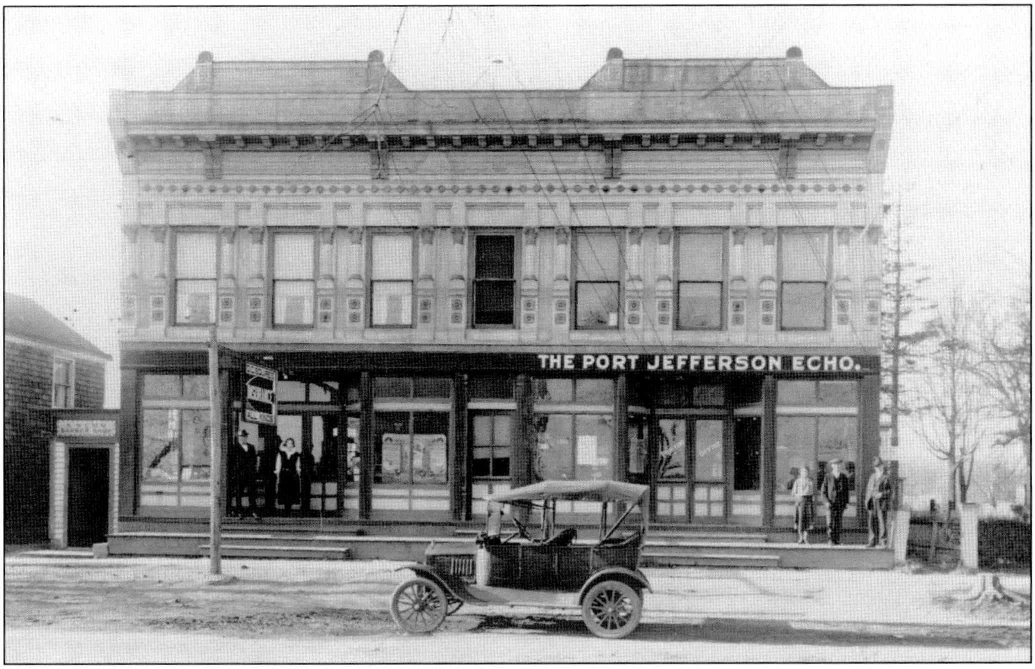

This impressive building stood near the railroad tracks and housed the *Port Jefferson Echo* newspaper, the Port Jefferson Station Post Office, and Charles A. Squires's real estate and insurance business. Squires was the major housing developer of Port Jefferson Station at the turn of the last century. The *Port Jefferson Echo* was one of two weekly newspapers covering Port Jefferson and vicinity at that time, the other being the *Port Jefferson Times*.

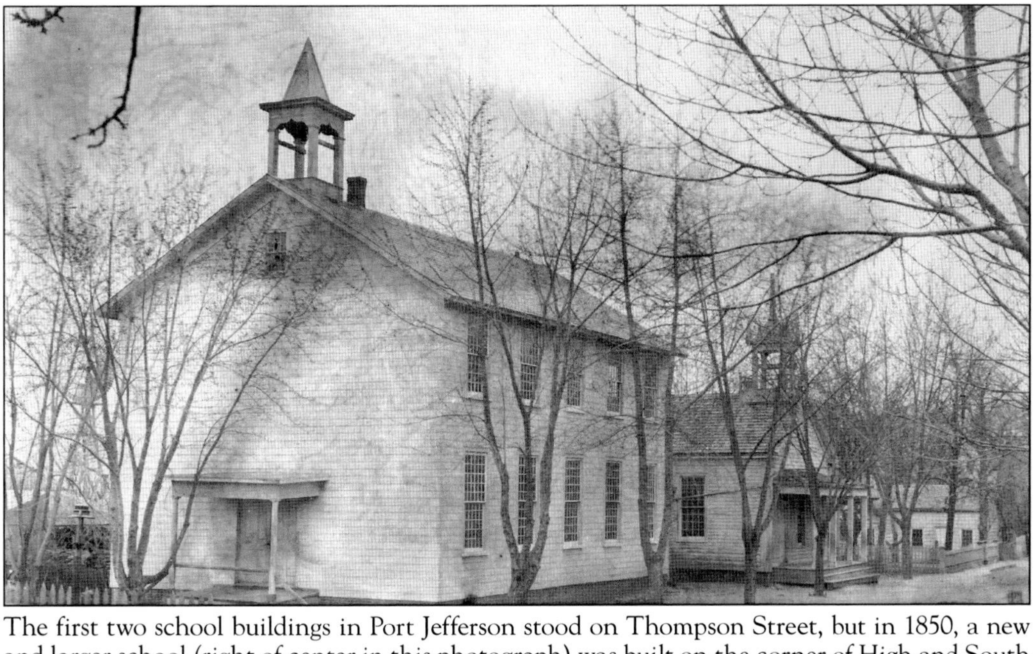

The first two school buildings in Port Jefferson stood on Thompson Street, but in 1850, a new and larger school (right of center in this photograph) was built on the corner of High and South Streets. Port Jefferson was growing so rapidly that by 1862, the two-story addition shown here was needed.

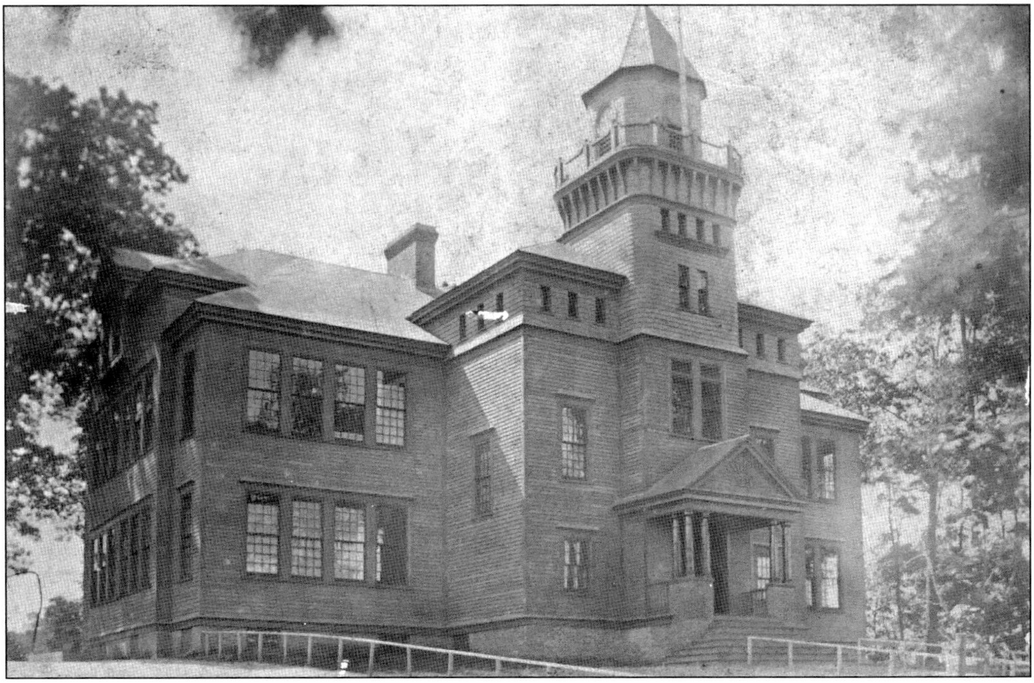

In 1890, the two school buildings shown in the previous photograph were replaced by this Victorian structure, built in Tuthill's Grove on Spring Street. This building housed all grades through high school. It burned down in July 1913 in a fast-moving and suspicious fire. By the time the firemen arrived, all that remained were the chimneys.

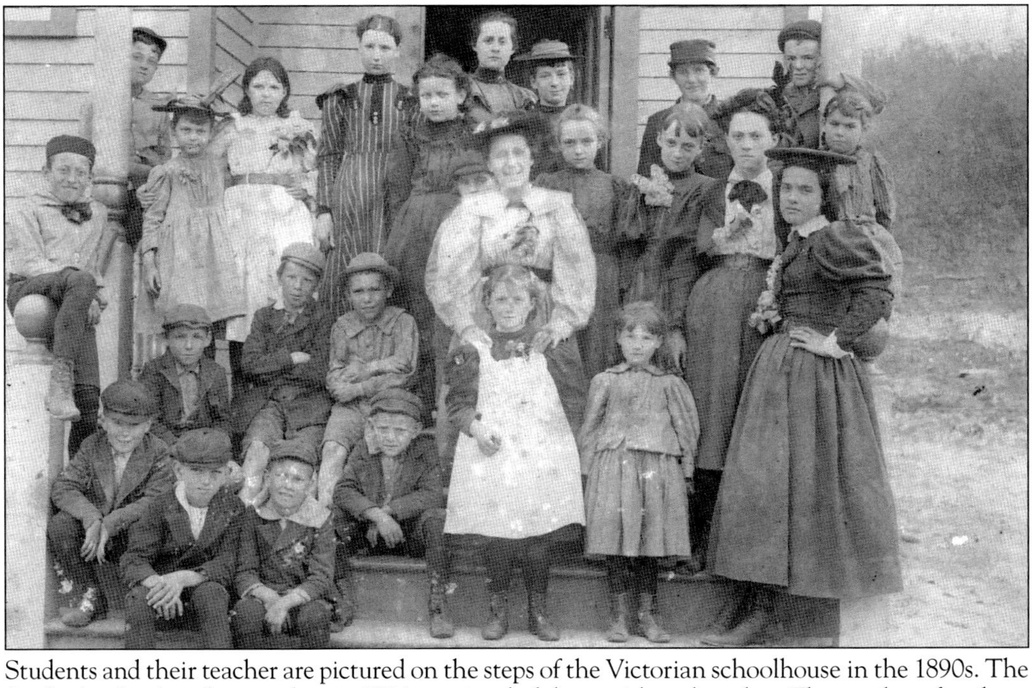

Students and their teacher are pictured on the steps of the Victorian schoolhouse in the 1890s. The first high school graduating class, in 1894, consisted of eleven girls and one boy. The number of students graduating varied greatly in the early years; sometimes there were none or only one or two.

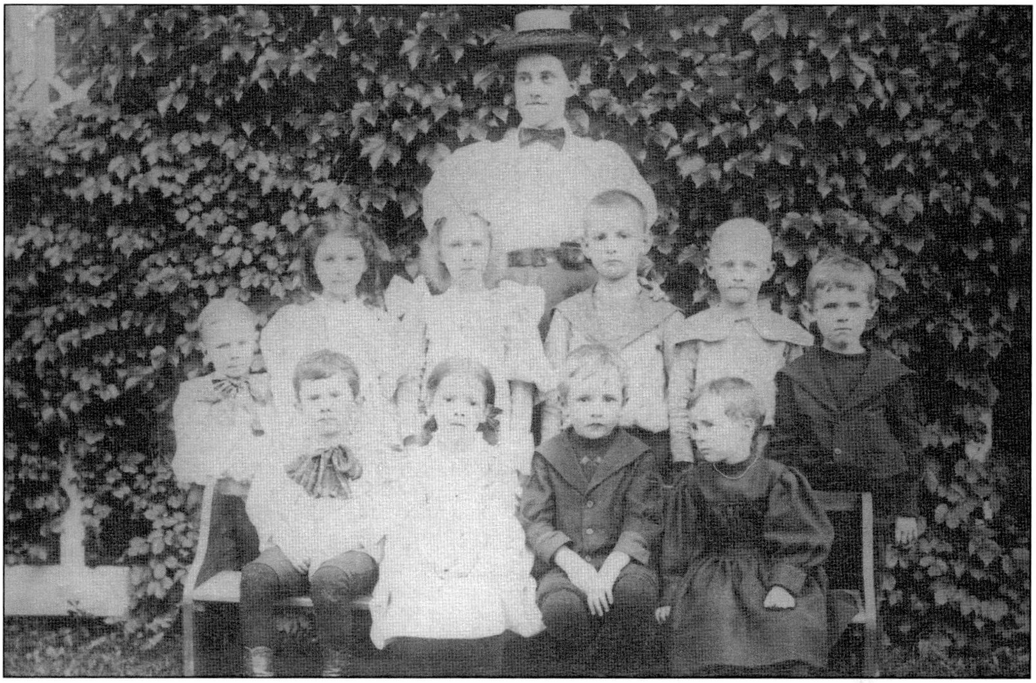

Port Jefferson's first kindergarten class is pictured here with its teacher, Sara Edwards, around 1897. The children include, from left to right, (first row) Chase Edwards, Helen Bayles, Manning Barr, and Liberty Barr; (second row) unidentified, Laura Davis, Hazel Spence, Rossiter Ritch, Ellsworth Conk, and Raymond Many. (Courtesy of Frances Child.)

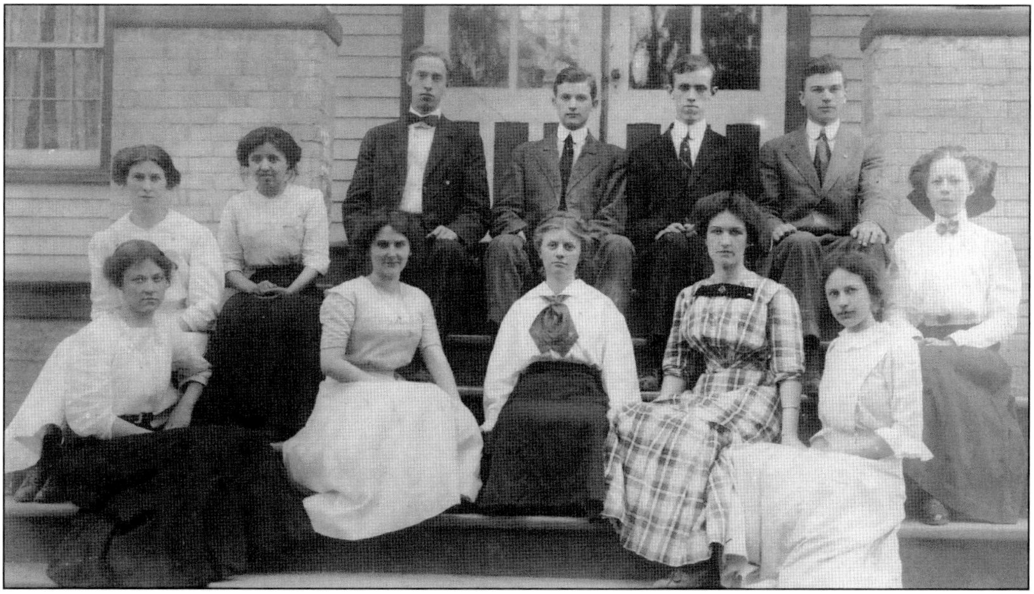

The class of 1911, shown here in front of the Victorian schoolhouse, consists of eight young women and four young men. As had been the custom for many years, their commencement was held at Athena Hall, which was handsomely trimmed with flowers in the class colors of white and gold. In a departure from earlier commencements, the ceremony featured a "decidedly entertaining" three-act high school comedy with music.

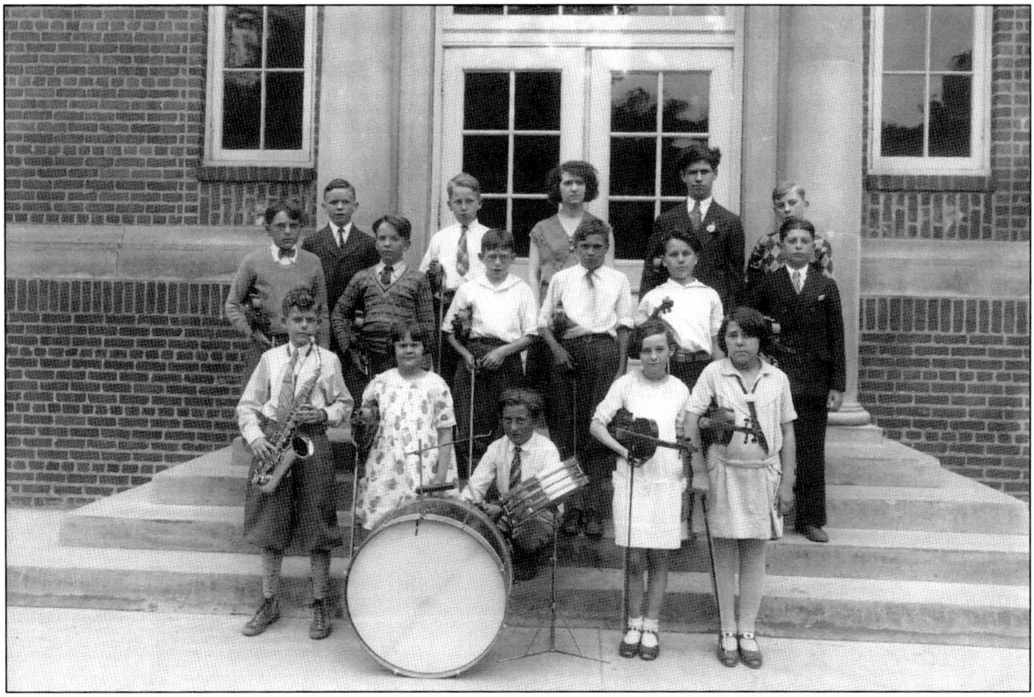

Posing here with their teacher, Norma Hosley, is the school orchestra in the late 1920s or early 1930s. Although school district policy prohibited married women from teaching, an exception was made for Hosley, who taught music in the schools for 40 years before retiring in 1970.

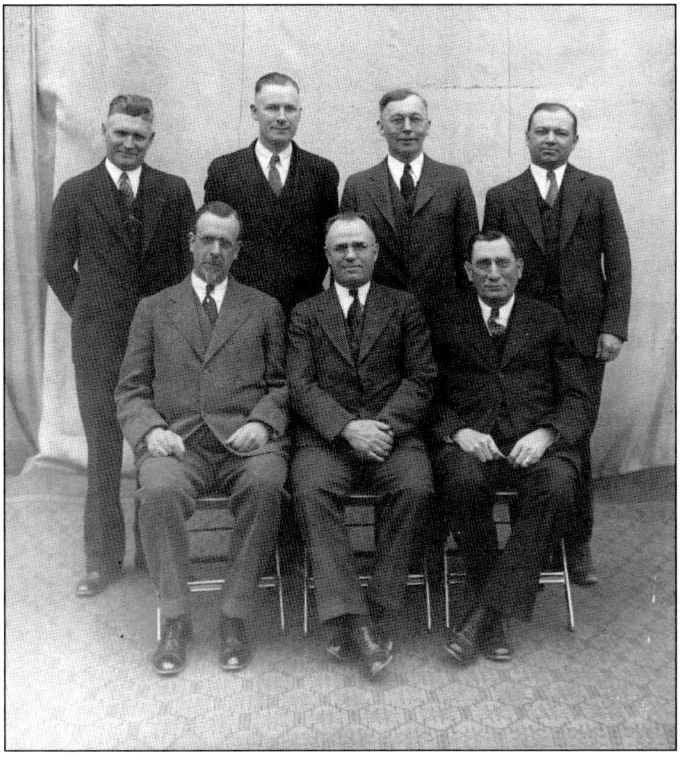

The 1935 board of education consists of, from left to right, (first row) H.H. Purvis, G.E. Woodard, and A.G. Loper; (second row) G.W. Johnston, R.L. Davis, A.E. Anderson, and C.W. Hansell. Woodard, the board president, was instrumental in financing and building the present high school, constructed on the old Plant Hotel property. When it opened in 1935, it was considered ultramodern and was equipped with the finest appointments. Until the late 1960s, the school educated all high school students in northern Brookhaven.

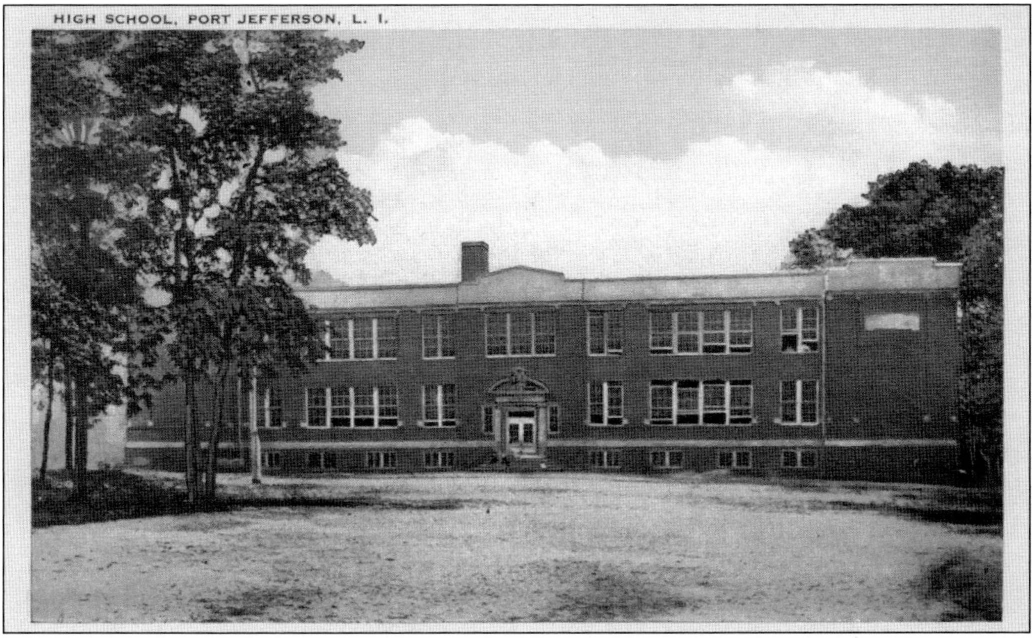

After the fire of 1913, classes were held in the basements of the Catholic, Baptist, and Methodist churches until this building was completed in 1914. It housed all grades until the new high school was opened in 1935. When it closed in 1992, this structure was among the oldest school buildings still in use in Suffolk County.

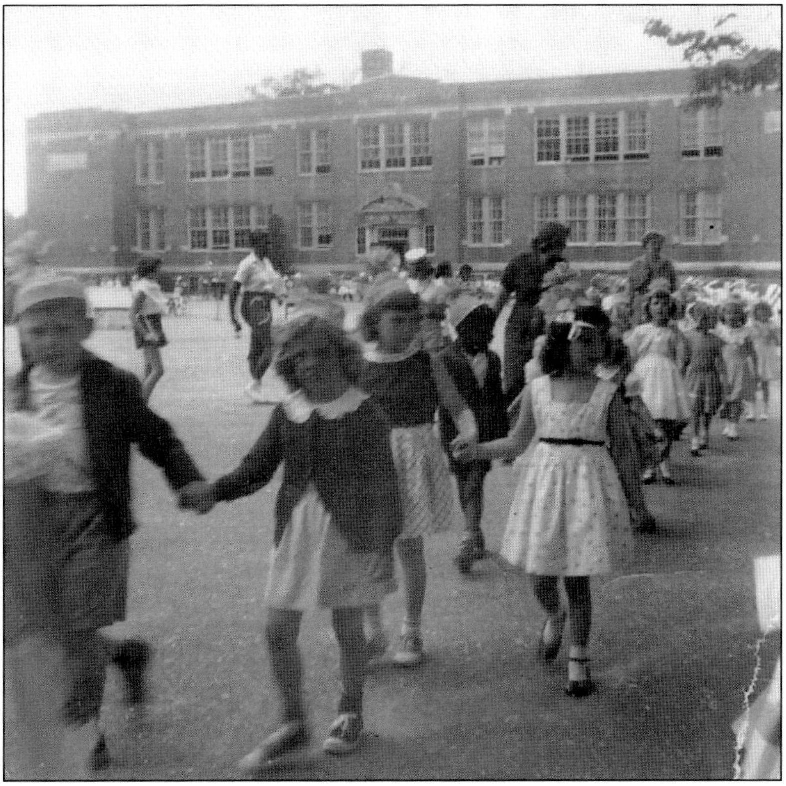

Elementary school students went to class in the 1914 building until the Scraggy Hill School was completed in 1958. From that year until 1992, the 1914 building served as the junior high school. Shown here are pupils on the first day of school in 1955. (Courtesy of Susan Bayles Fox.)

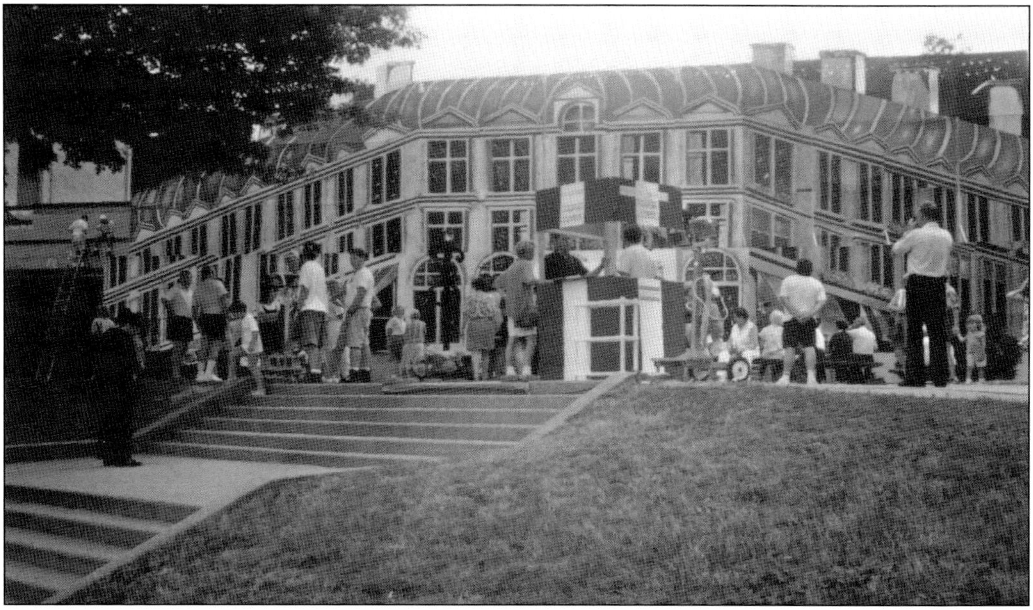

For more than 50 years, the parents of Port Jefferson high school seniors have carried on the tradition of transforming the high school, inside and out, to reflect the year's prom theme. From October, when the secret theme is chosen, until the Monday after graduation in June, the parents work secretly to surprise the students. Then, on prom night, the whole community turns out to watch the new graduates walk down the red carpet and marvel at the transformation. These photographs show the 1992 Paris-themed prom, complete with an Eiffel Tower made of duct tape. Recent themes have included Cirque de Royale, Pirates of Port Jefferson Harbor, Passport to America, Royal Game of Life, and Harry Potter. (Both, courtesy of Beth Pranzo.)

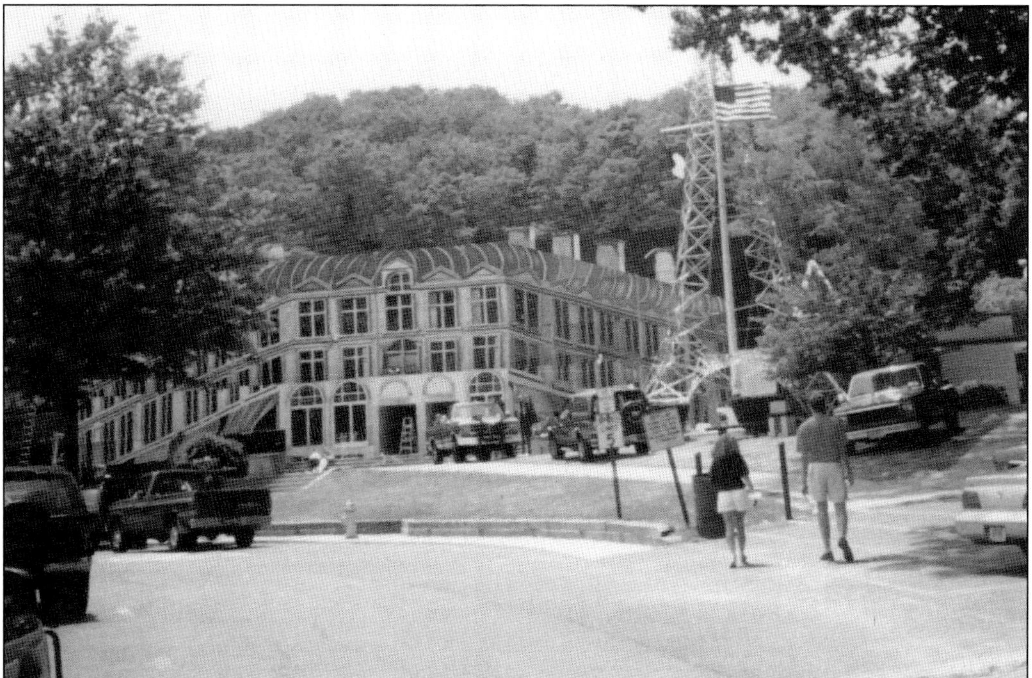

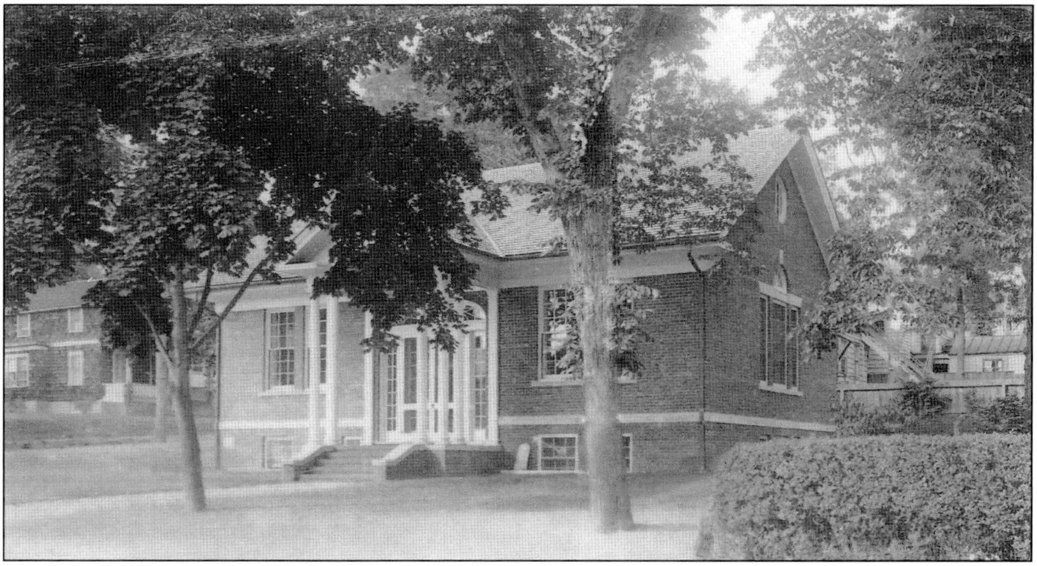

The Port Jefferson Free Library was organized by the Ladies Literary Society in 1908. After renting space above a store, the board of trustees, which included many of the town's leading citizens, purchased the Good Templars Hall next to the Baptist church in 1911. Efforts to build a permanent library were unsuccessful, until property on the corner of East Main and Thompson Streets was acquired in 1924, the house on it moved, and the cornerstone laid in December of that year. The Arthur S. Greene photograph above shows the library shortly after it opened in 1925. The library continued to outgrow its space, and major additions were completed in 1967 and 1997. Today, the library serves Port Jefferson, Belle Terre, Miller Place, and Mount Sinai with outstanding facilities, collections, and services, including Our Living Heritage. (Both, courtesy of Port Jefferson Free Library.)

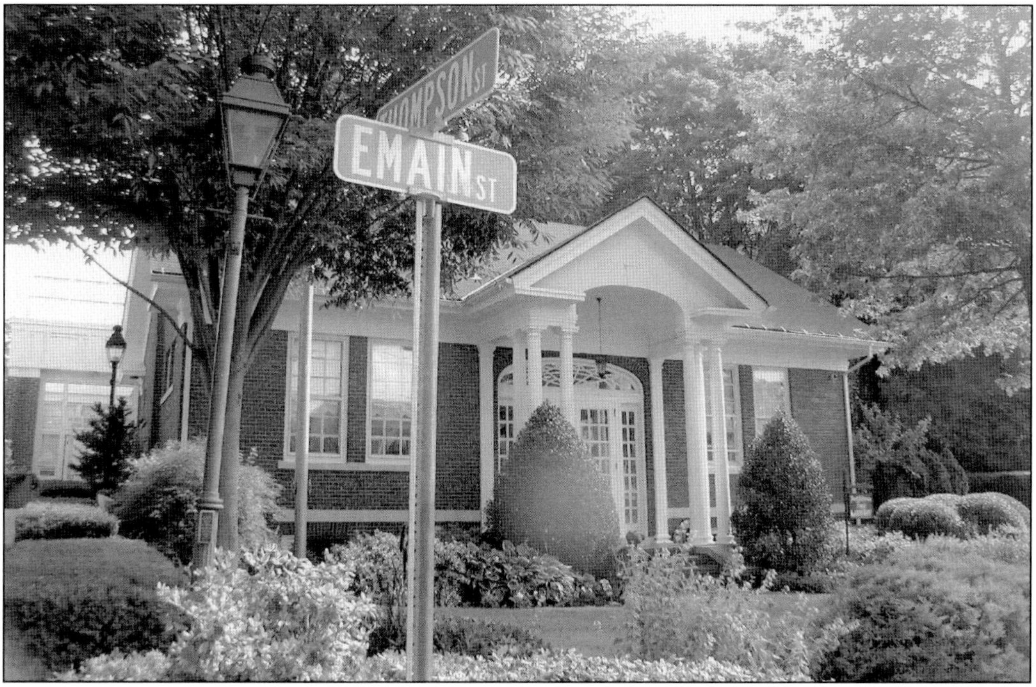

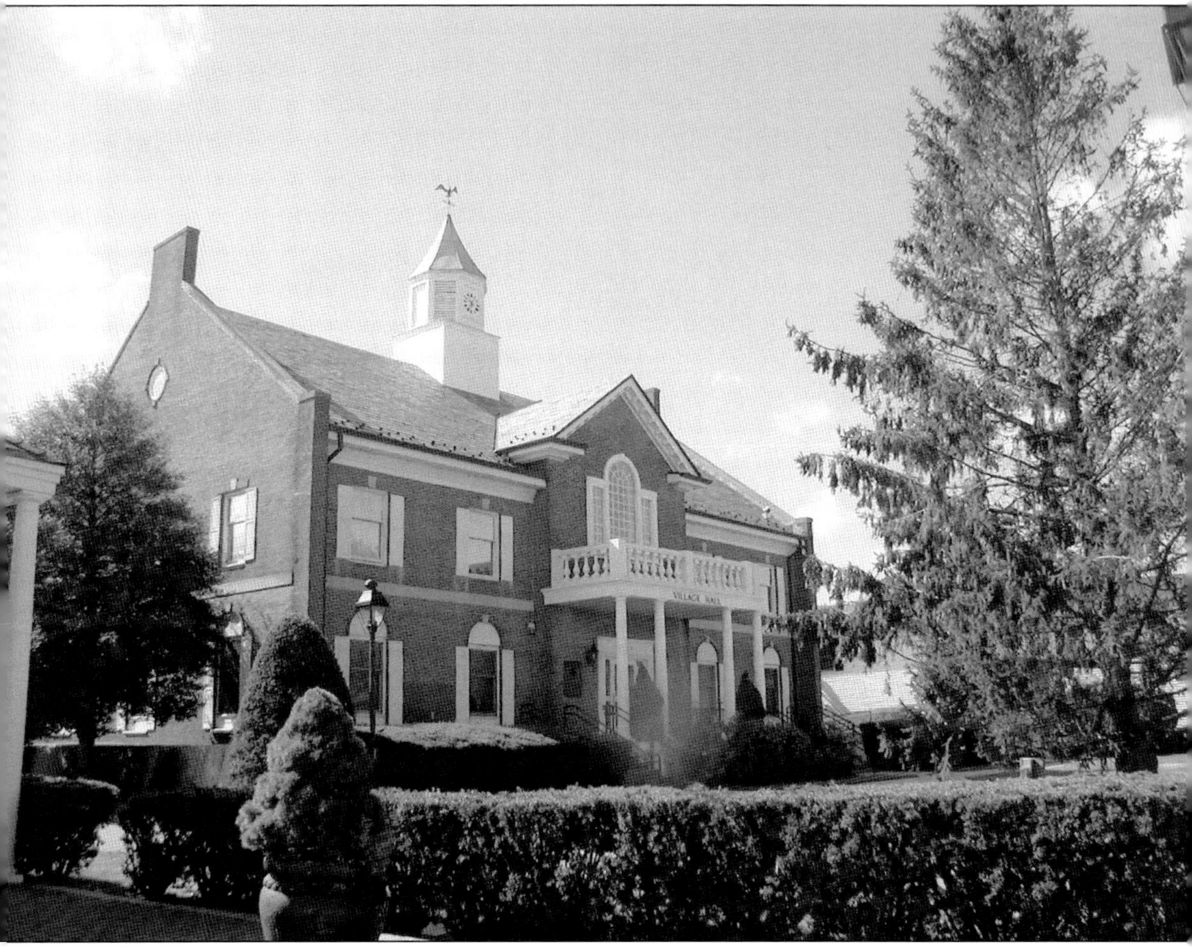

In the middle years of the 20th century, Port Jefferson found that its previously busy downtown was no longer the shopping hub for surrounding communities that it had been, as more and more businesses preferred to be closer to major highways. Although a modern marina was constructed in 1957, other efforts at revitalization were stymied by lack of cooperation from the Town of Brookhaven. The overindustrialization of the harbor was another issue over which local residents felt they had no control. For these and many other reasons, a proposal for home rule was put before the voters and was passed. On April 12, 1963, Port Jefferson officially became an incorporated village. Shortly thereafter, construction began on the imposing Georgian-style village hall shown here. It was built on the site of the Loper Brothers Lumber Yard on West Broadway and opened in 1967. (Courtesy of Port Jefferson Free Library.)

Six

Port at Play

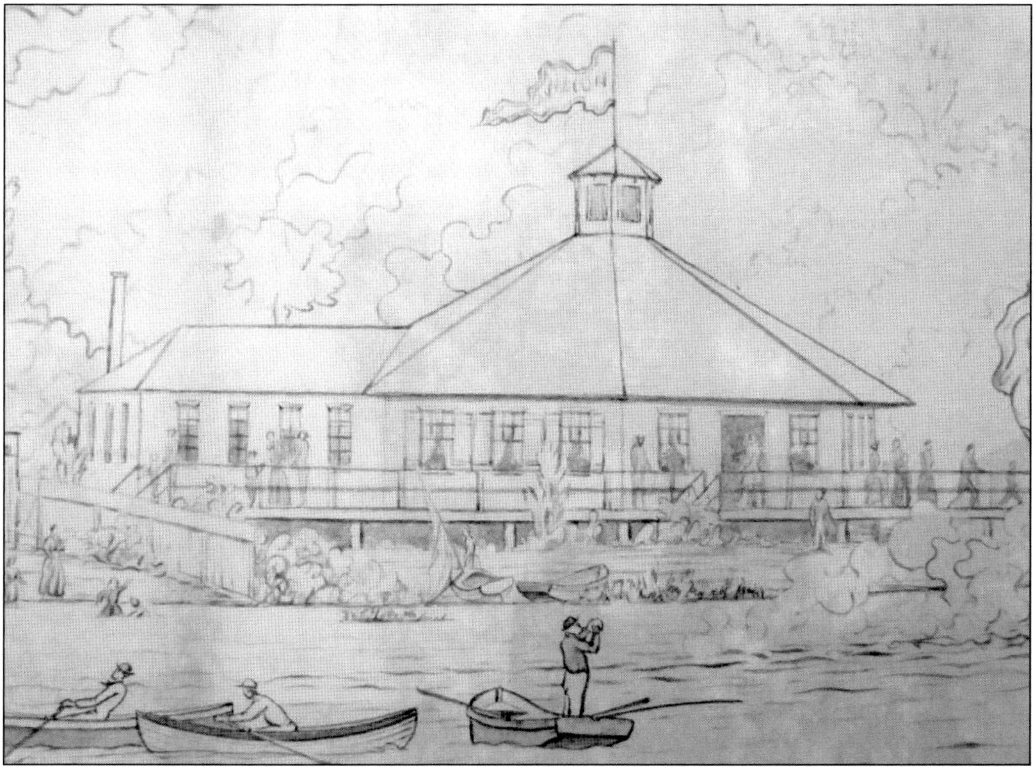

California Grove and Pavilion was located on the west side of the harbor and developed by the ferry company to attract tourists. Its name derived from the seemingly "great" distance between it and Port Jefferson proper. P.T. Barnum spoke at the gala opening in 1885. California Grove hosted carnivals, clambakes, fireworks displays, and reunions. The pavilion staged dances and band concerts. The attraction closed in 1899.

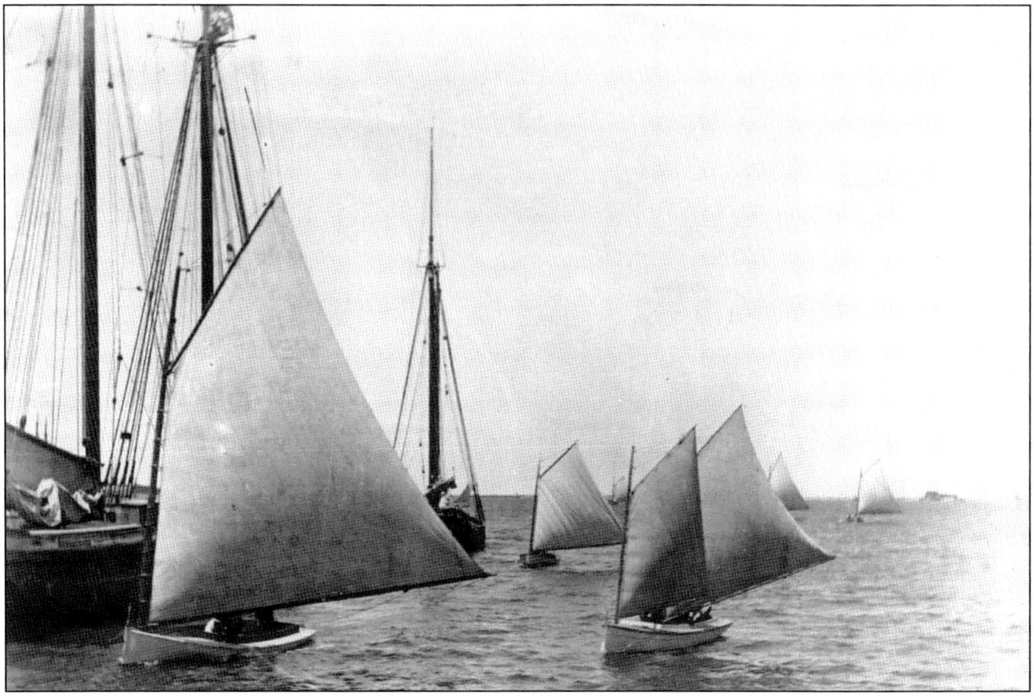

Shown here is a scene from the popular catboat races. These boats were built for Petit's Pine Bluff Camp, located on the west side of the harbor in Poquott. The catboat races occurred during Port Jefferson's Old Home Week celebration. The Petit camp was established in 1890 in order to "develop healthy boys with strong character." It closed in 1934.

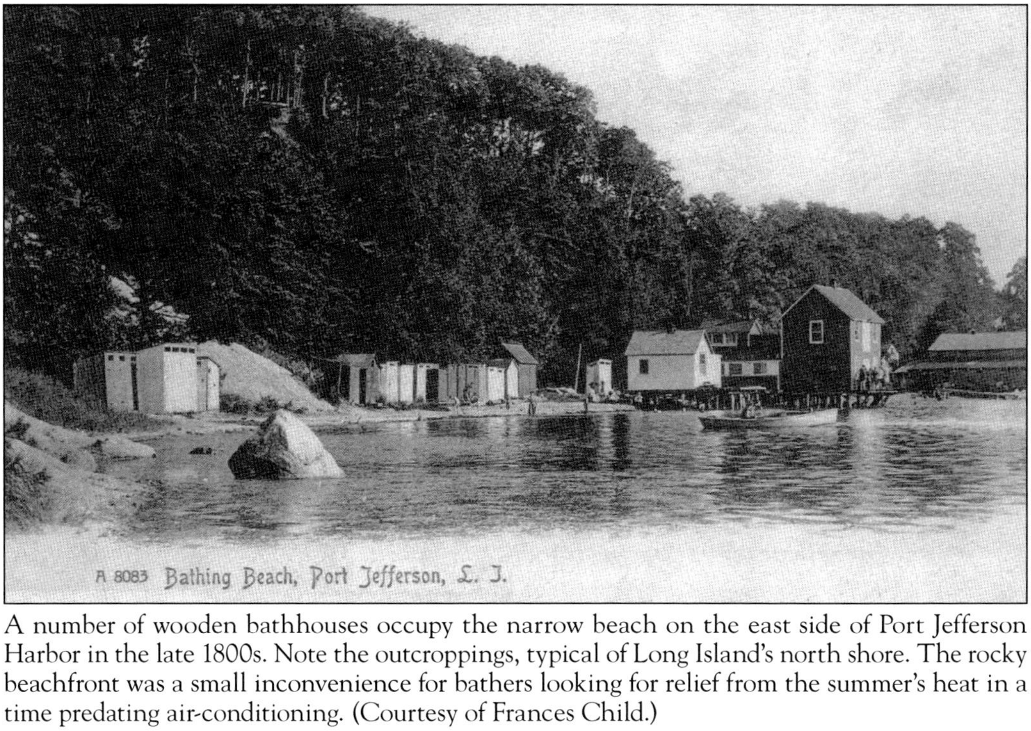

A number of wooden bathhouses occupy the narrow beach on the east side of Port Jefferson Harbor in the late 1800s. Note the outcroppings, typical of Long Island's north shore. The rocky beachfront was a small inconvenience for bathers looking for relief from the summer's heat in a time predating air-conditioning. (Courtesy of Frances Child.)

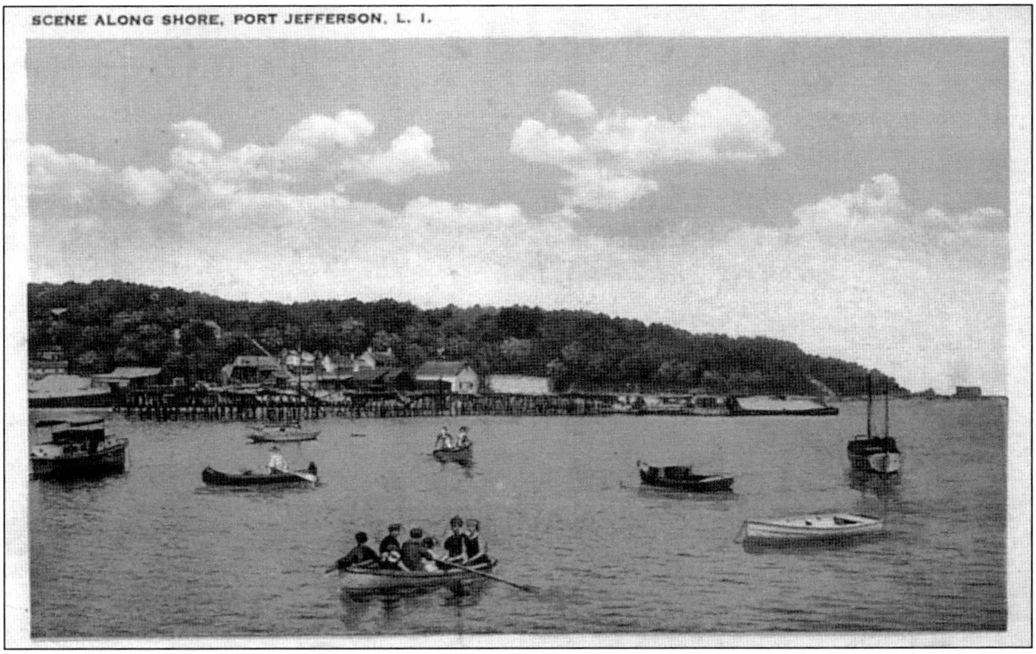

Schooners, yachts, and cargo ships were not the only seaworthy vessels to be found in Port Jefferson's protected harbor. This view looking west depicts people in canoes and rowboats enjoying a day out on the water. Manufacturers of small sailing craft were well represented among the shipbuilding enterprises of the village. (Courtesy of Frances Child.)

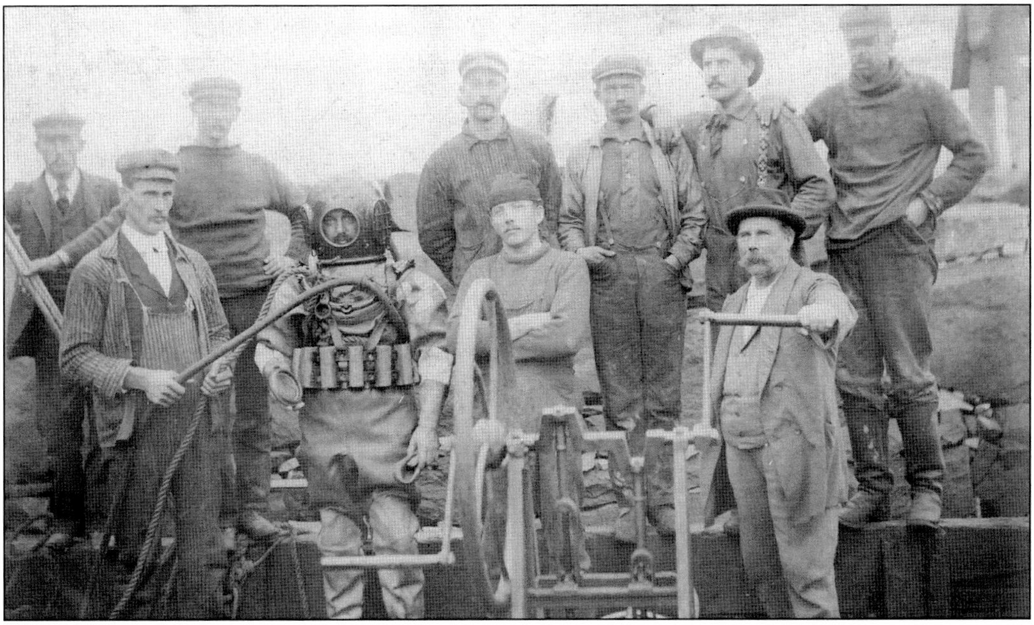

Not only was there a variety of activity on the surface of the water, but, as this 1896 photograph attests, there was also some action below the waterline. The unidentified man in the cumbersome diving suit is the 19th-century version of an underwater explorer, appearing quite different from the modern scuba diver. He is totally dependent on his crew for a steady supply of oxygen once he plunges below the surface.

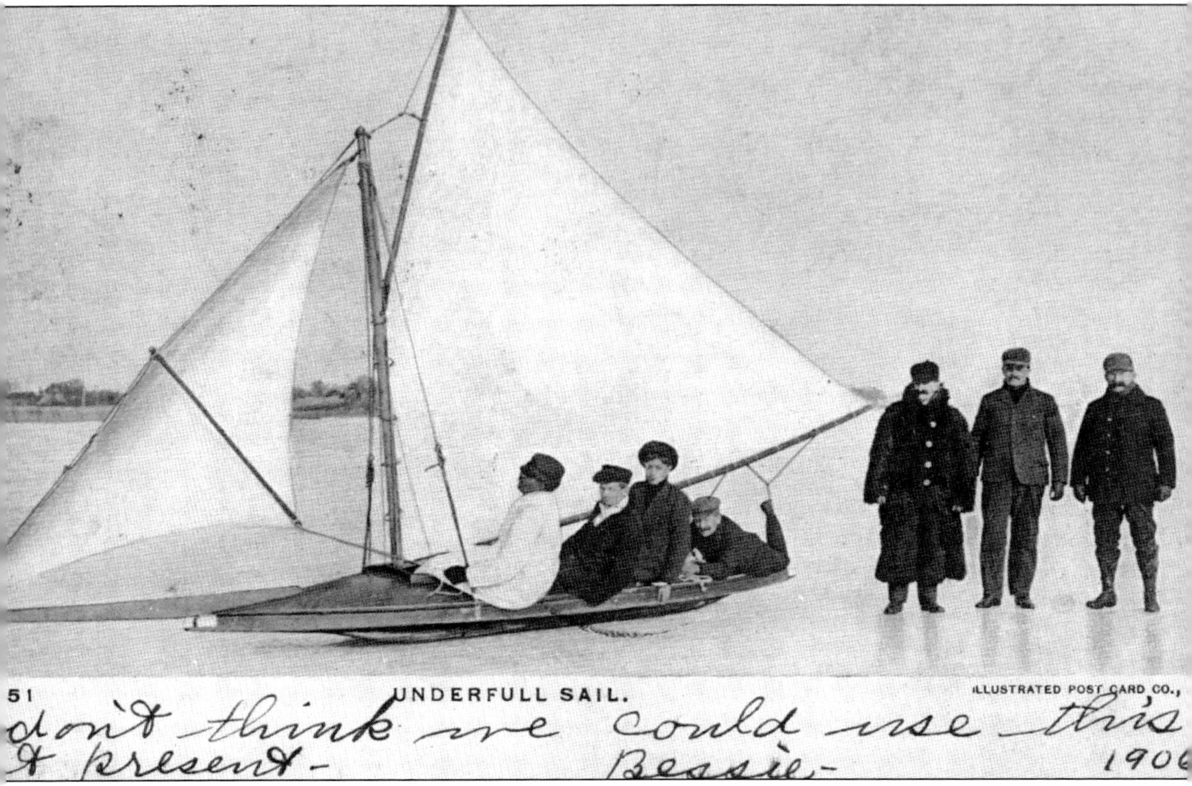

Sailing upon its placid surface was not the only recreational activity the harbor provided the residents of Port Jefferson. In this 1906 photograph, iceboaters test their mettle against Mother Nature's deep freeze during a prolonged cold spell. Skimming across the slippery surface was not for the faint of heart. With a trailing breeze, these lightweight craft flew effortlessly across the ice. Most people were content to lace on their skates and enjoy the rare experience of skating upon the harbor instead of swimming in it. While the freezing of the harbor might have been a special treat for some, for those whose livelihood depended upon free, unfrozen access to Long Island Sound and beyond, the sight of ice-skaters and iceboaters was not a happy one.

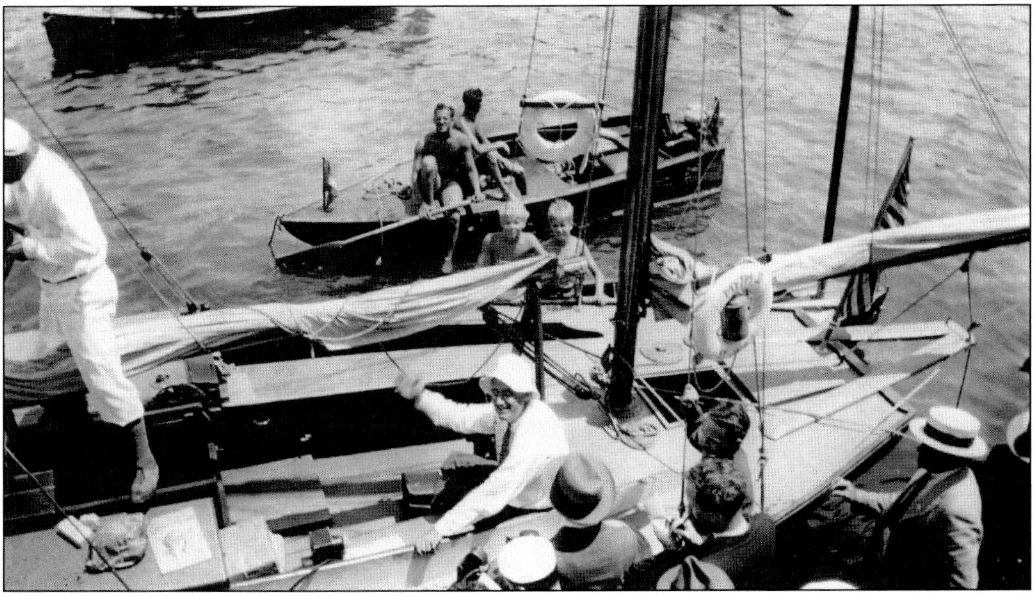

Franklin Roosevelt, governor of New York and the recently nominated Democratic Party candidate for president, is shown here on the yawl *Myth II*, waiting to shove off on a vacation with his sons in July 1932. Among the large crowd that had gathered, two local boys, Randall Woodard and Gilbert Kinner (in the center of the picture directly above Roosevelt), approached the yawl in their sailboat and got to shake Roosevelt's hand, a moment that is immortalized in the newsreels of the time.

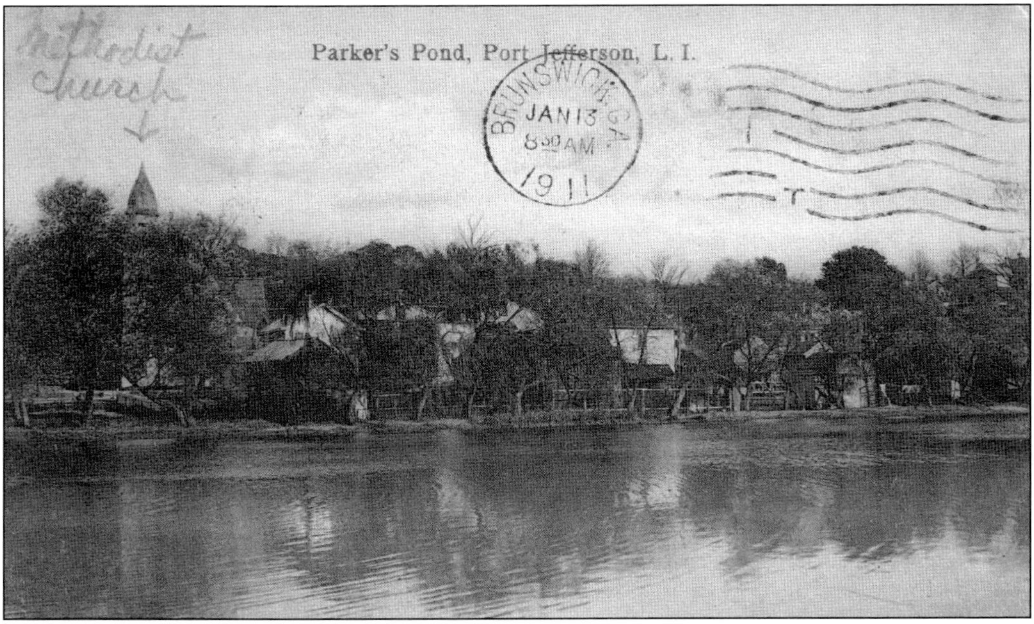

When the harbor was not frozen over, Port Jefferson's favorite ice-skating spot was Parker's Pond, also known as Crystal Lake. This beautiful freshwater pond was situated on the west side of Main Street, behind the present firehouse and across from the Methodist church. It was owned by A.J. Parker, a tombstone sculptor who supplemented his income by cutting ice from the pond during the winter. (Courtesy of Frances Child.)

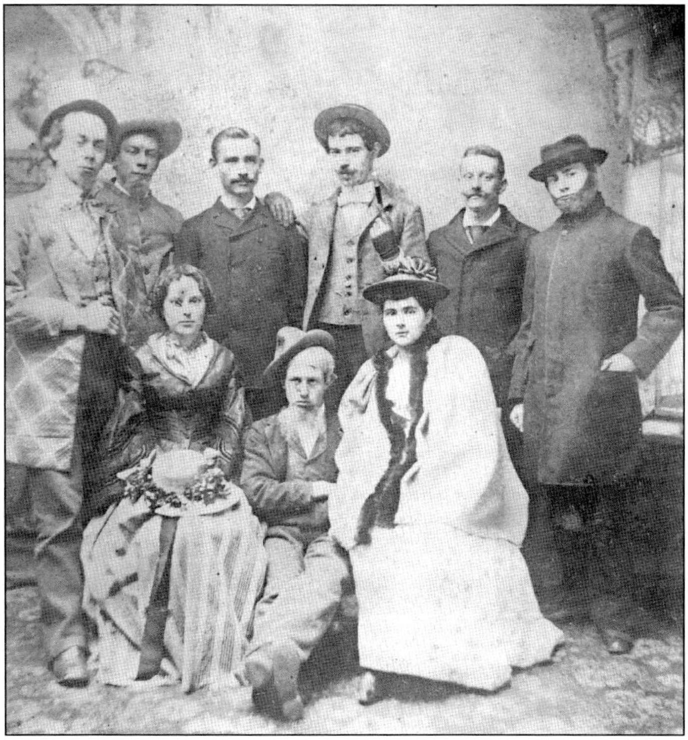

One of the precursors of the modern productions now performed at Theatre Three was a group of actors who called themselves the Pastime Dramatic Society of Port Jefferson. Founded in 1891, the group staged productions at Athena Hall, now Theatre Three. The troupe members are pictured here in rehearsals for their presentation of the play *Hick'ry Farm* in 1892. (Courtesy of Frances Child.)

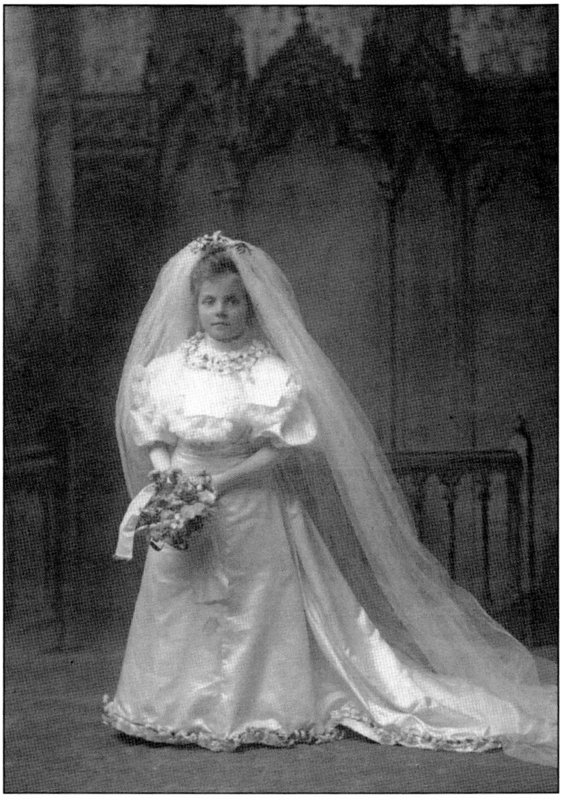

Florence Grace McKave, eight years old, is dressed for her role in a Tom Thumb wedding. These ceremonies, popular in the early part of the 20th century, consisted of children under 10 years of age playing different members of a wedding party. P.T. Barnum was responsible for the first one, when he promoted the nuptials of actual little person and circus performer "Tom Thumb" (Charles Stratton) and his little-person bride, Lavinia Warren, in 1863.

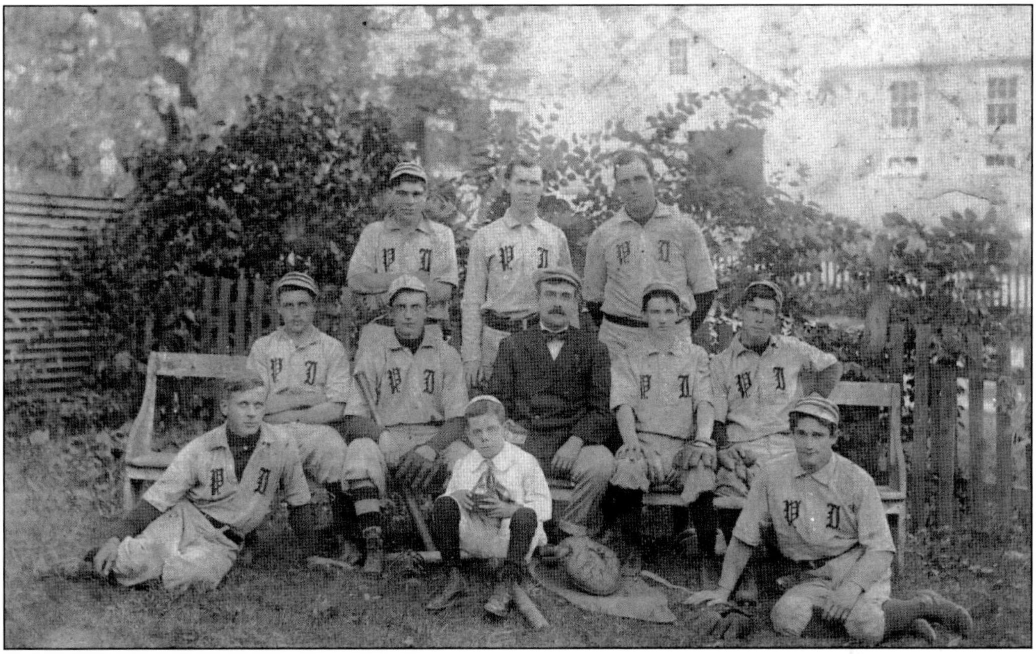

The Port Jefferson village baseball team poses for a picture with its mascot, George Platt (center), in the early 20th century. Baseball was the popular town sport of the time, and this team provided the community with a source of pride and identity. It played its home games on a field in Port Jefferson Station, drawing crowds in the hundreds to witness players' feats on the diamond.

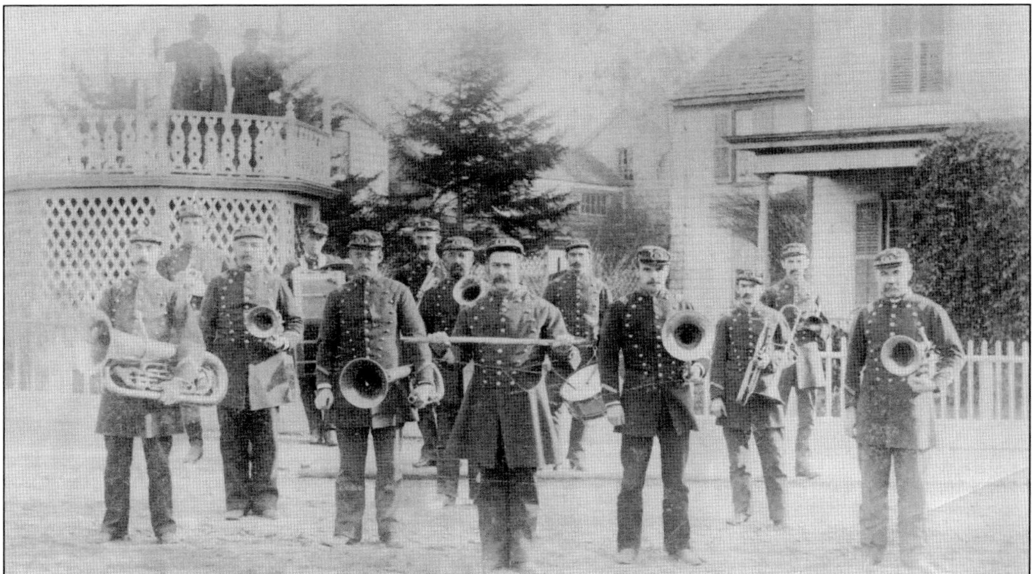

The Port Jefferson Brass Band is shown standing in Hotel Square in the late 1800s. Community bands were prevalent during this period, as they provided one of the only local sources of entertainment. Bands played at patriotic ceremonies, parades, picnics, and political rallies. Their repertoire consisted of popular songs of the day as well as the marches of John Phillip Sousa. The Port Jefferson Brass Band advertised itself as available for "music for all occasions" and performed frequently at Athena Hall and California Grove. (Courtesy of Frances Child.)

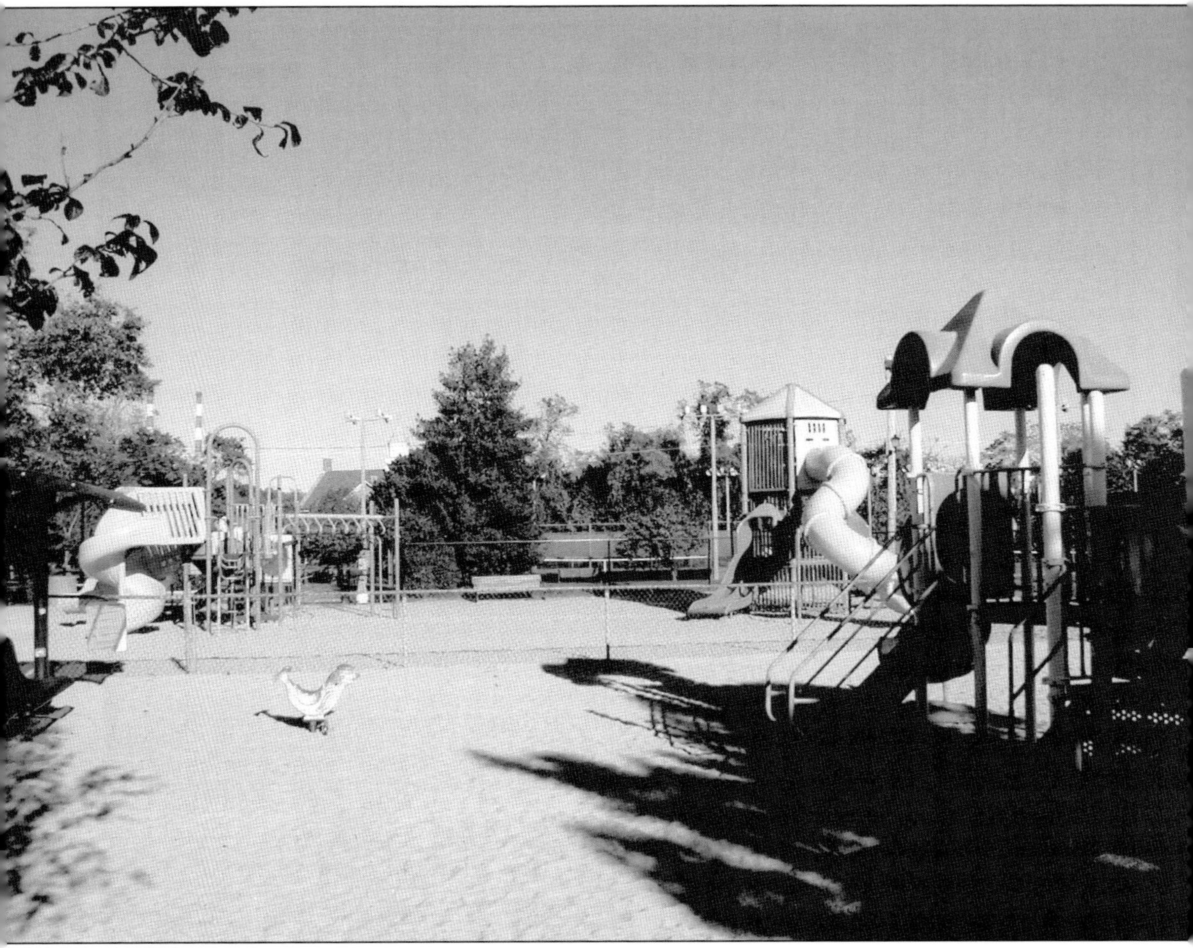

In the 21st century, Port Jefferson continues to offer its citizens many recreational opportunities. In 1969, handball and tennis courts were constructed in the Meadows Playground behind Village Hall, on land that was once part of the drowned meadow. One of the most popular recreational facilities in the Meadows is the playground shown here, popularly called "Rocketship Park." Flag football, baseball, softball, and soccer teams play on the Caroline Avenue fields on land acquired by the village in 1968. Indoor sports are enjoyed in the gymnasium of the old junior high school on Spring Street. The village beaches offer two miles of shoreline on Long Island Sound for swimming, fishing, and strolling. The Port Jefferson Country Club at Harbor Hills, which traces its origin to the Belle Terre course of 1908, offers an 18-hole golf course and eight tennis courts. The newest addition to Port Jefferson's recreational facilities is the Village Center, offering classes for children and adults and ice-skating in the winter months. (Courtesy of Port Jefferson Free Library.)

Seven

CELEBRATIONS

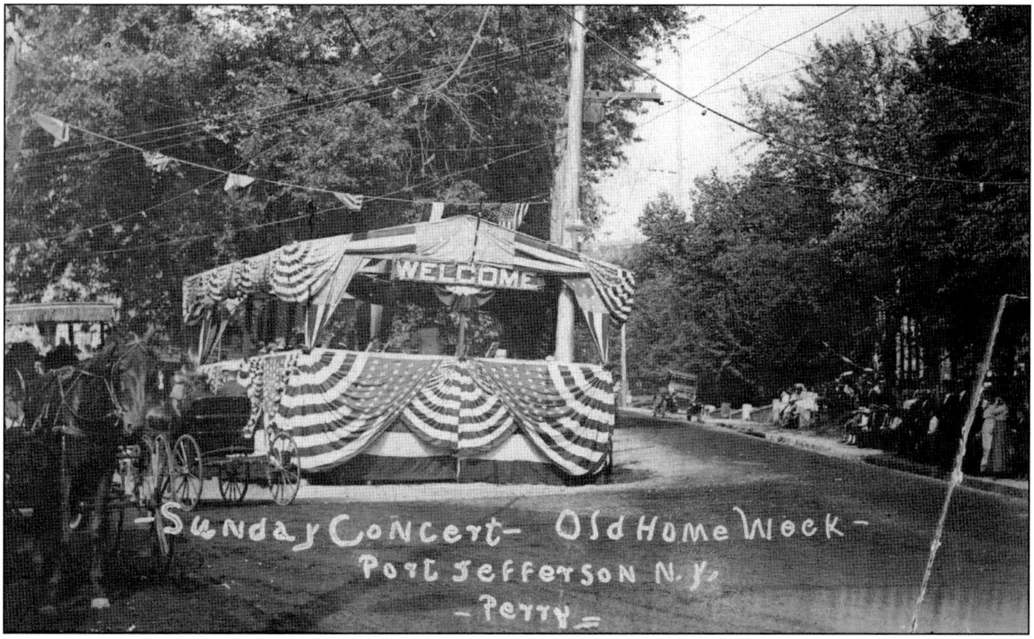

Initiated by the local Business Men's Association to promote commerce, Old Home Week was first celebrated in 1908. The village's buildings were bedecked in patriotic bunting, and a festive atmosphere prevailed. Among the events were concerts, boat races, dances, sporting events, and hot-air balloon displays. This photograph shows the reviewing stand at the corner of East Main and Prospects Streets as the crowd awaits a musical presentation.

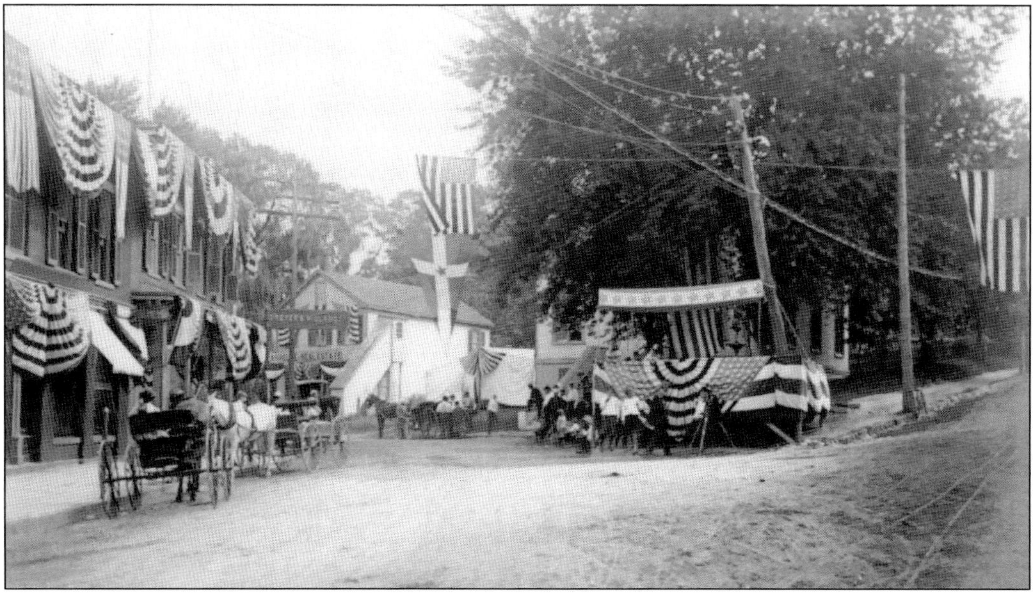

This view is looking down East Main Street, with Prospect Street on the right. The decorative flags and bunting of Old Home Week hang from the stores on the left, which include the Dreyer and McDermott store. The top of the Biddle Fountain is visible through the reviewing stand. The prolific local photographer Arthur S. Greene is standing at the tripod in front of the stand in this 1908 photograph.

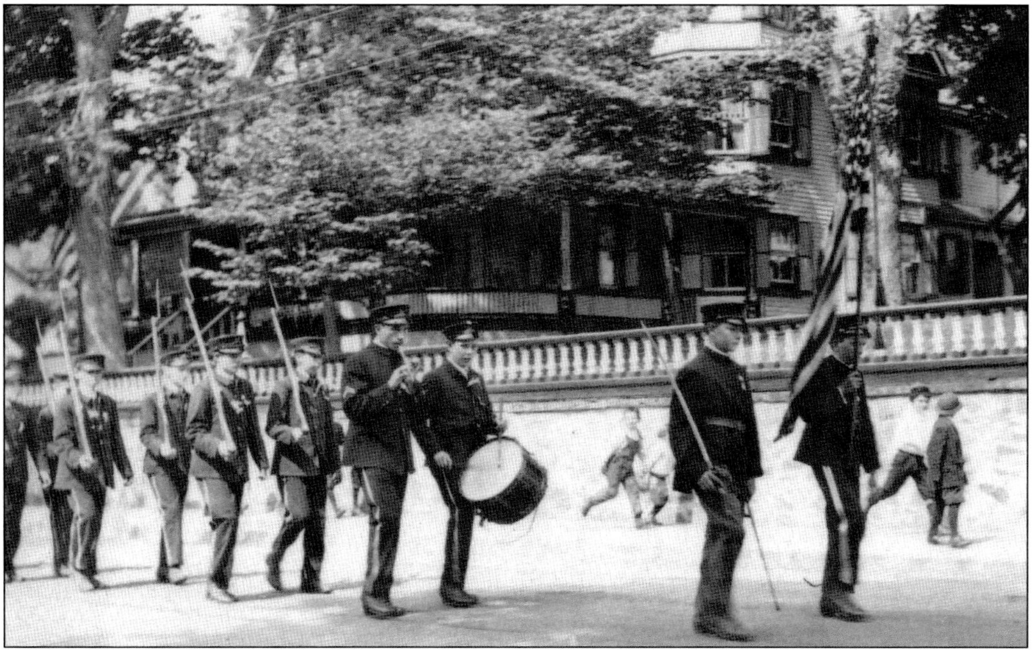

The local chapter of the Boys Brigade of America marches down Main Street during Old Home Week in 1911. This Christian organization was a forerunner of the Boy Scouts. Started in England, its purpose was to teach young men discipline and to promote patriotism. The boys attended services together, performed military drills, and participated in community activities. Note their youthful followers on the sidewalk.

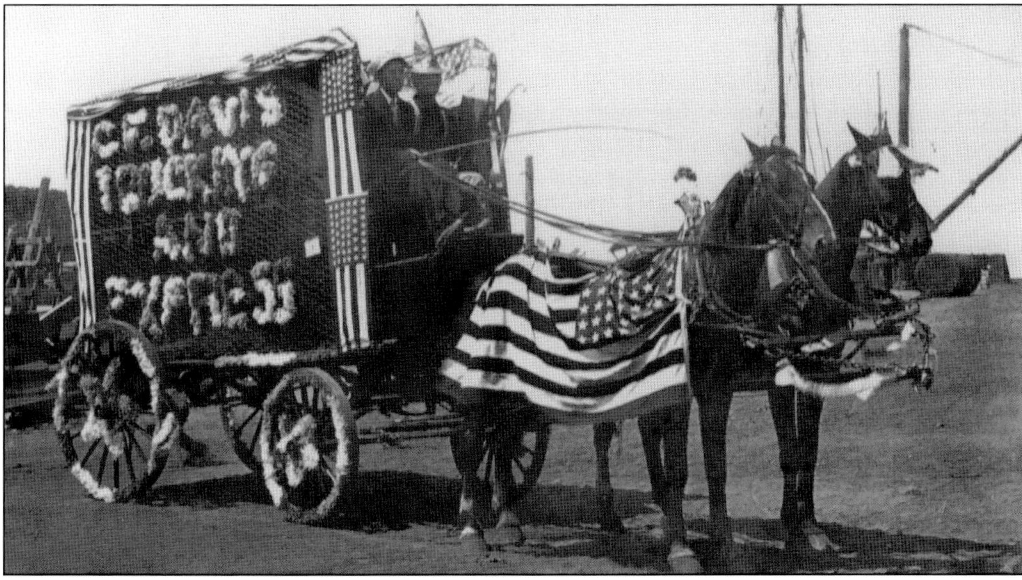

Prizes were given to parade participants during Old Home Week. Categories included the most tastefully decorated automobile, the best team of workhorses, and the best driving horse attached to a runabout. The winner for best-decorated float was this entry of the C.F. Davis Trucking and Express Company.

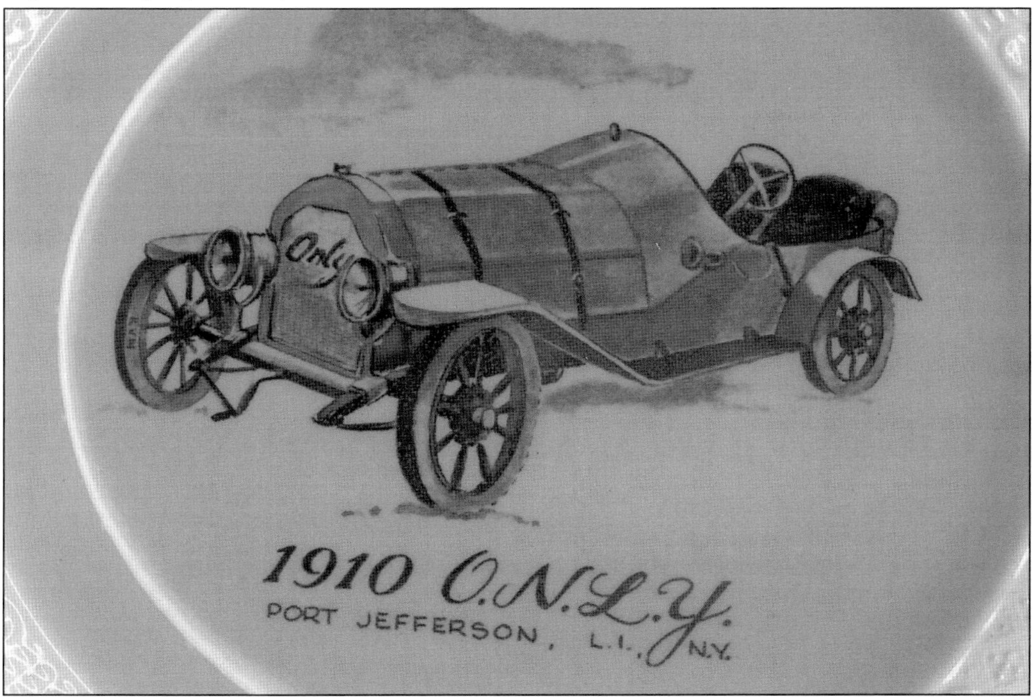

Beginning in 1910, the Automobile Club of Port Jefferson sponsored races up steep East Broadway. Subsequent editions of the race, known as the Hill Climb, were staged in 1911 and 1924, with locally produced cars acquitting themselves very well. The O.N.L.Y. car, shown here on a commemorative plate, was a one-cylinder vehicle that could reach a speed of 60 miles per hour. In the first Hill Climb, it finished second to a 200-horsepower Fiat.

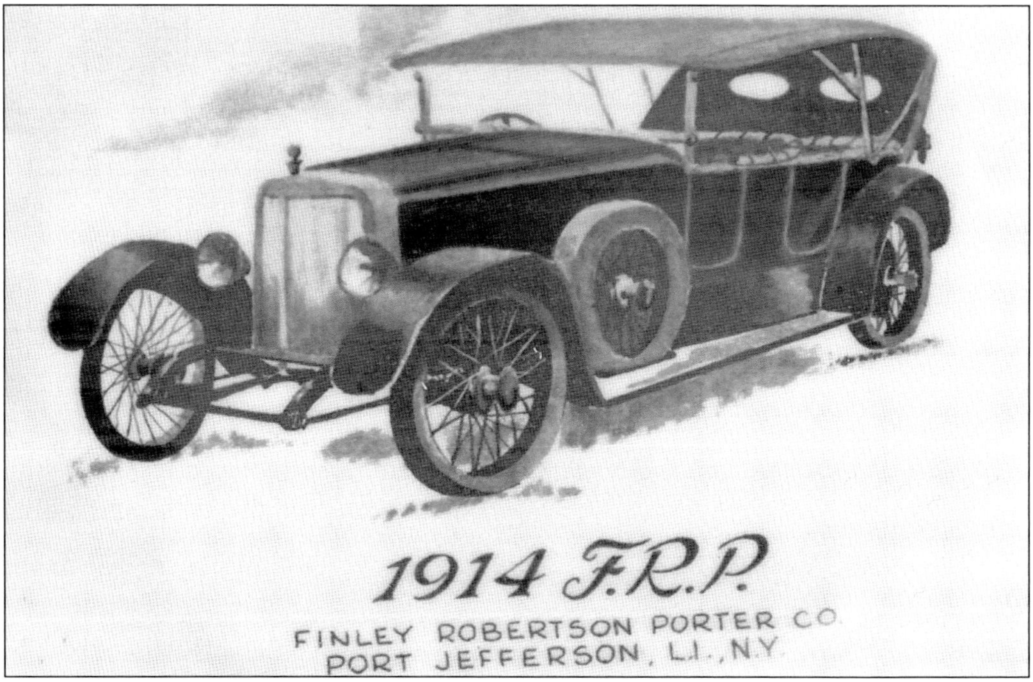

Finley Robertson Porter was an innovative automobile designer who manufactured his FRP car in Port Jefferson for a brief time. With its 125-horsepower engine enabling it to achieve speeds of up to 80 miles per hour, the FRP was promoted as "America's Foremost Pleasure Car." Its high cost proved prohibitive, and only about a dozen were produced over a two-year span. One of the surviving FRPs is shown in the below photograph, with local Allison Vandall at the wheel. On Thanksgiving Day in 1924, he drove this modified version of a 10-year-old FRP to victory in the Port Jefferson Hill Climb. The race attracted participants from all over the world. Vandall triumphed over the Lexington Minute Man Six entry, which had been the winner of the Pikes Peak Hill Climb in Colorado. He won $500 for his effort and garnered a great deal of pride for the Port Jefferson automobile industry.

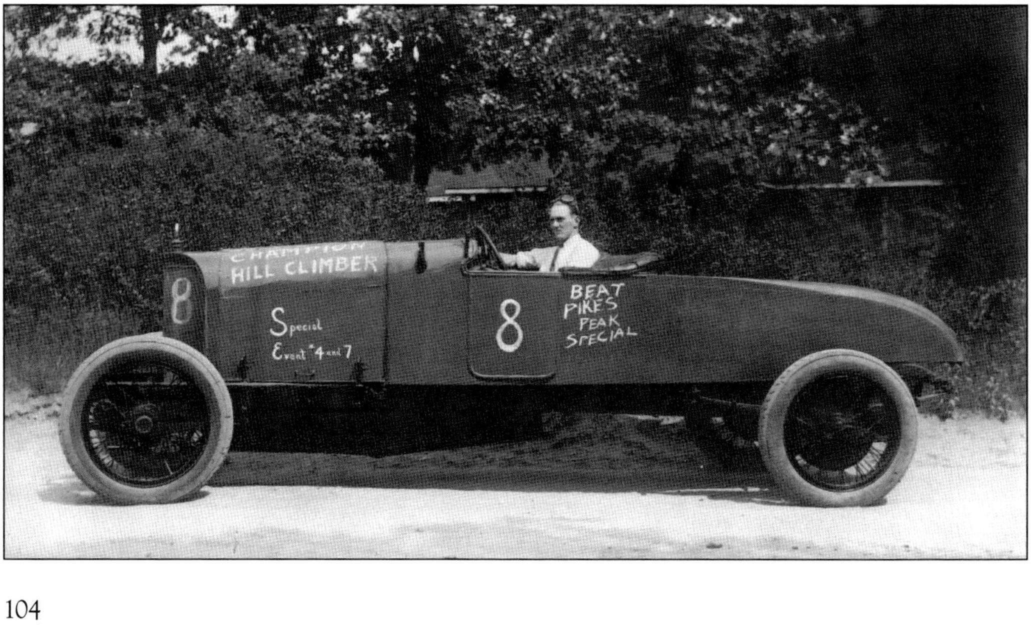

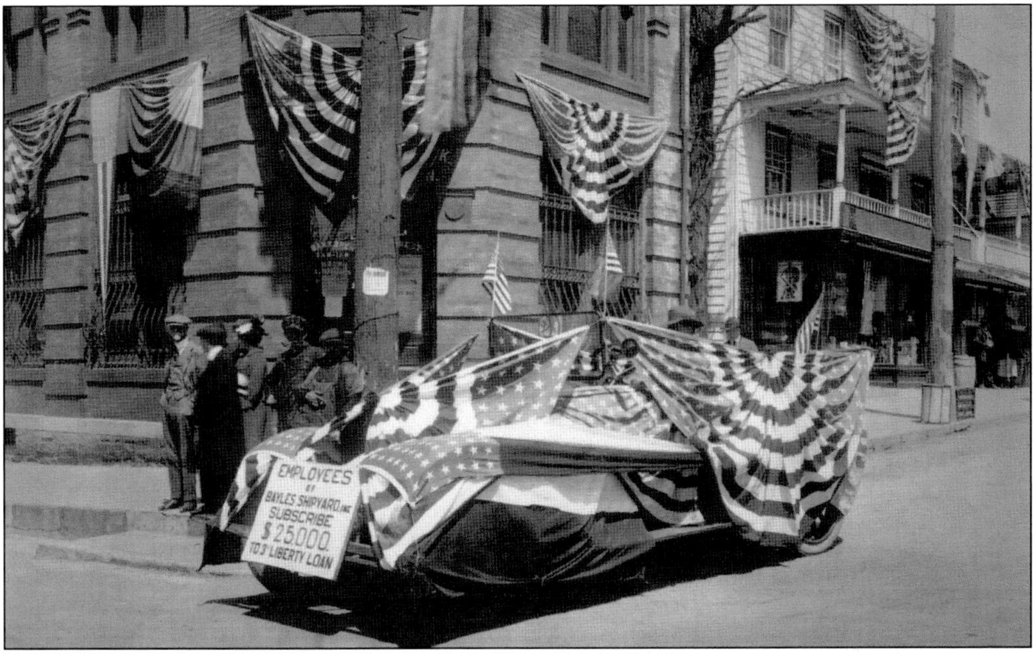

It is April 26, 1918, and the Bayles Shipyard employees have patriotically decorated this vehicle in red, white, and blue in order to promote the government's Liberty Loan program. Citizens were encouraged to purchase war bonds to help defray the cost of US involvement in World War I. The Liberty Loan car float is turning from East Main Street on to Main Street, passing in front of the First National Bank of Port Jefferson. The Port Jefferson Hotel is in the background.

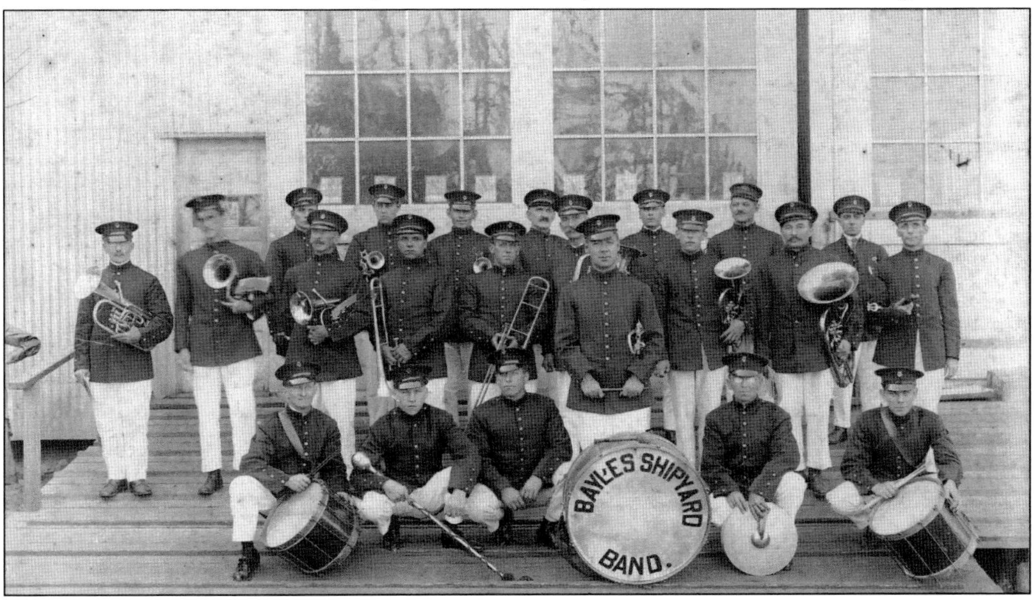

The Bayles Shipyard Band poses for a portrait in the yards around 1918. Made up of approximately 20 to 25 pieces, mainly brass and percussion, the band performed at ship launches as well as parties and dances. The band also performed on a bandstand on the shipyard's grounds. The Bayles Shipyard Jazz Band received a favorable mention in the local newspaper after it performed in the Grand Ballroom of the Plant Hotel in 1919.

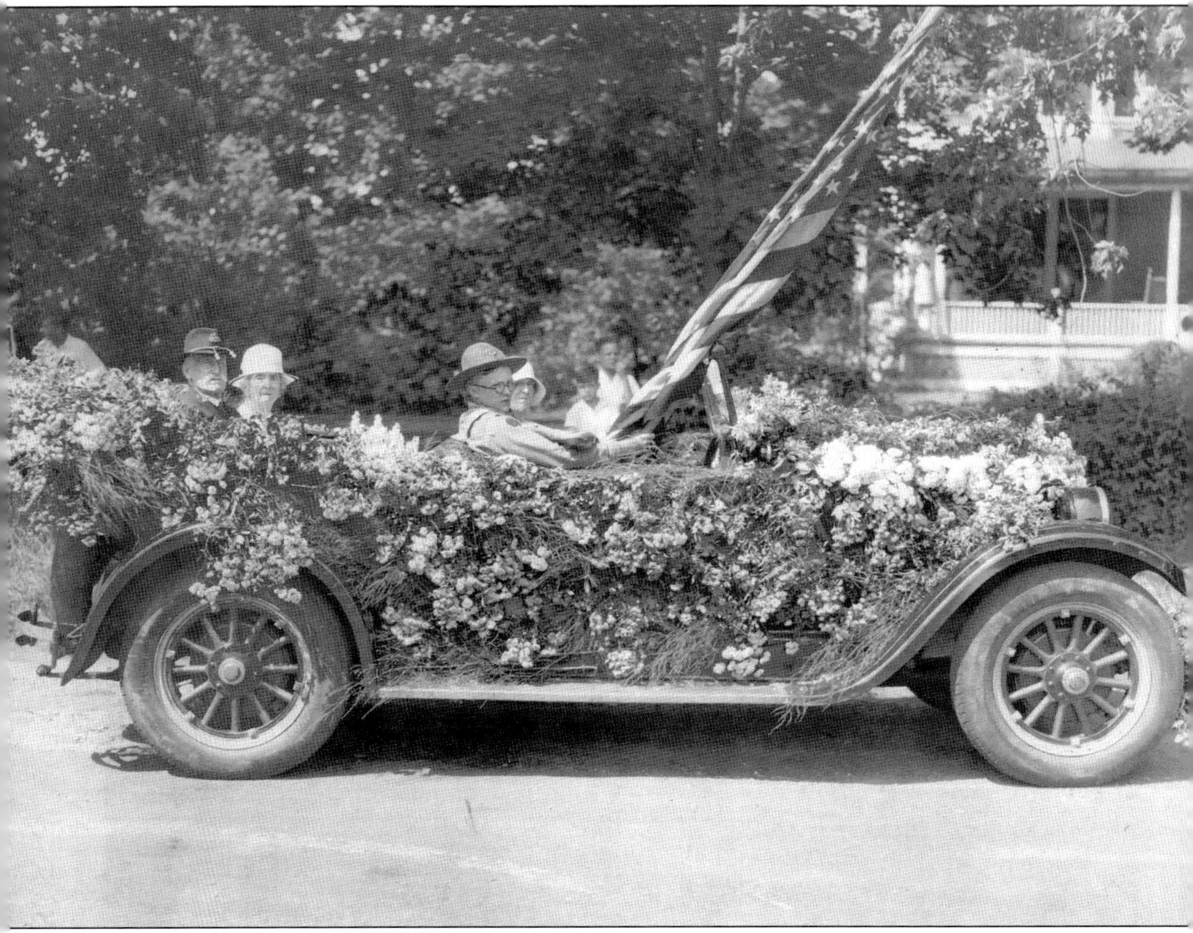

Abram and Marian Bentley are shown in the 1919 Fourth of July Parade. Bentley was a Civil War veteran from New Jersey who came to Port Jefferson with his wife in 1866 to work in Effingham Tuthill's carriage factory, the first and foremost of Port Jefferson's carriage makers. Although he was only 22, he was already experienced in the trade, having served as an apprentice for six years before joining the Army. With two partners, he started his own carriage business in 1874, and by 1886, he had become the sole owner of an establishment considered the most complete in Suffolk County. Both Bentleys were very active community members. When Abram died in June 1934 at the age of 89, just two months after his wife, he was the last surviving member of the Lewis O. Conklin Post of the Grand Army of the Republic.

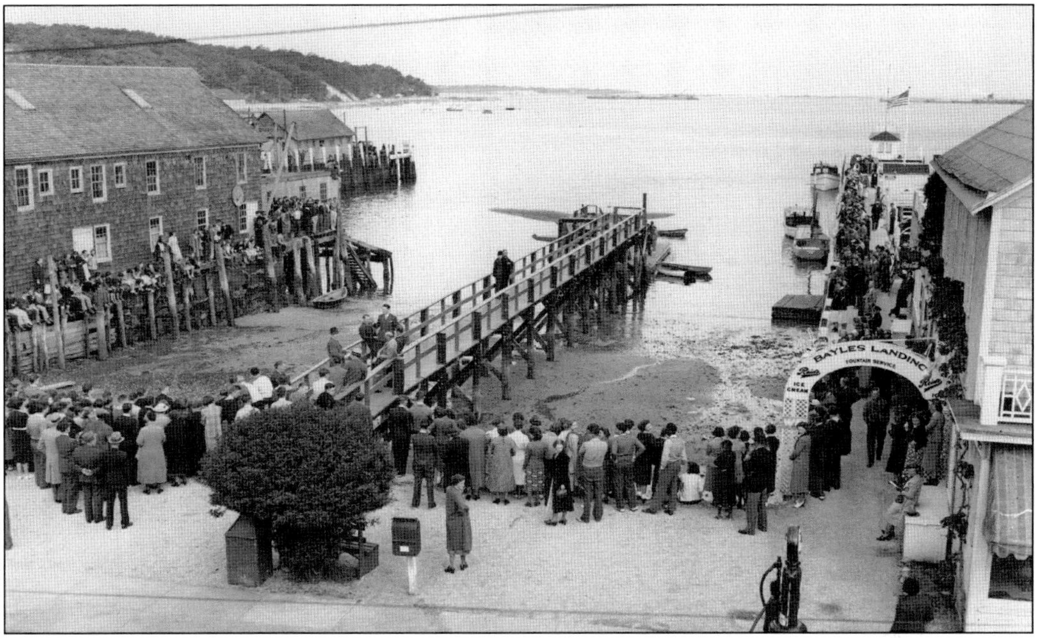

In 1938, the country was still in the depths of the Depression. In order to assist the still-developing air transport industry through the tough times, President Roosevelt and Postmaster General James Farley launched a promotion they called National Air Mail, held between May 15 and 21. Each citizen was encouraged to either mail or receive an airmail letter during that seven-day period. A new 6¢ airmail stamp was issued. Thursday, May 19, was the designated day when 1,700 special one-day-only flights would carry those letters. As seen in these photographs, a large crowd has come to Bayles Landing to witness the first airmail flight from Port Jefferson. In the above photograph, the seaplane's wings are barely visible beyond the end of the dock. It was estimated that during the week, over sixteen million letters and nine million parcels were transported. In the photograph below, East Broadway runs behind the crowd of what look to be mainly high school students.

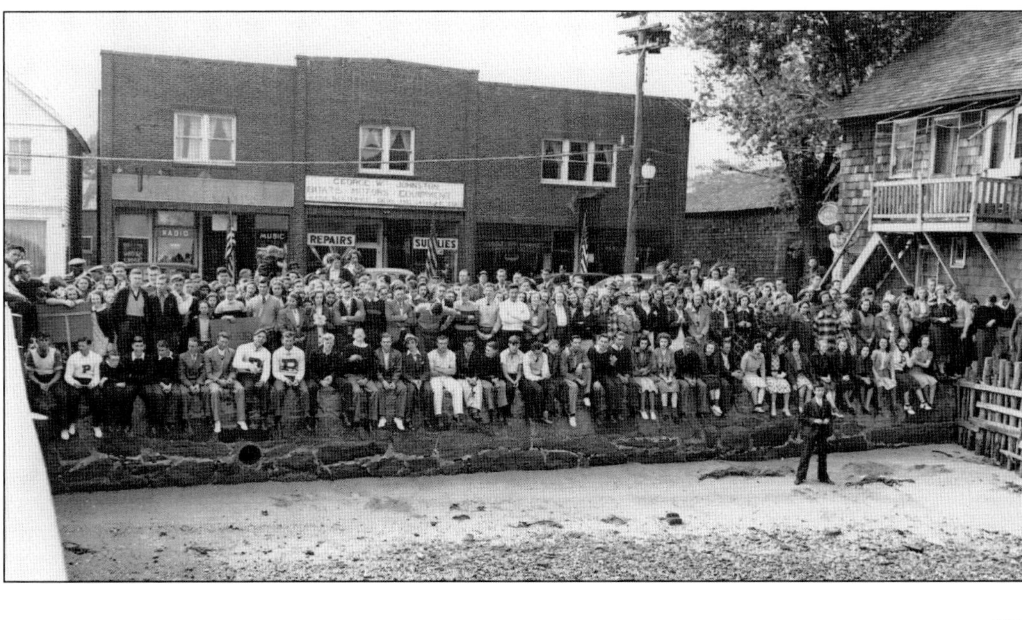

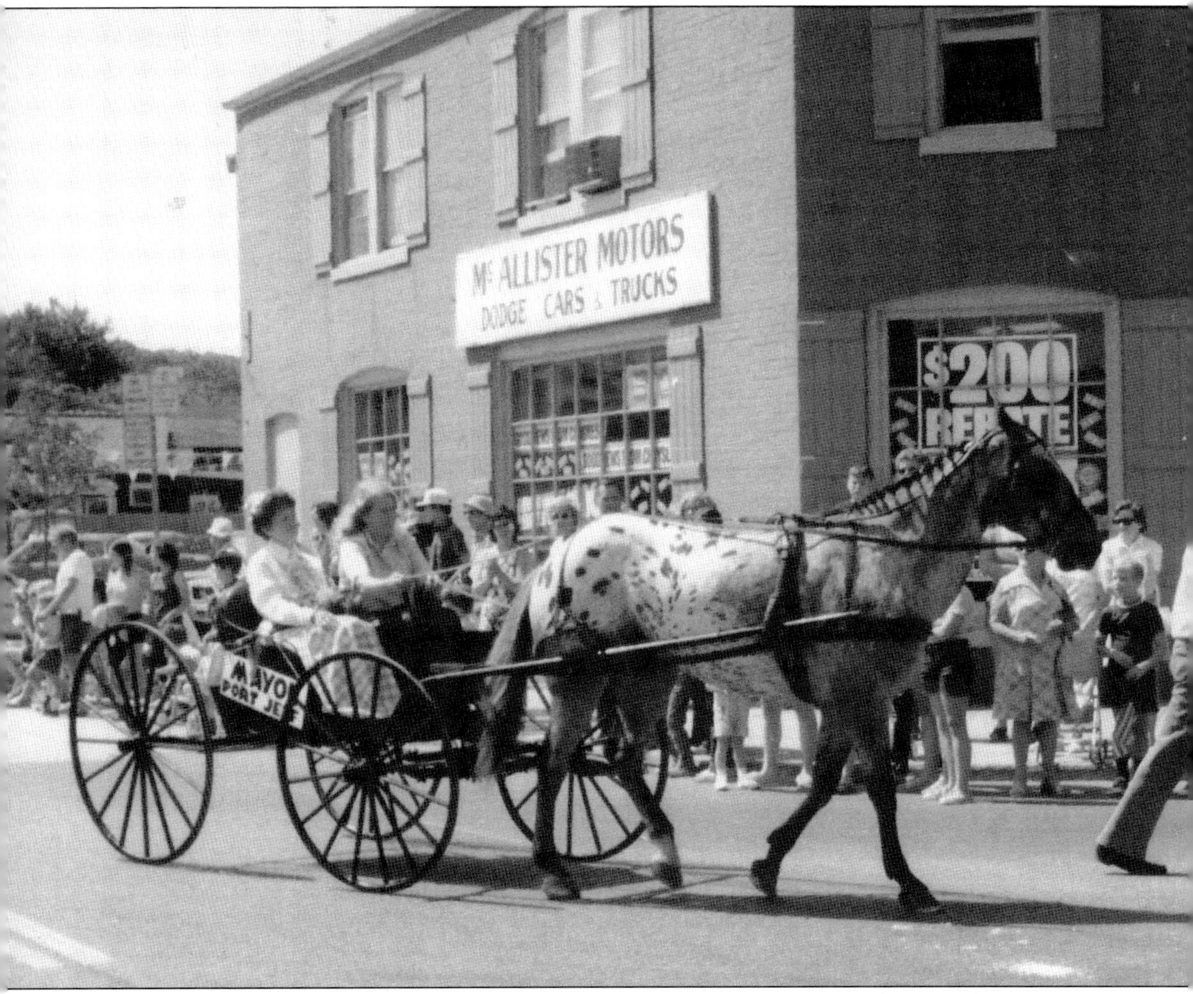

In the 1976 Bicentennial Parade on Main Street, Port Jefferson mayor Sandra Swenk experiences a ride in a 19th-century mode of transportation as she passes a dealership of the preferred choice of the 20th century. The appearance of a horse-drawn carriage pays homage to one of Port Jefferson's major industries of the 1800s besides shipbuilding. Named after the third president and one of the Founding Fathers, the village, like many communities across the United States, showed its true red, white, and blue colors in celebrating the country's 200th anniversary. Two tall ships visited, and there were whaleboat races in the harbor. Reflecting the events of Old Home Week, an old-fashioned field day was staged, featuring bike, sack, and three-legged races along with a tug-of-war competition and, of course, a gala parade and fireworks.

Eight

Leading Men and Ladies

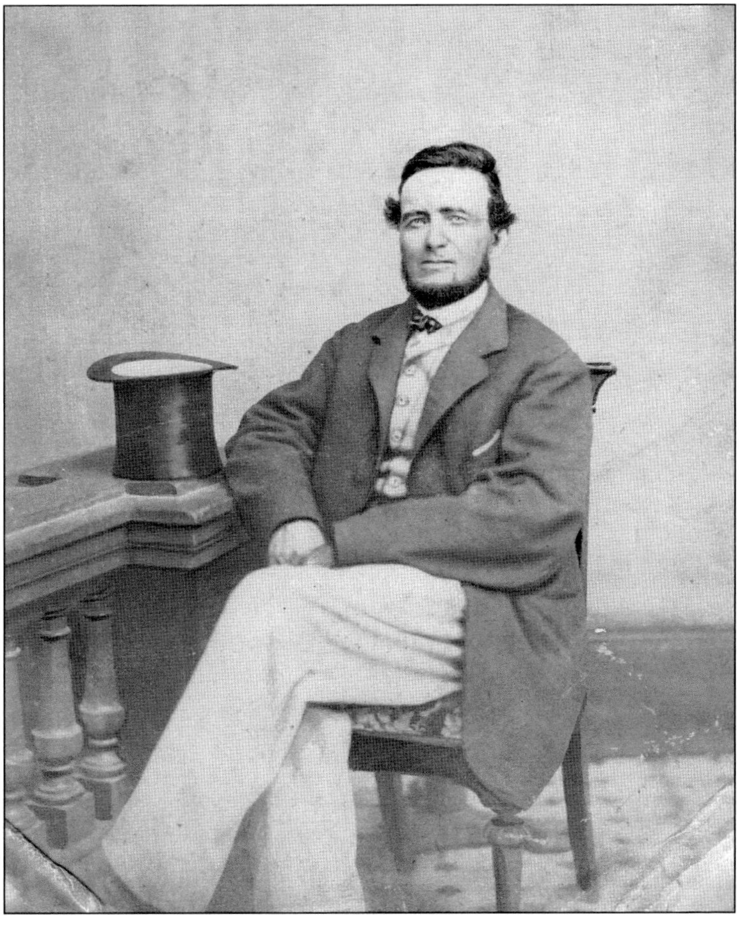

James Madison Bayles, son of Elisha Bayles, the patriarch of the shipbuilding Bayleses, was born in Port Jefferson in 1815 at Cookie Hill. He spent his teenage years as a crew member on a number of ships before going into shipbuilding in 1836. He found he had a natural affinity for ship construction. His intolerance of poor workmanship and his attention to detail earned the business a reputation for quality craftsmanship. (Courtesy of Frances Child.)

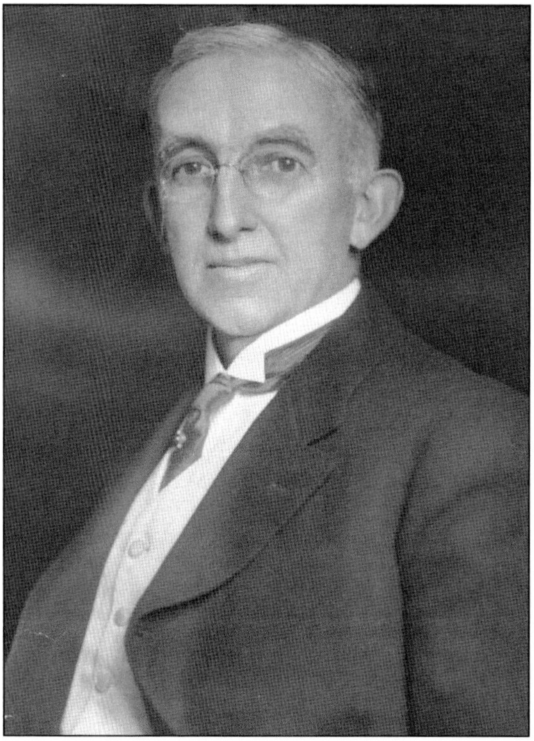

Hamilton Tooker Bayles (1852–1922), the fourth son of James M. Bayles, was a partner in the Bayles Chandlery with his brother G. Frank Bayles until the shipyard was purchased by the government in 1917. He served as president of the Town Board of Trustees and was treasurer of the Port Jefferson Fire Department and the Cedar Hill Cemetery Association. (Courtesy of Frances Child.)

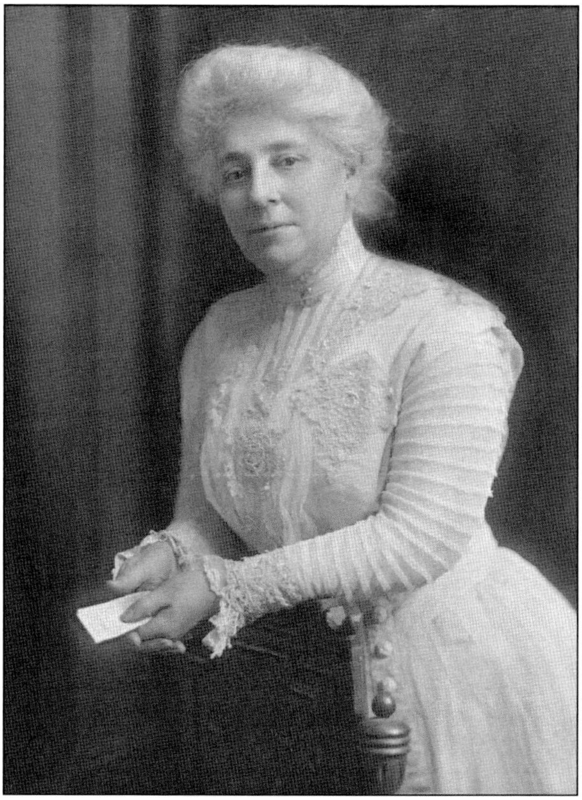

Rosalia Horton Bayles was the wife of Hamilton Tooker Bayles. Born in 1856, she was one of the most active women in Port Jefferson, having been a member of the Village Improvement Society, the Belle Terre and Suwassett Garden Clubs, and the Ladies Literary Society, which would go on to found the library in 1908. (Courtesy of Frances Child.)

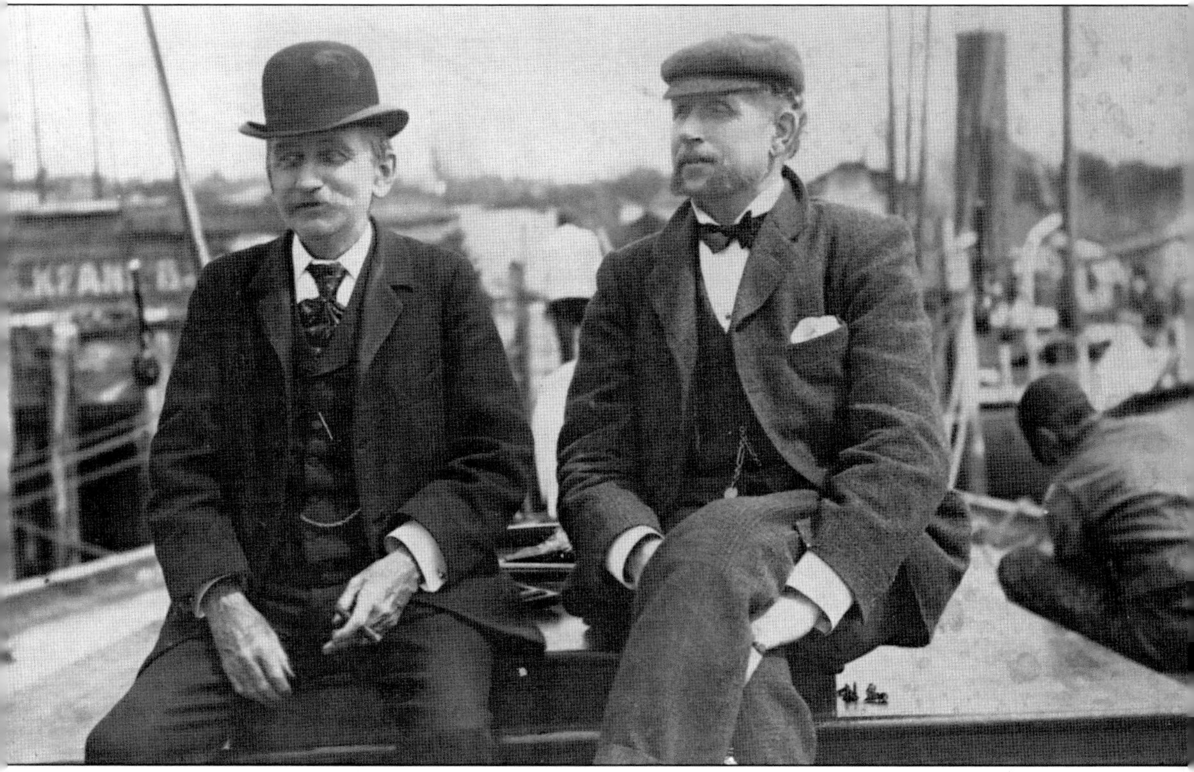

James Eban Bayles (1841–1929) became a partner with his father in J.M. Bayles & Son in 1862, at the age of 21. Known as "Boss Jim," he built more than 80 vessels, from barks and schooners to motor yachts, in the yard next to the house where he was born. His ships were famous for their speed, carrying capacity, and "fine outline." The Bayles yard also specialized in repairing and overhauling yachts and became one of the largest such businesses in the country. In addition to being Port Jefferson's foremost shipbuilder, Bayles also served as Brookhaven town supervisor (1884–1888), leader of the Democratic Party, trustee of the school district, charter member of the fire department, and founding trustee of the Port Jefferson Free Library. He is shown here, with derby, around 1910 with his friend, Capt. John Marshall.

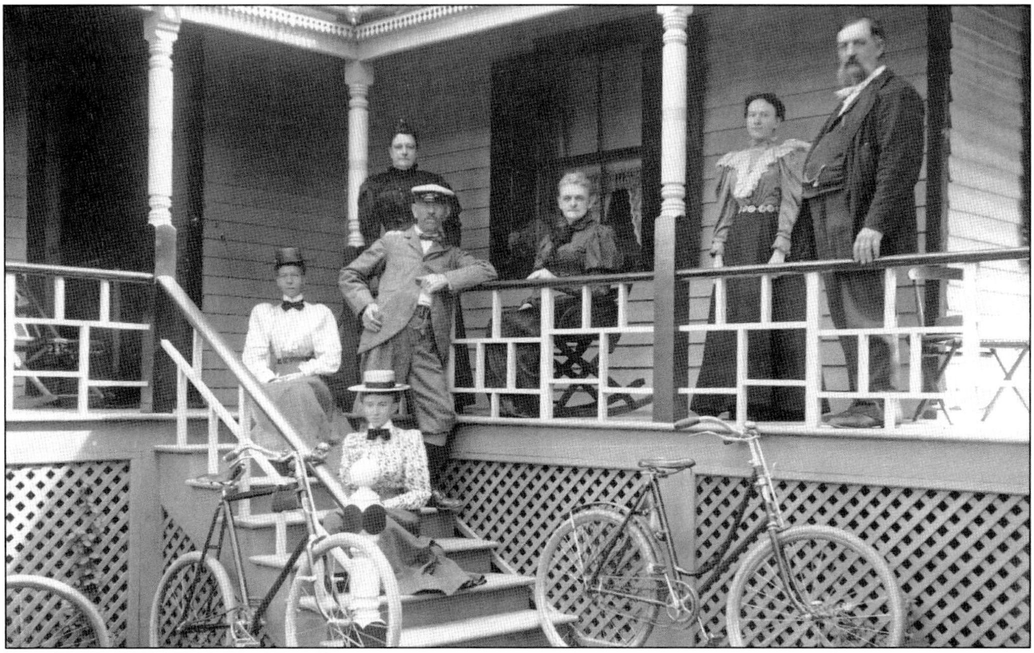

Capt. John "Jack" Tooker (standing on stairs) was born into one of the most famous seafaring families of Port Jefferson. Returning from a long voyage in the late 1890s, he received word that war was about to break out between the United States and Spain and became worried that he might be attacked. Approaching the New Jersey coast, Tooker thought himself home free, only to spy a fast-approaching unidentified ship. It turned out to be a US Navy cruiser.

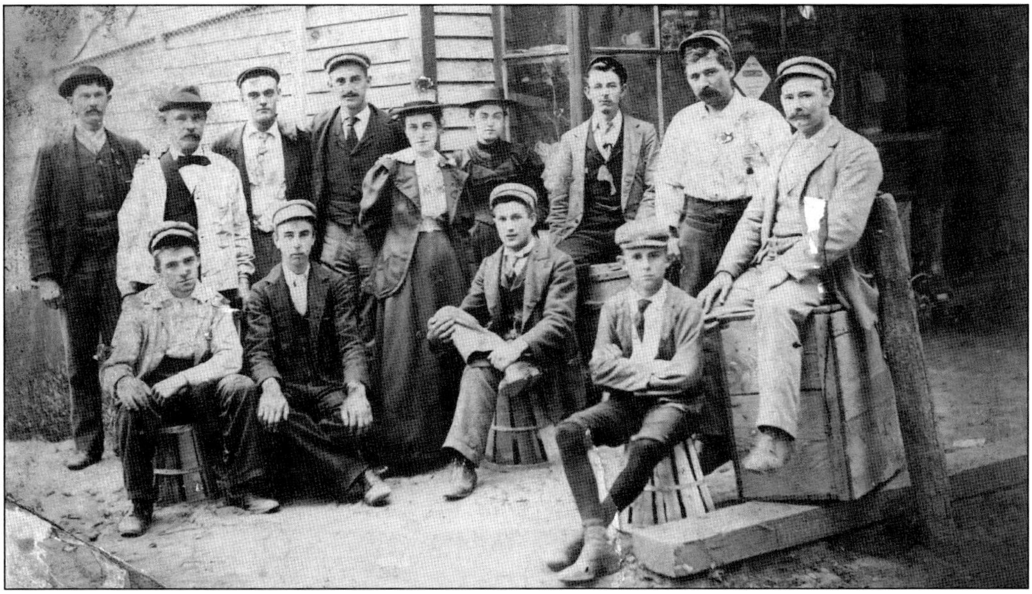

Orange T. Fanning was an influential business force in the community. His various interests included a coal and lumber business, a general store, and a wagon and carriage repository. He served as president of both the First National Bank and the ferry company. He also had a hand in organizing the first telephone company in the village. Some of his employees pose outside of his general store.

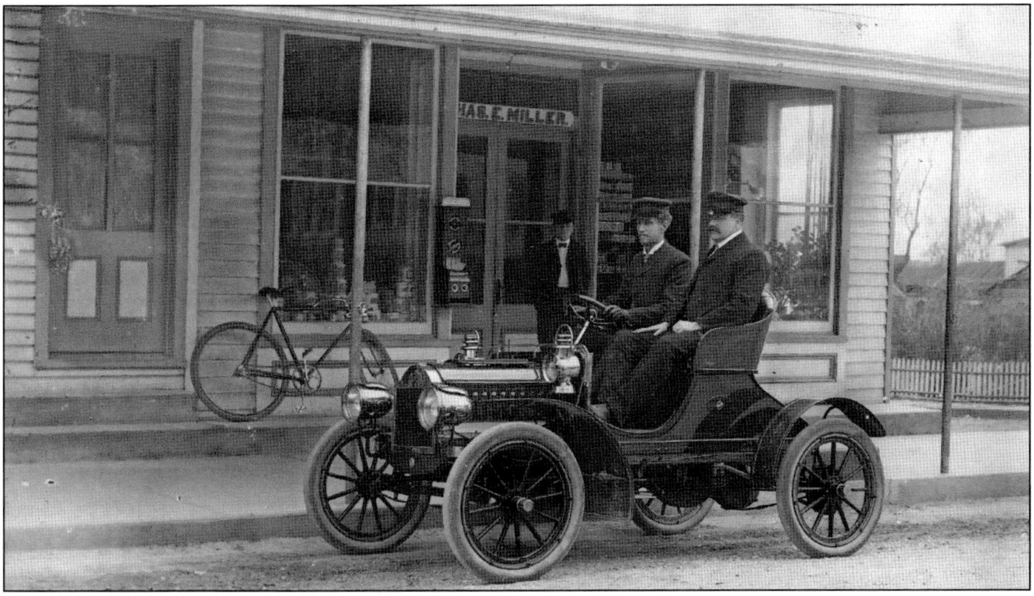

Charles E. Miller (at the wheel) and Capt. Albert L. Haskell are parked in front of Miller's grocery store, located on the southwest corner of Main Street and Maple Place. Miller had been a clerk on the ferry *Nonowantuc*, and Haskell was a luxury boat captain who skippered William K. Vanderbilt Jr.'s yacht, *Tarantula*.

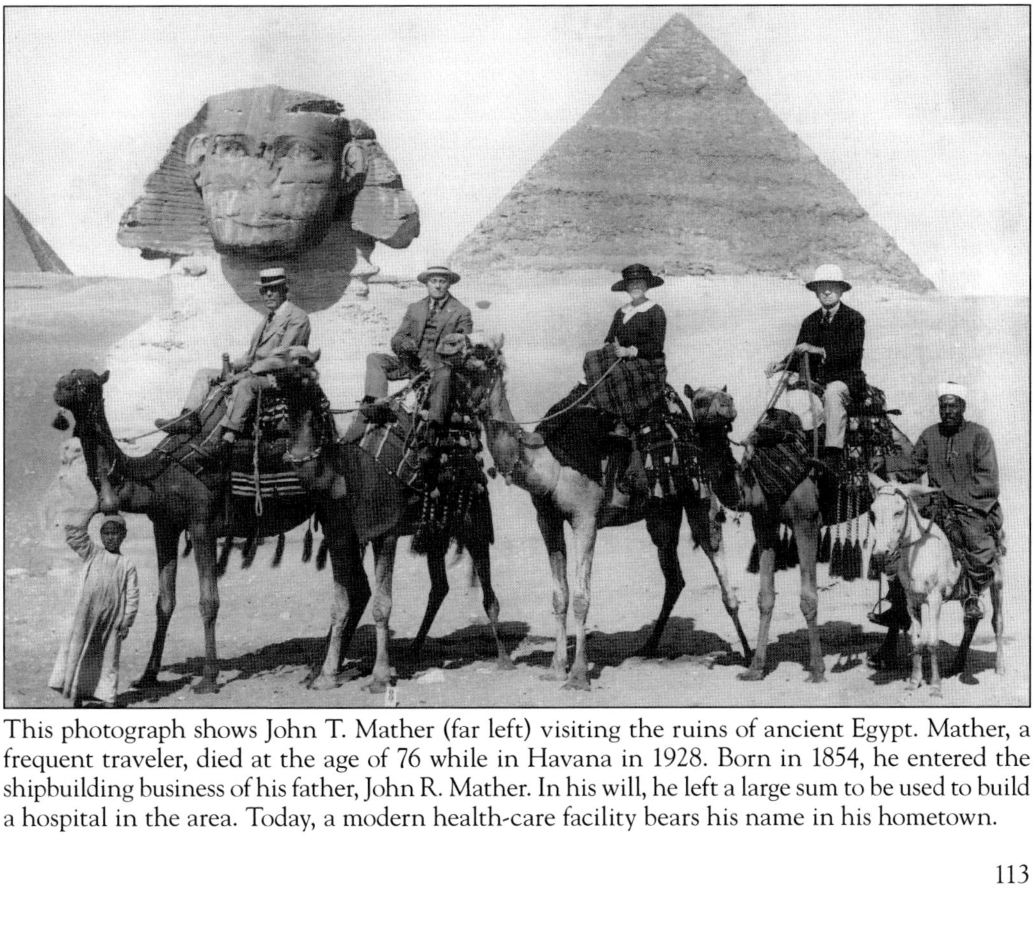

This photograph shows John T. Mather (far left) visiting the ruins of ancient Egypt. Mather, a frequent traveler, died at the age of 76 while in Havana in 1928. Born in 1854, he entered the shipbuilding business of his father, John R. Mather. In his will, he left a large sum to be used to build a hospital in the area. Today, a modern health-care facility bears his name in his hometown.

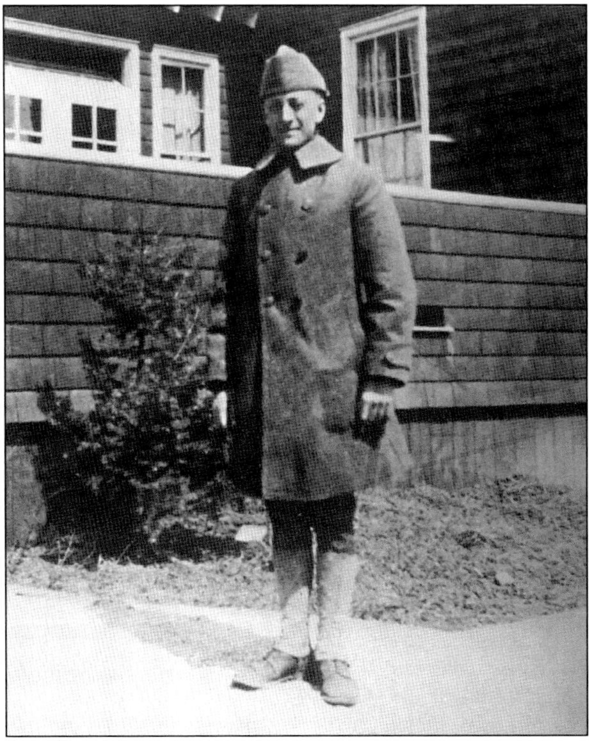

Irving Wilson Ritch Jr., a member of a prominent local family, poses in his uniform at Camp Upton, Yaphank, in 1918. Corporal Ritch was the first Port Jefferson serviceman killed in action in World War I, falling at the Battle of Argonne Forest in September 1918. The Wilson Ritch Post of the American Legion is named in his honor.

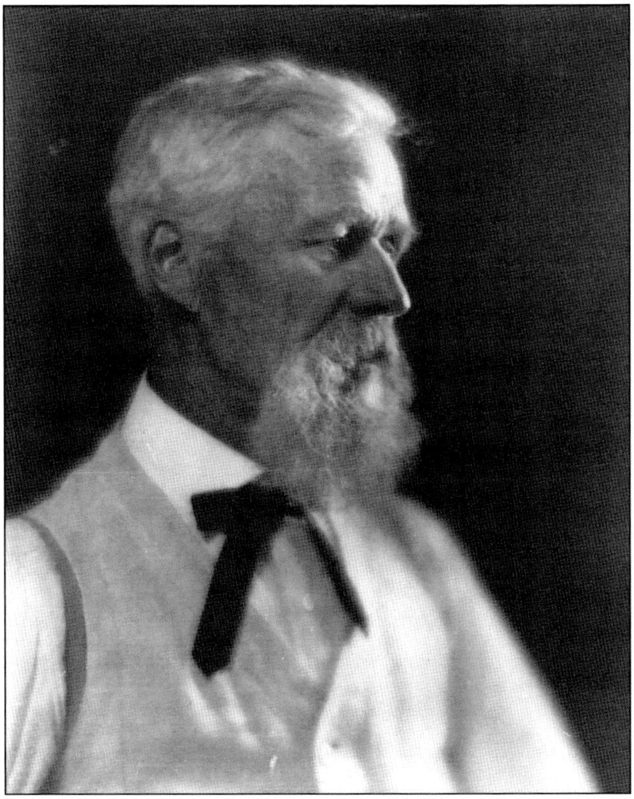

William Moore Davis (1829–1920), a native of Setauket, was apprenticed to Port Jefferson shipbuilder William Henry Darling, but he was always interested in painting and drawing. By 1861, he had formed a friendship with renowned Stony Brook artist William Sidney Mount, who, until his death in 1868, continued to give Davis advice and encouragement. From 1862 to 1872, Davis kept a studio on Broadway in New York City, but in the latter year he returned to Port Jefferson for good.

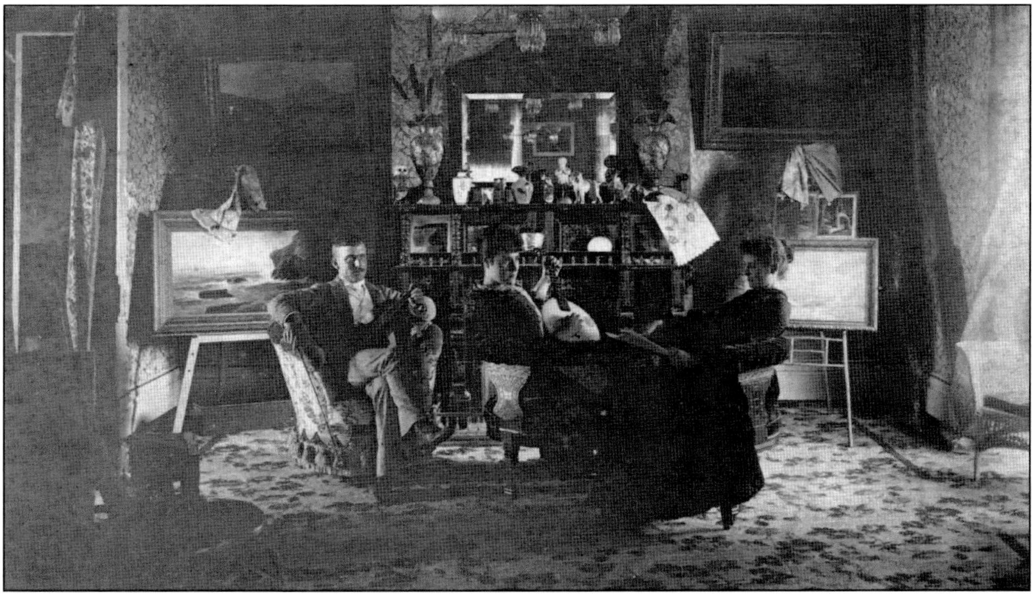

Some of William M. Davis's paintings can be seen in this photograph of the artist at home. For many years, he maintained a studio on the west side of East Main Street, where he also sold artists' supplies. He exhibited at the National Academy of Design and the Brooklyn Art Association throughout the 1860s to popular and critical acclaim, but in later years, his exhibits were confined to the local area.

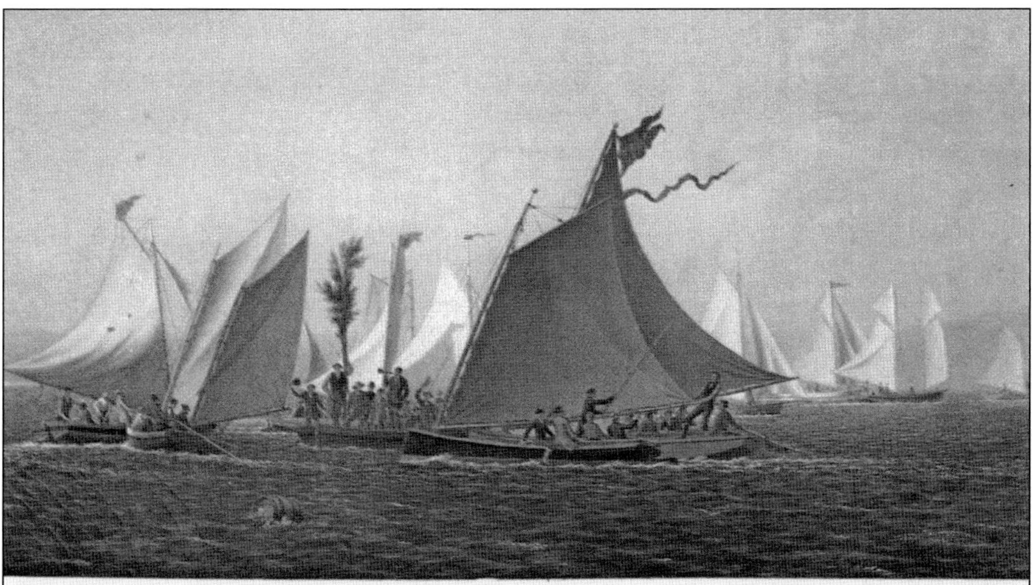

Davis's early shipbuilding training is evident in his many paintings of maritime subjects, including *The Sharpie Race*, shown here. Sharpie boats were designed for oystering in shallow waters. In this oil painting, Capt. Charles Tooker is depicted holding aloft the pine branch that marks the finish line of the race.

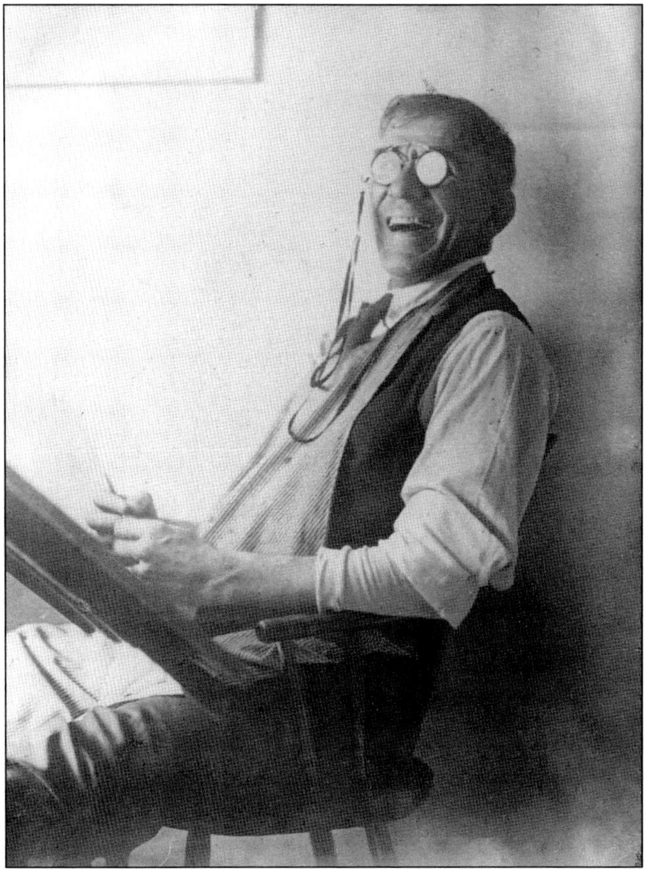

Drawn by the varied scenery and seafaring atmosphere of Port Jefferson, artist Leon Foster Jones, a New Hampshire native, and his wife, Josephine, settled in the village in 1912. His subjects included the fast-disappearing shipbuilding industry, the decaying hulls of sailing ships, and old houses and mills. Many of his works are displayed in the Port Jefferson Free Library. He died at Mather Hospital in 1940. (Courtesy of Frances Child.)

This watercolor painting of the derelict hull of an old schooner in Setauket Harbor, entitled *Scott's Cove,* dates from 1928. Davis and Jones were the subjects of a show, "Two Artists from Port Jefferson," at the Long Island Museum in 1993. (Courtesy of Port Jefferson Free Library.)

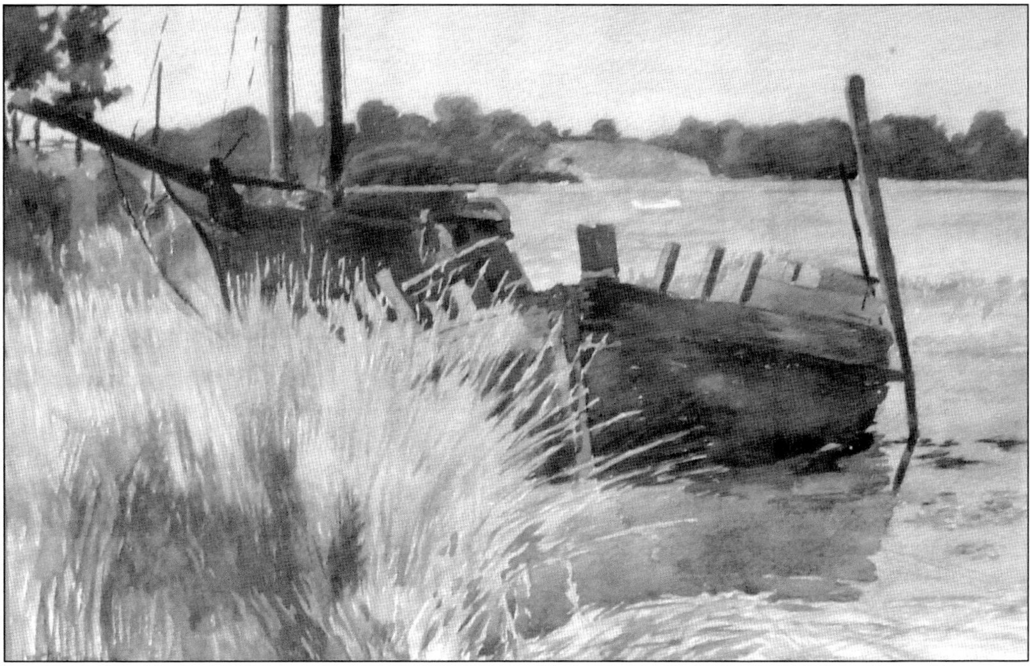

The area on the west side of the village, south of the harbor, was from an early date known as Brick Hill or Brick Kiln, because of the large clay deposits sometimes used to make bricks. In the 1860s, the area began to be developed for residences, and in 1873, circus impresario P.T. Barnum (shown at right at about that time period) continued this trend by buying up a number of parcels, constructing roads, and building houses, including one for himself, although he never lived in it. By 1880, he had abandoned the project, but the chief artery through the area is still called Barnum Avenue. Ship captains, in particular, were attracted to the area, and many spacious and attractive homes grace Barnum and streets to the west. (Right, courtesy of the Barnum Museum, Bridgeport, Connecticut, 2001.2.2-1.)

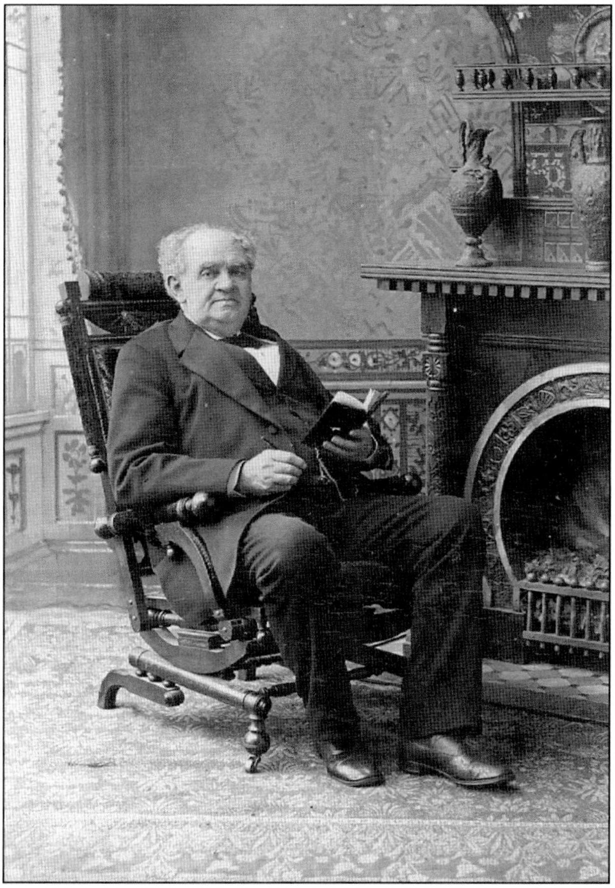

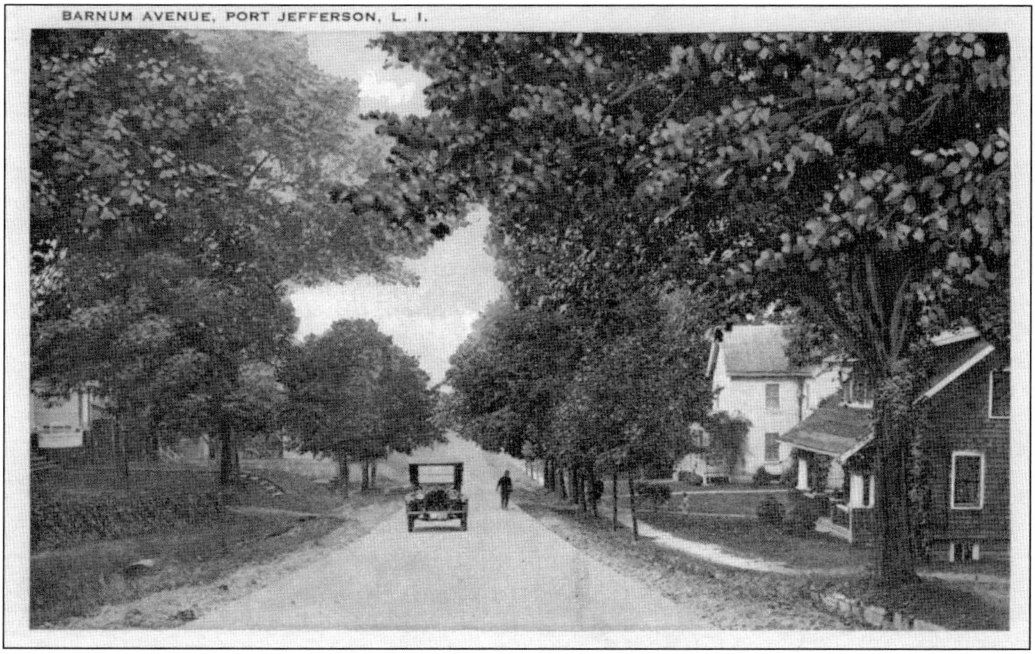

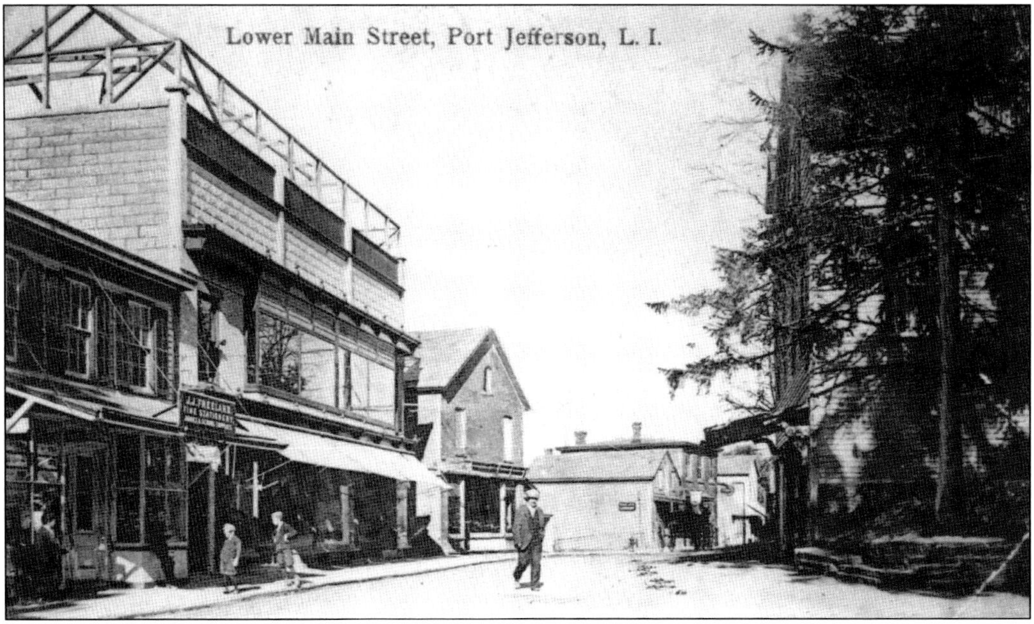

Arthur S. Greene, Port Jefferson's most prolific photographer, came to the village in 1894. A year later, he opened his own studio above the Norton store on East Main Street, shown here on the left. During his long career, he took tens of thousands of photographs, thus preserving the history of northern Brookhaven.

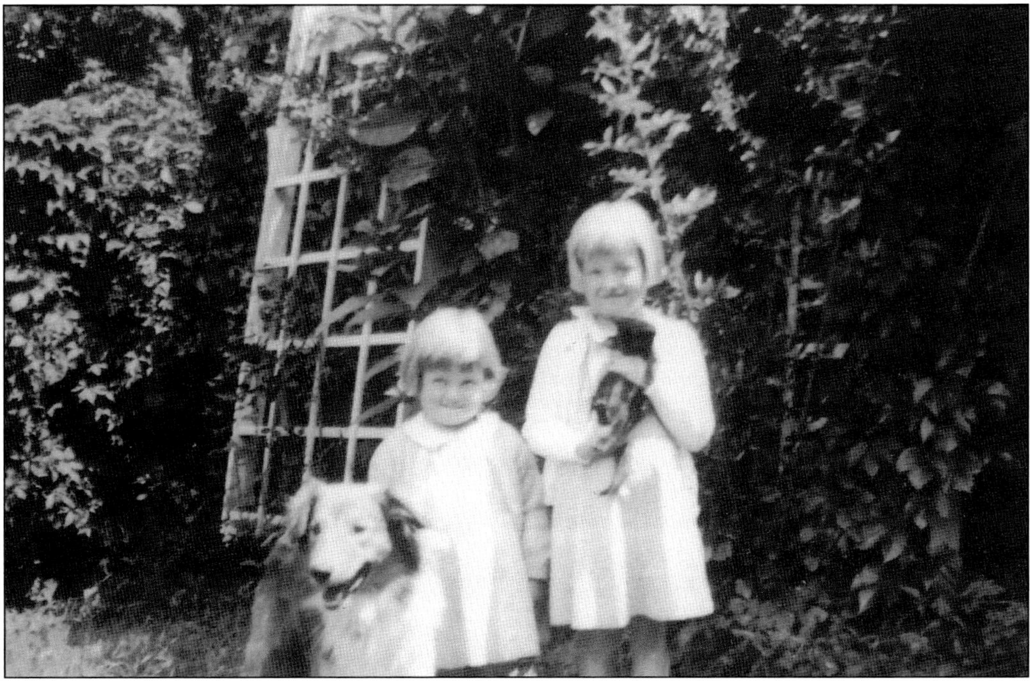

Sandra (Clarke) Swenk (left) and her older sister Nancy pose in the backyard of the Mather House (now home of the historical society) with their longtime pet dog Mack. Sandra would grow up to become Port Jefferson's mayor, from 1971 to 1977. She was the first woman ever elected mayor of a Long Island village. This photograph is from the 1940s. (Courtesy of Sandra Swenk.)

Nine

Belle Terre

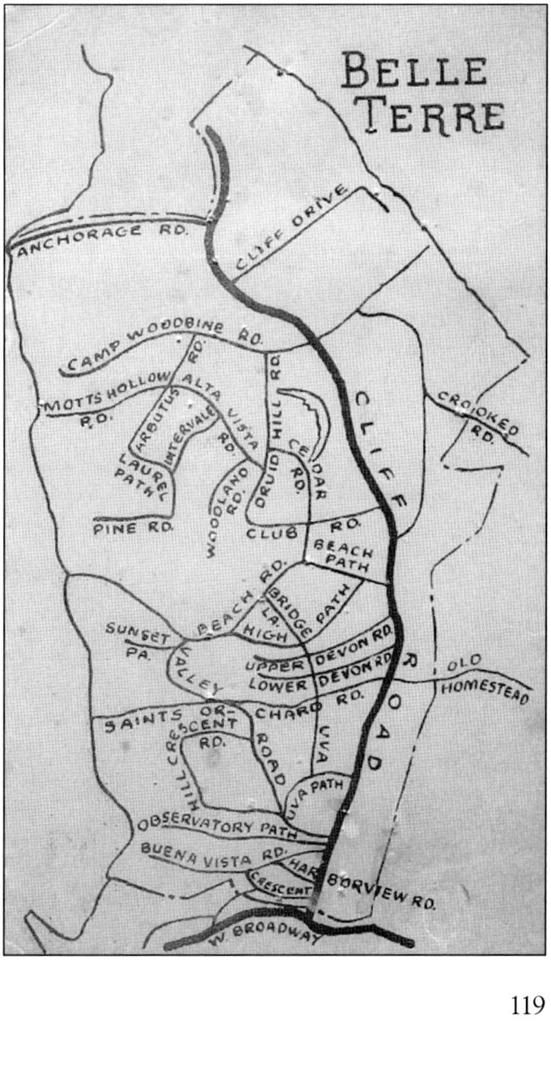

Belle Terre, an area to the east of Port Jefferson Harbor on Mount Misery Neck, is an incorporated village that shares Port Jefferson's school district and zip code. The inspiration for Belle Terre was Tuxedo Park in upstate Orange County, a country resort for New York blue bloods. Belle Terre was sometimes described as "The Tuxedo of Long Island." An early map shows the picturesque road names planned for the community. (Courtesy of Port Jefferson Free Library.)

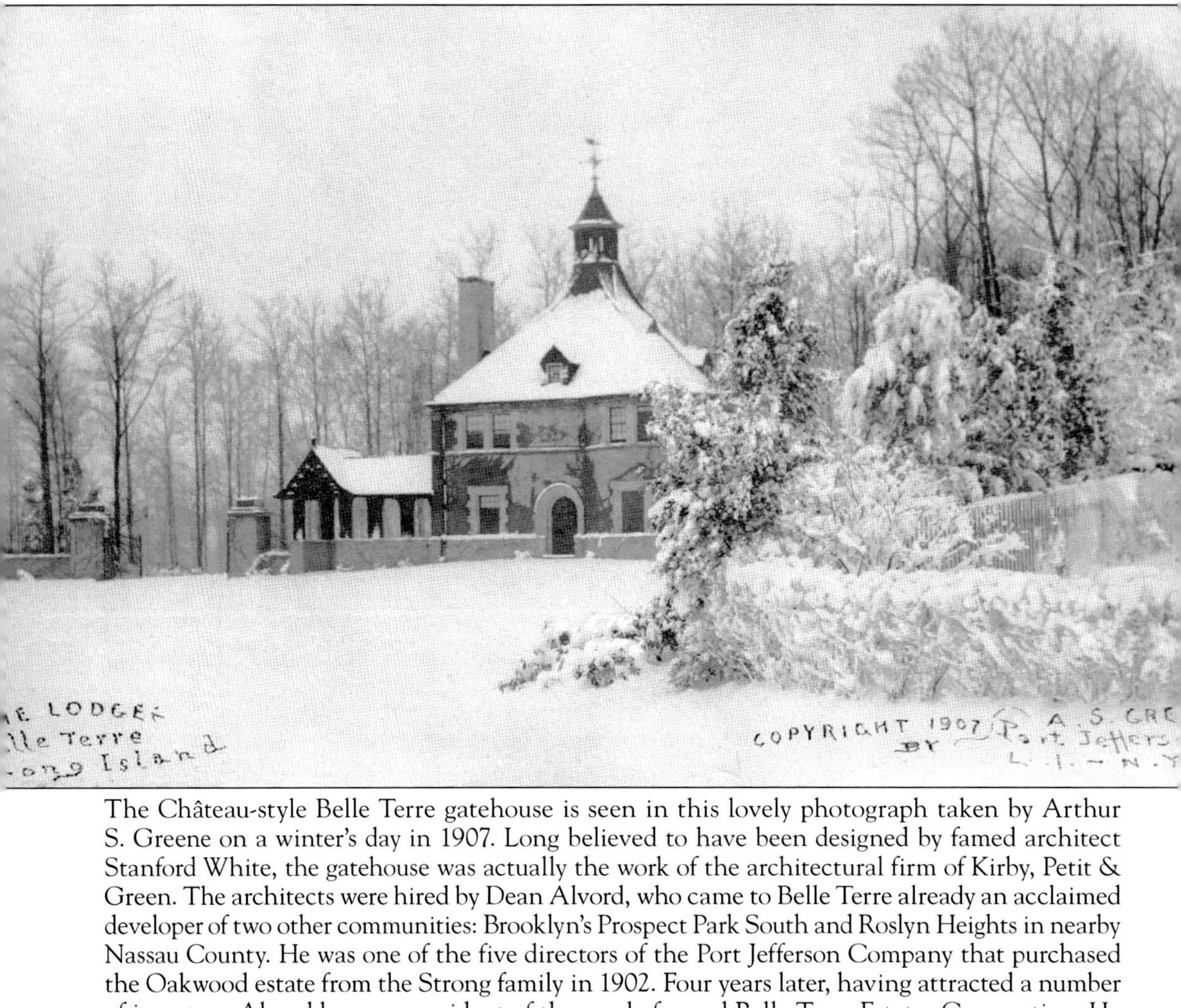

The Château-style Belle Terre gatehouse is seen in this lovely photograph taken by Arthur S. Greene on a winter's day in 1907. Long believed to have been designed by famed architect Stanford White, the gatehouse was actually the work of the architectural firm of Kirby, Petit & Green. The architects were hired by Dean Alvord, who came to Belle Terre already an acclaimed developer of two other communities: Brooklyn's Prospect Park South and Roslyn Heights in nearby Nassau County. He was one of the five directors of the Port Jefferson Company that purchased the Oakwood estate from the Strong family in 1902. Four years later, having attracted a number of investors, Alvord became president of the newly formed Belle Terre Estates Corporation. He then began promoting the development as the ideal setting on which to build a home. Additional incentives included exclusive use of a luxurious clubhouse, golf course, and bridle paths. (Courtesy of the Belle Terre Archive.)

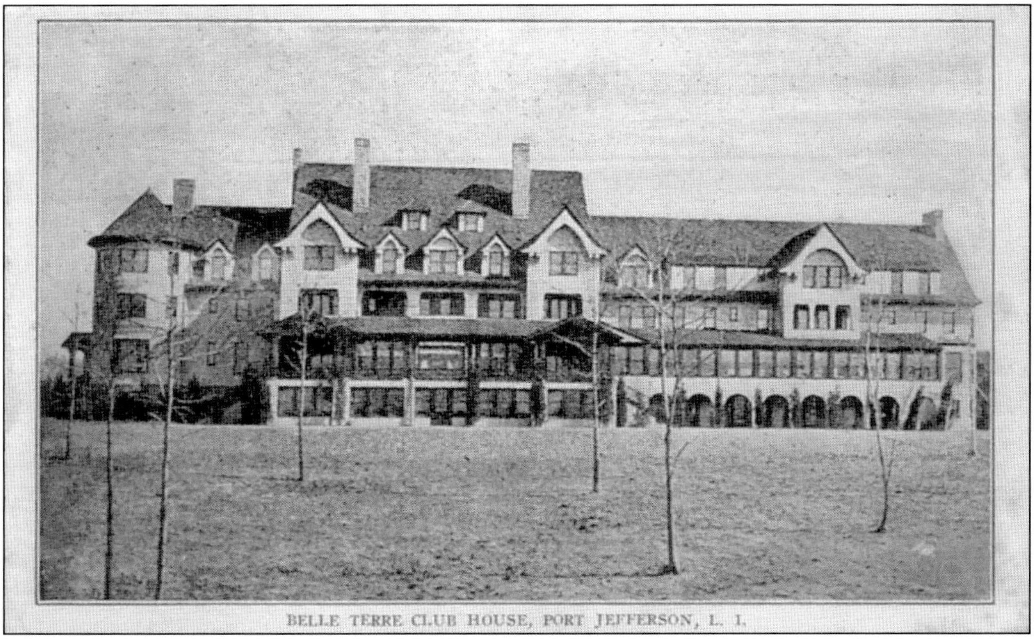

The centerpiece of Belle Terre was the private Belle Terre Club (1906), also a Kirby, Petit & Green design. It had rooms for 100 guests, each with its own fireplace, electric lighting, and telephone service. Members included Vanderbilts, Astors, and Whitneys. In 1934, the clubhouse burned down in a spectacular fire that could be seen for miles. (Courtesy of Frances Child.)

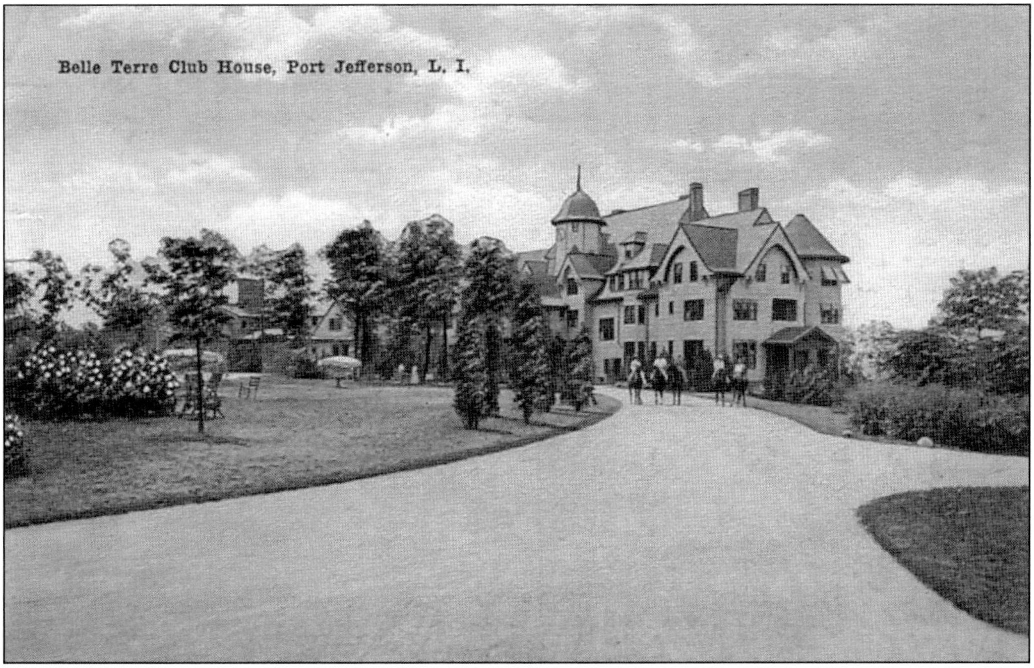

Club amenities abounded. The dining room, serving gourmet meals, could seat 200. Riding was available on 60 miles of bridle paths and roads. The club also had tennis courts, croquet grounds, bowling greens, and a billiard parlor. Guests could also choose to sit on the spacious porch, enjoy the views of Port Jefferson Harbor, and listen to an orchestra. (Courtesy of Frances Child.)

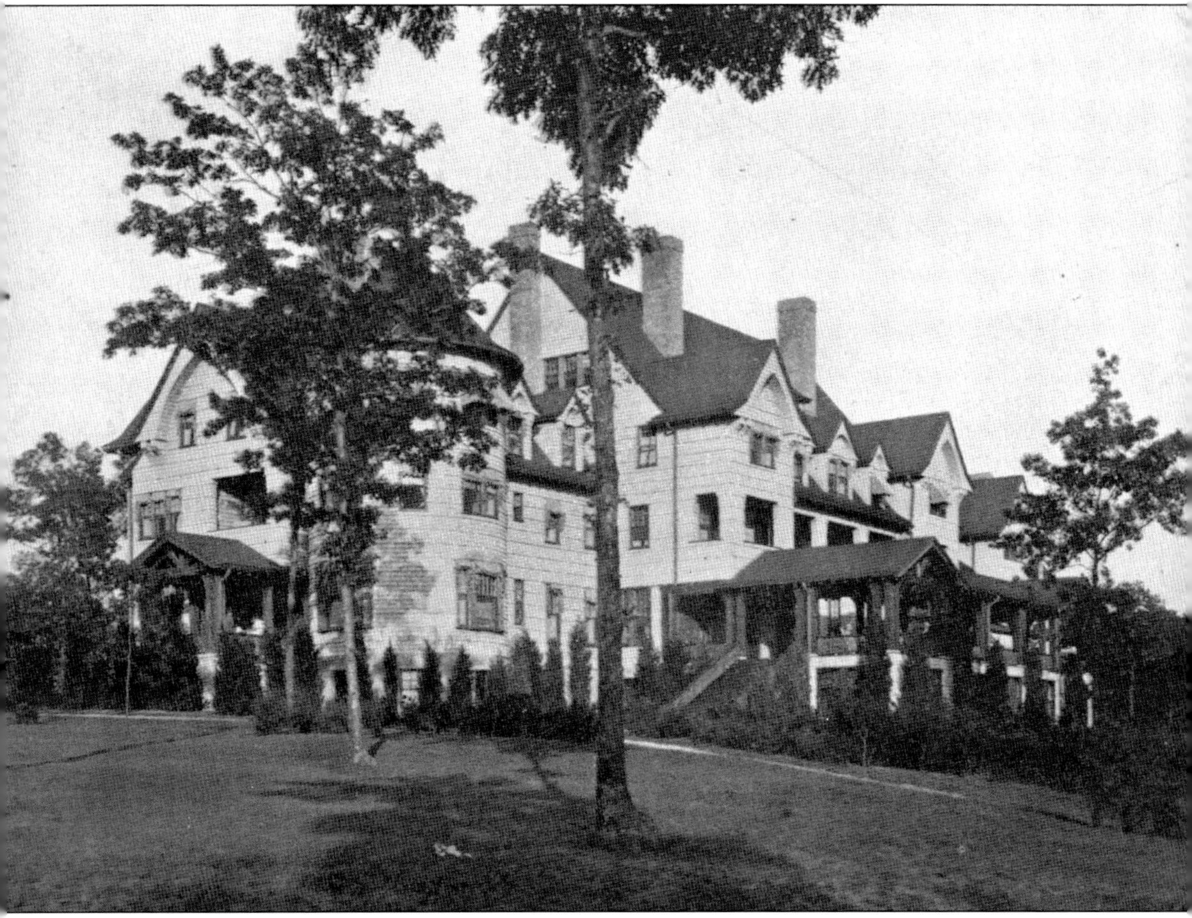

The clubhouse, set high on a bluff overlooking Port Jefferson Harbor, was clearly visible from the water. Promotional literature emphasized its healthful location. The exterior of the clubhouse was designed to resemble an old English inn. Many of the larger private homes in the community also looked as though they would have been at home in the English countryside, while the smaller six-to-eight-room bungalows had a more contemporary, Craftsman appearance. Belle Terre Estates was meant to be an exclusive community for a congenial group of well-heeled New Yorkers. The sales brochure touts its single, gated entrance, its three sides surrounded by water, and its distance from New York City, "just sufficient to remove it from the intrusions of the excursion element." It was also meant to be self-sufficient, with its own water supply, electric plant, and farm and garden. (Courtesy of the Belle Terre Archive.)

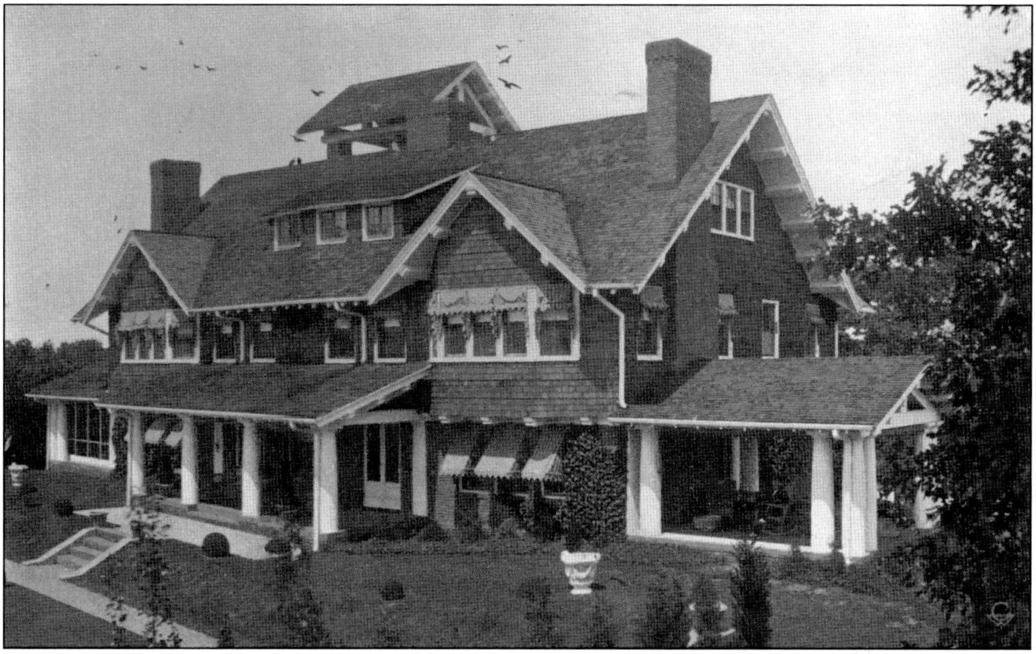

Nevalde, Dean Alvord's own estate, built in 1909, was also designed by Kirby, Petit & Green. The columns on the wide porches shared the distinctive design—smooth on the lower one-third and fluted above—with that chosen by the architects for the pergolas and the train station. (Courtesy of the Belle Terre Archive.)

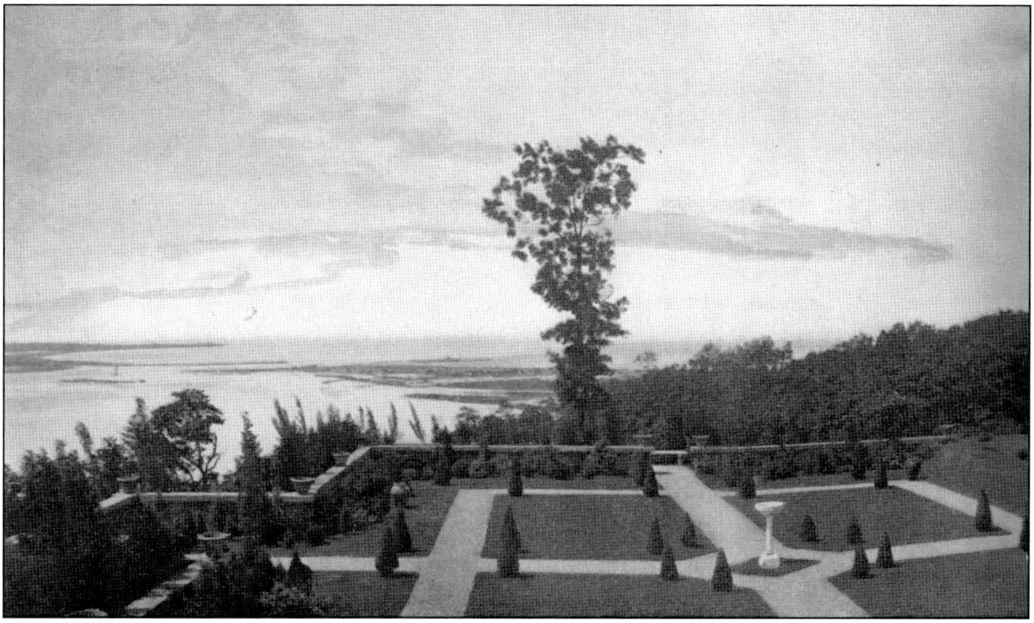

This is a view of the formal gardens of Nevalde, with Port Jefferson Harbor and Long Island Sound in the background. Unfortunately, Belle Terre Estates, of which Alvord had become the president in 1906, went into receivership in 1913. Large tracts of land, still undeveloped, were sold to sand-mining interests, and the views that Alvord and others had enjoyed were marred by dredging. (Courtesy of the Belle Terre Archive.)

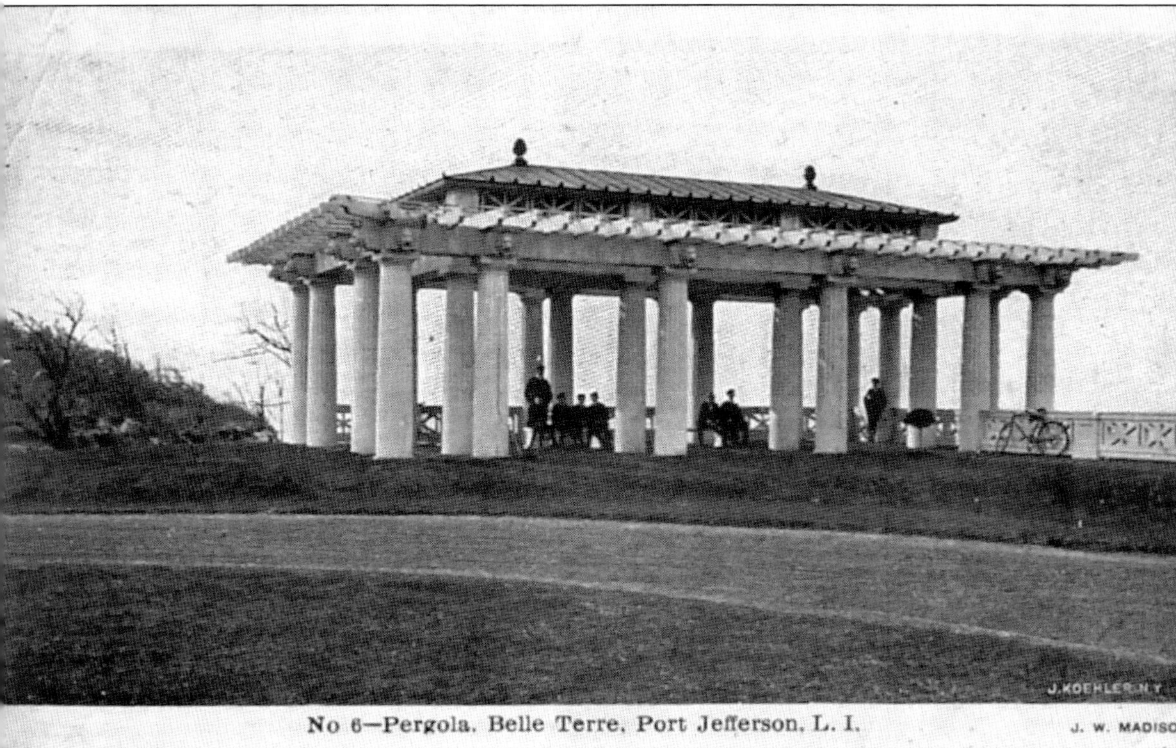

Kirby, Petit & Green designed two pergolas for the end of Cliff Road to provide residents and guests with unobstructed views of the harbor and the sound. Ralph Peters, president of the Long Island Rail Road and a member of the club, had arranged for private railcars to take members and prospective members to Port Jefferson. Belle Terre Road was built at this time to connect the Belle Terre gatehouse with the railroad station. Columns matching those of the pergolas were added to the station. These station columns still exist, but, unfortunately, the pergolas do not. They were built very close to the edge of the bluff, and by 1933, erosion and weather had taken their toll. The pergolas had to be demolished. (Courtesy of Frances Child.)

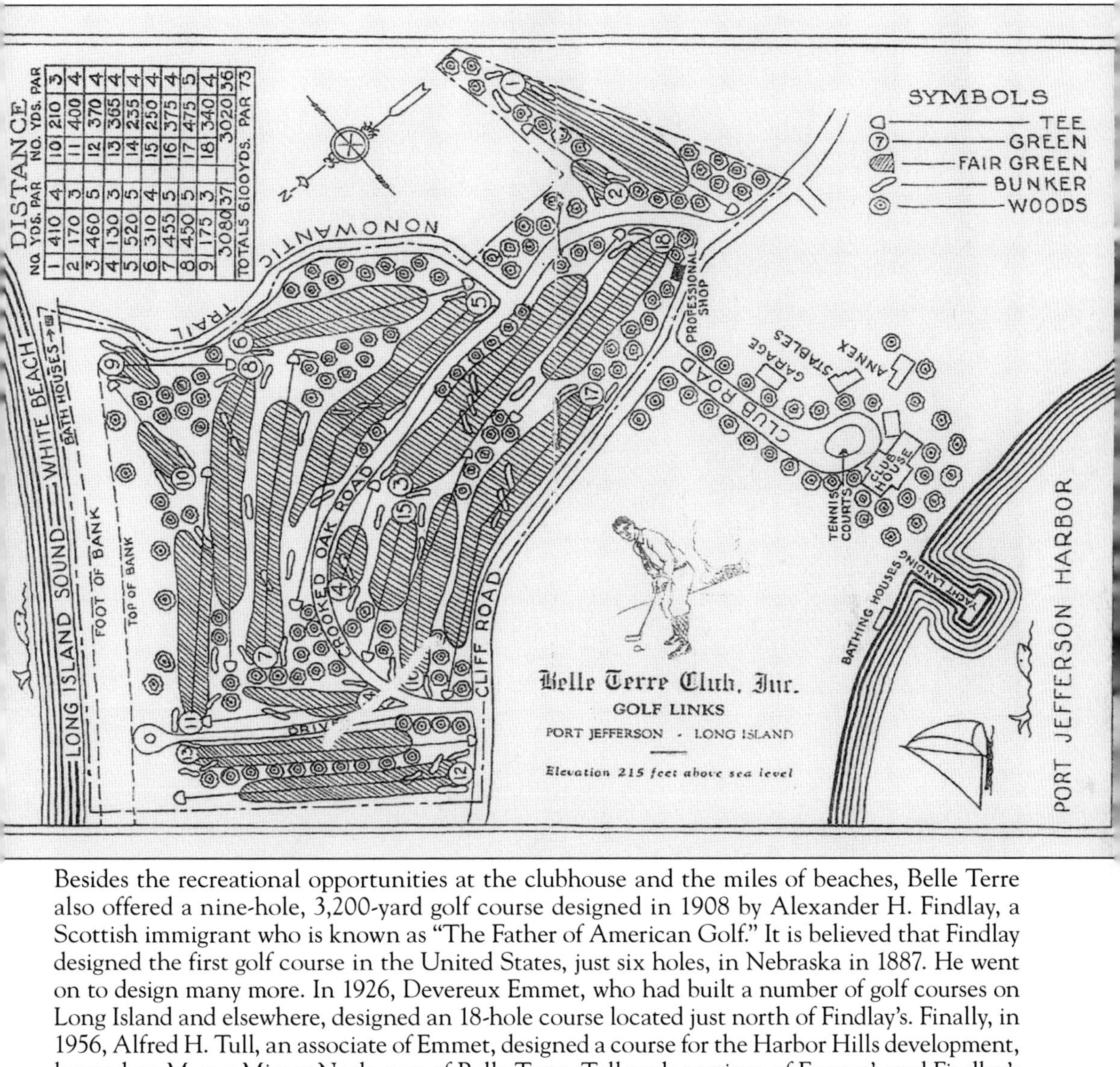

Besides the recreational opportunities at the clubhouse and the miles of beaches, Belle Terre also offered a nine-hole, 3,200-yard golf course designed in 1908 by Alexander H. Findlay, a Scottish immigrant who is known as "The Father of American Golf." It is believed that Findlay designed the first golf course in the United States, just six holes, in Nebraska in 1887. He went on to design many more. In 1926, Devereux Emmet, who had built a number of golf courses on Long Island and elsewhere, designed an 18-hole course located just north of Findlay's. Finally, in 1956, Alfred H. Tull, an associate of Emmet, designed a course for the Harbor Hills development, located on Mount Misery Neck, east of Belle Terre. Tull took portions of Emmet's and Findlay's courses and created the 18-hole course known today as Port Jefferson Country Club at Harbor Hills. (Courtesy of the Belle Terre Archive.)

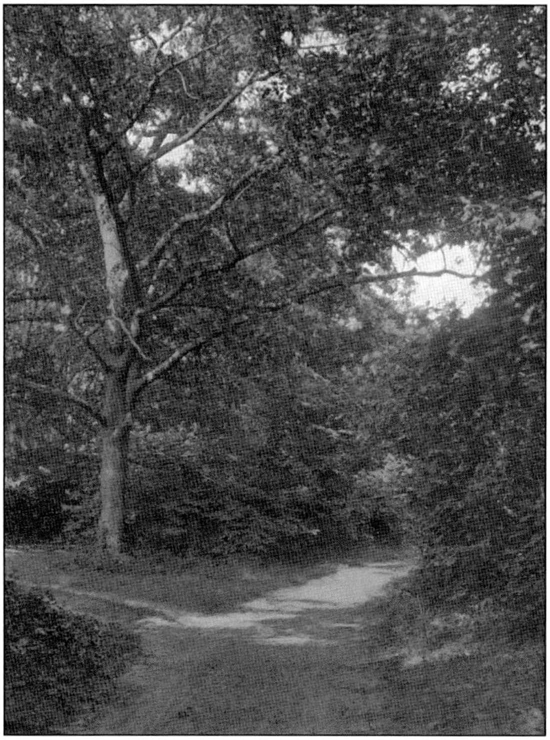

Efforts were made to enhance the grounds of Belle Terre Estates and make them as picturesque as possible. Shady bridle paths, such as this one, were lined with mountain laurel. These paths led to nooks and overlooks for riders and walkers alike, such as Druid's Hill, Giant's Cradle, and Sentimental Rock. (Courtesy of the Belle Terre Archive.)

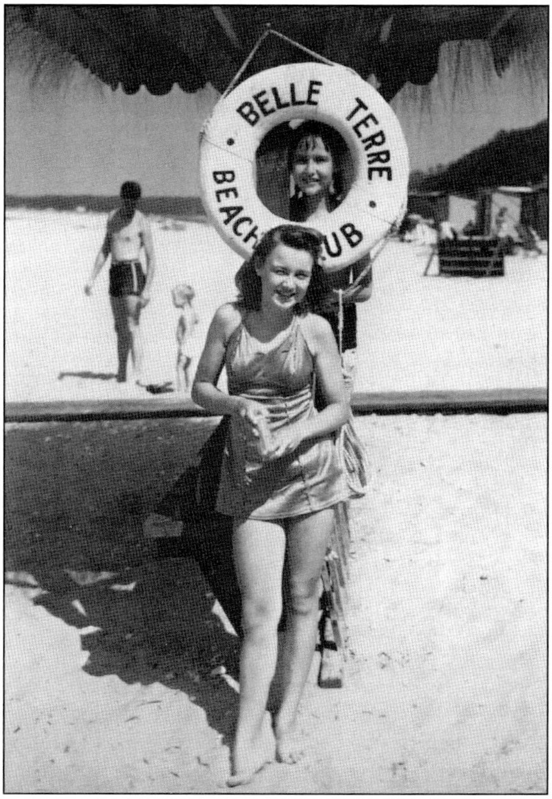

The sand-mining companies that bought much of Belle Terre in the 1910s and 1920s gouged out great portions of the shoreline. After Belle Terre was incorporated in 1931 and expelled the sand miners and dredgers, the beaches were once again open for recreation, more houses were built, and the area became as pleasant a residential community as Dean Alvord could have imagined. The two young sisters pictured here enjoy the beach in 1941.

Bibliography

Bone, Frederick W. *The Sands of Time: A History of the Sand and Gravel Operations in Port Jefferson and Nearby Harbors*. East Setauket, NY: Three Village Historical Society, 1998.

Brady, Kenneth C. *Arthur S. Greene, 1867–1955: The Life and Work of a Long Island Photographer.* Landover, MD: Colortone Press, 1999.

Child, Frank and Frances. *The Search for the Schooner* Palestine. Port Jefferson, NY: Danfords Inn, Marina, Executive Conference Center, for the Port Jefferson Historical Society, 1989.

Hefner, Robert J. *Historic Resources Survey, Port Jefferson, New York: Phase One: Reconnaissance Survey*. East Hampton, NY: R.J. Hefner, 1998.

Historical Society of Greater Port Jefferson. *Port Homes: Historical Homes of Port Jefferson*. Port Jefferson, NY: The Society, 2002.

Michos, Mildred, comp. *People of Port Jefferson: A Collection of Biographies, Newspaper Articles, Genealogies, and Notices about People of Port Jefferson* (computer disc). Port Jefferson, NY: M. Michos, 1998–2004.

Sisler, Patricia Hansell and Robert Sisler. *The Seven Hills of Port: A Documented History of the Incorporated Village of Port Jefferson*. Port Jefferson, NY: P.H. Sisler and R. Sisler, 1992.

Sisler, Robert. *Port Jefferson Area's First Century on Wheels, 1850s to 1950s: The Port Jefferson and Northern Brookhaven Transportation Hub, Vehicle Manufacturers, Dealers, and Owners*. Setauket, NY: Printing Spectrum, 2007.

Sisler, Robert and Patricia. *Those Half Thousand Great Ships Built in Port Jefferson*. Port Jefferson, NY: Printing Spectrum, 1997.

Sisler, Robert and Patricia Hansell Sisler, comps. *204 Clippings on Port Jefferson Area History including Local Scientists at RCA as Printed in the* Port Jefferson Record *and* Port Times-Record. Port Jefferson, NY: R. Sisler, 2001.

Welles, Gordon and William Proios. *Port Jefferson: Story of a Village*. Port Jefferson, NY: Historical Society of Greater Port Jefferson, 1977.

In addition, the newsletter of the Historical Society of Greater Port Jefferson and the websites of the Port Jefferson Village Digital Archive and the Suffolk County Historic Newspapers have been invaluable.